# Visual Cryptography for Image Processing
# and Security

Feng Liu · Wei Qi Yan

# Visual Cryptography for Image Processing and Security

Theory, Methods, and Applications

Second Edition

 Springer

Feng Liu
The State Key Laboratory of Information
  Security
Institute of Information Engineering
Chinese Academy of Sciences
Beijing
China

Wei Qi Yan
School of Computer and Mathematical
  Sciences
Auckland University of Technology
Auckland
New Zealand

ISBN 978-3-319-23472-4      ISBN 978-3-319-23473-1    (eBook)
DOI 10.1007/978-3-319-23473-1

Library of Congress Control Number: 2014945954

Springer Cham Heidelberg New York Dordrecht London

Printed on acid-free paper

Springer International Publishing AG Switzerland is part of Springer Science+Business Media
(www.springer.com)

# Preface

Visual cryptography is a secret sharing technique which allows the encryption of a secret image among a number of participants. The beauty of visual cryptography scheme (VCS) is its decryption of the secret image requires neither cryptography knowledge nor complex computation. Compared to the traditional secret sharing schemes, it encrypts a large amount of secret information, i.e. an entire image where its content is versatile. The Visual Cryptography Scheme (VCS) has been applied to secret sharing, information hiding, identification/authentication, copyright protection, etc. The second edition of this book mainly focuses on fundamental concepts, theories and practice of visual cryptography, designs, constructions and analysis of visual cryptography schemes and the related applications.

A construction of a general access structure VCS by applying (2, 2)-VCS recursively is presented in this book at first. Compared to many of the known VCS, the presented VCS has smaller pixel expansion and average pixel expansion, and larger contrast in most cases. According to the constructions, a general access structure VCS is constructed by only applying (2, 2)-VCS recursively, regardless whether the underlying operation is OR or XOR. This result is most interesting, because the construction of VCS under the operation XOR for general access structure has never been claimed to be possible before.

For the designs and analysis of VCS, an embedded extended visual cryptography scheme (Embedded EVCS) is introduced where its shares are all meaningful images rather than noise. The embedded EVCS applies the embedded technique and halftone technique. Compared to some of the known EVCS's, the scheme has the following advantages: (1) It deals with grey-scale level input images; (2) It has small pixel expansion; (3) It generates a general access structure EVCS and is always unconditionally secure; (4) Each participant only receives one share; (5) It is flexible in the sense that there exist two trade-offs between the share pixel expansion and the visual quality of the shares; between the secret image pixel expansion and visual quality of the shares.

Various VCS problems will be discussed in this book. One of typical problems is alignment. Evidences shows that the original secret image is able to be recovered visually when one of the transparencies is shifted by at most $m - 1$ sub-pixels, and the average contrast becomes $\overline{\alpha} = \frac{(m-r)\cdot e}{m^2\cdot(m-1)}$. The study is based on a deterministic visual cryptography scheme, and the shifted scheme is a probabilistic visual cryptography scheme with less average contrast but still visible.

Correspondingly, the smallest pixel expansion and largest contrast of $(2, n)$-VCS under XOR operation are analyzed in this book. The values of the smallest pixel expansion, the largest possible contrast, the largest contrast, the smallest possible pixel expansion, and the concrete constructions are provided as well. The chapter also shows that, construction of the basis matrix of contrast optimal $(2, n)$-VCS is equivalent to construction of the maximum capacity binary codes with specific parameters, hence the known constructions of the maximum capacity binary code (constant weight or not constant weight) is able to be applied to construct contrast optimal $(2, n)$-VCS optionally. The book shows that $(k, n)$-VCS presented by Droste in 1996 is a $(k, n)$-VCS that works both under OR and XOR operations. This advantage brings more convenience to the participants. Furthermore, a method to reduce the pixel expansion of $(k, n)$-VCS is presented. The method significantly reduces the pixel expansion compared to that of the $(k, n)$-VCS proposed by Tuyls. A construction of concolorous $(k, n)$-VCS where the shares are concolorous is also introduced in this book. The book proves that the concolorous $(k, n)$-VCS does not exist with odd $k$, and proposes a construction of concolorous $(k, n)$-VCS with even $k$. The concolorous $(k, n)$-VCS is able to be used to protect the shares from being stolen by hidden cameras.

In this edition, we correct the typos and mistakes of the last edition as well as add new contents. We contribute 2D barcode for authentication of VC shares and Braille for authentication of VC shares to this new edition. We combine the content of VC authentication and VC cheating prevention together and put them into a new chapter. We also provide questions and exercises which are put at the rear of each chapter for those interested readers.

In general, this book addresses the fundamental problems of visual cryptography from the aspects of theory and practice, which is beneficial for the community to get a better understanding of this media based security technology. Hence the book will potentially have a broad impact across a range of areas including document authentication and cryptography. The book could be used as a reference for the potential researchers and students who have the intention to deeply study visual cryptography.

June 2015                                                                         Feng Liu
                                                                                 Wei Qi Yan

# Acknowledgments

We thank support from our families, we appreciate the work from our colleagues and students who were working with us together in the past a few years. We thank the readers who provided constructive suggestions for this book.

# Contents

# About the Authors

**Prof. Feng Liu** State Key Laboratory of Information Security, Institute of Information Engineering, Chinese Academy of Sciences, Beijing China.

Dr. Liu received his bachelor degree in Computer Science from Shandong University and his Ph.D. degree in Information Security from Institute of Software (IOS), Chinese Academy of Sciences (CAS). He is currently a Full Professor with the State Key Laboratory of Information Security (SKLOIS), Institute of Information Engineering (IIE), Chinese Academy of Sciences (CAS). Meanwhile Professor Liu is serving as director of the Executive Office of SKLOIS, his research interests include strategic and economic aspects of information security, visual cryptography, network security and formal analysis of security protocols, etc.

**Dr. Wei Qi Yan** School of Computer and Mathematical Sciences, Auckland University ofTechnology, Auckland New Zealand.

Dr. Yan received his Ph.D. in Computer Engineering from Institute of Computing Technology (ICT), Chinese Academy of Sciences (CAS). Dr. Yan's expertise is in digital security and forensics, he is leading the Computer and Communication Security research group with the Auckland University of Technology (AUT). Dr. Yan is the Editor-in-Chief (EiC) of the International Journal of Digital Crime and Forensics (IJDCF). Dr. Yan was an Exchange Computer Scientist between the Royal Society of New Zealand (RSNZ) and the Chinese Academy of Sciences (CAS), he is the Chair of the ACM Multimedia chapter of New Zealand, a Member of the ACM, a Senior Member of the IEEE, TC members of the IEEE. Dr. Yan is an Adjunct Professor with Ph.D. supervision of the State Key Laboratory of Information Security (SKLOIS) China, a Visiting Professor of the University of Auckland (New Zealand) and the National University of Singapore (Singapore) in Computer Science. Dr. Yan is a Fellow of the Higher Education Academy (HEA), UK.

# Acronyms

| | |
|---|---|
| ACM | Advanced Color Model |
| AP | Authorized Pixel |
| APE | Average Pixel Expansion |
| BIBD | Balance Incomplete Block Design |
| BSS | Binary Secret Sharing |
| CEVCS | Color Extended Visual Cryptography Scheme |
| CIVCS | Cheating Immune Visual Cryptography Scheme |
| CM | Color Model |
| CMY | Cyan, Magnet, Yellow |
| CVCS | Color Visual Cryptography Scheme |
| DVCS | Determinate Visual Cryptography Scheme |
| EVCS | Extended Visual Cryptography Scheme |
| HVS | Human Visual System |
| OTA | Online Trustable Authorization |
| PVCS | Probabilistic Visual Cryptography Scheme |
| RGB | Red, Green, Blue |
| SCM | Successful Cheating Method |
| VC | Visual Cryptography |
| VCM | Visual Cryptography Model |
| VCS | Visual Cryptography Scheme |
| $2^V$ | Power set of the set V |
| $\emptyset$ | Empty set |
| $cl(C)$ | The closure of the closed set $C$ |
| $\Gamma_{Qual}$ | Set of the qualified set |
| $\Gamma_{Forb}$ | Set of the forbidden set |
| $m$ | The minimum qualified set |
| $M$ | The maximum qualified set |
| $GF(2)$ | Galois field of order 2 |
| $w(v)$ | Hamming weight of the vector $v$ |
| $OR$ | $OR$ operation |

| | |
|---|---|
| *XOR* | Exclusive operation |
| *NOT* | NOT operation |
| $\alpha$ | Contrast |
| $m, m'$ | Pixel expansion |
| $R(A, P)$ | The dark ratio of the Subset $A$ in the full set $P$ |
| $R(P)$ | The average ratio of all the subset of the full set $P$ |
| $lcm(a, b)$ | Least common multiple of $a$ and $b$ |
| $gcd(a, b)$ | Greatest common divisor between $a$ and $b$ |
| $M_0 \| M_1$ | Concatenation of matrix $M_0$ and matrix $M_1$ |
| $max(\cdot)$ | Function $max(\cdot)$ |
| $min(\cdot)$ | Function $min(\cdot)$ |

# Chapter 1
# Introduction

## 1.1 Introduction

Visual cryptography (VC) was originally invented and pioneered by Moni Naor and
Adi Shamir in Eurocrypt 1994 [10, 22], which decodes concealed images without
any cryptographic computations. It works as follows, a secret image is chosen and
using VC techniques, it is encrypted into a number of pieces (known as shares).
When these shares are printed onto transparencies and stacked together (physically
superimposed), our human eyes do the decryption. This allows an average person
to use the system without any knowledge of cryptography and without performing
any computations whatsoever. This is the advantage of VC over the other popular
cryptographic schemes. The image consists of black-and-white pixels. The original
secret image is recovered by superimposing the two shares. The underlying operation
of such scheme is OR. The below Fig. 1.1 is the original secret image to be shared,
Fig. 1.2 is the restored secret image with 2 times expansion.

    The secret image is composed of black-and-white pixels. The original secret image
is recovered by superimposing two share images together. The underlying operation
of such a scheme is the logical operation OR. Generally, a $(k, n)$-VCS takes a secret
image as input, and outputs $n$ share images that satisfy two conditions: (1) any $k$
out of $n$ share images can recover the secret image; (2) any less than $k$ share images
cannot get any information about the secret image. There are four features of VCS:

- The VCS is for image encryption and decryption;
- Without complicate computation, the decryption is performed using our human
  vision system, the operation is fast, no information exchanges and communications
  between VCS shares;
- It is a secret sharing system;
- It is one pad system, satisfies unconditionally secure;

© Springer International Publishing Switzerland 2015
F. Liu and W.Q. Yan, *Visual Cryptography for Image
Processing and Security*, DOI 10.1007/978-3-319-23473-1_1

**Fig. 1.1** Original secret image

**Fig. 1.2** Restored secret image

Therefore the VCS is simple, it does not need any decryption devices and computations, several transparencies are enough to get the secret. However, VCS could deal with huge volume of picture data compared to the text encryption, because the encrypted object is a picture, the information range is much wide.

However, traditional cryptography needs computer participation, since the traditional encryption is based on the limitations of current time frame and computing resources. A computer has to be supported by software such as operating system and applications, and hardware such as CPU, memory, etc. This makes computers are not a secure computing device, since virus, worms, malware, and backdoors could be used to steal secure information. But VCS could avoid this weakness and guarantee the security computations such as encryption and decryption.

VCS could combine with the recent new technologies such as digital watermarking. A watermark is a very small piece of identification, it could be embedded and extracted in real time. VCS shares could be used as watermarks and identify copyright or ownerships in network, internet, and cloud environment since the size is quite small.

The new recent research directions include optimization of contrast [2–6, 9–11, 16, 17, 25], pixel expansion [13, 15, 18, 25, 32], constructions of general VCS structure [14, 18, 27, 30], color visual cryptography [13, 26, 30], VCS schemes for meaningful images [18, 28], applications of VCS [19], VCS immunity and cheating prevention [12, 15, 19, 20, 23, 24], etc. We will organize our book in this order to address each chapter.

## 1.2 Access Structure

VCS is a secret sharing scheme for images, the scheme is built on access structure, hence we provide the definition of access structure first. In a secret sharing scheme, suppose all the participants of an access structure form a set $V = \{1, 2, \ldots, n\}$. The specification of all qualified and forbidden subsets of participants constitutes an access structure $(\Gamma_{Qual}, \Gamma_{Forb})$. Denote it as the set of qualified sets (the participants in a qualified set collaboratively recover the secret image) and $\Gamma_{Forb}$ as the set of forbidden sets (the participants in a forbidden set cannot recover the secret image). Obviously, we have $\Gamma_{Qual} \cap \Gamma_{Forb} \neq \emptyset$. In VC, we only take the access structure $\Gamma_{Qual} \cup \Gamma_{Forb} = 2^V$ into consideration, where $2^V$ is the power set of $V$, i.e., the set of all the possible subsets of $V$. The set $\Gamma_{Qual}$ is monotone because of that, if a part of the participants in a set $B \in \Gamma_{Qual}$ recover the secret image, then obviously all the participants in $B$ should recover the secret image as well. We define $\Gamma_m = \{A \in \Gamma_{Qual} : \forall B \tilde{\subseteq} A \Rightarrow B \tilde{\in} \Gamma_{Qual}\}$ and $\Gamma_M = \{A \in \Gamma_{Forb} : \forall B \tilde{\supseteq} A \Rightarrow B \tilde{\in} \Gamma_{Forb}\}$.

We call $\Gamma_m$ *the minimal qualified access structure*, and a subset $A \in \Gamma_m$ is called *the minimal qualified set*. We call $\Gamma_M$ the maximal forbidden access structure, and a subset $B \in \Gamma_M$ is called the maximal forbidden set. For any $C \subseteq 2^V$, define $cl(C) = \{B \subseteq V : \exists A \in C, s.t. B \supseteq A\}$. We call $cl(C)$ the closure of $C$. Since $\Gamma_{Qual}$ is monotone, then $cl(\Gamma_m) = \Gamma_{Qual}$. This means that the qualified access structure $\Gamma_{Qual}$ and the minimal qualified access structure $\Gamma_m$ are determined by each other. Similarly, $\Gamma_M$ and $\Gamma_{Forb}$ are determined by each other as well. Furthermore, because $\Gamma_{Forb} = 2^V \setminus \Gamma_{Qual}$, we have that $\Gamma_m$ and $\Gamma_M$ can be determined by each other.

Particularly, we call a qualified set $B \in \Gamma_M$ that has the largest cardinality *the maximum qualified set* of $\Gamma_m$. Formally, the maximum qualified set $B$ satisfies $|B| = max\{|Q|, Q \in \Gamma_m\}$. Note that, the maximum qualified set of $\Gamma_m$ may not be $V$, and there may be several maximum qualified sets in $\Gamma_m$.

It should be pointed out that the threshold access structure is a special case of the general access structure [1], because a threshold $(k, n)$ access structure is a general access structure with the constraints: $\Gamma_m = \{B \subseteq V : |B| = k\}$ and $\Gamma_M = \{B \subseteq V : |B| = k - 1\}$.

In VCS, there is a secret image which is encrypted into some share images. The secret image is called the original secret image for clarity, and the share images are the encrypted images (and are called the transparencies if they are printed out). When a qualified set of share images (transparencies) is stacked together properly, it gives a visual image which is almost the same as the original secret image, we call this the recovered secret image. In the case of black-and-white images, the original secret image is represented as a pattern of black-and-white pixels. Each of these pixels is divided into sub-pixels which themselves are encoded as black and white to produce the share images. The recovered secret image is also a pattern of black-and-white sub-pixels which should visually reveal the original secret image if a qualified set of share images is stacked. In this chapter, we will focus on the black-and-white images, where a white pixel is denoted by the number 0 and a black pixel is denoted by the number 1. We notice that the definitions of VCS under OR and XOR operations are quite similar. We will give some definitions about VC under the operation "·", which is either the OR operation or the XOR operation.

## 1.3 Fundamental $(k, n)$-VCS

For a vector $v \in GF^m(2)$, denote $w(v)$ as the Hamming weight of the vector $v$, i.e., the number of nonzero coordinates in $v$. A $k$ out of $n$ VCS, denoted by $(C_0, C_1)$, consists of two collections of $n \times m$ binary matrices $C_0$ and $C_1$. To share a white (respectively, black) pixel, a dealer (the one who sets up the system) randomly chooses one of the matrices, called a share matrix, in $C_0$ (respectively, $C_1$) and distributes its rows (representing a pattern of sub-pixels in the share image) to the $n$ participants of the scheme, i.e., giving row $i$ to participant $i$. More precisely, we give a formal definition of $(k, n)$-VCS as follows:

**Definition 1.1** (*Fundamental VCS*) Let $k, n, m, l$ and $h$ be nonnegative integers satisfying $2 \leq k \leq n$ and $0 \leq l \leq h \leq m$. The two collections of $n \times m$ binary matrices $(C_0, C_1)$ constitute a VC scheme $(k, n)$-VCS if there exists a value $\alpha > 0$ and satisfies:
(1) **Contrast**. Any $k$ participants is able to recover the secret image by stacking (the "·" operation) their share images. More precisely, for any $s \in C_0$, the stacking (the "·" operation) of any $k$ out of the $n$ rows of $s$ satisfies $w(v) \leq l$, where the operation stands for the underlying operation OR or XOR. And $v$ is a resultant vector that satisfies $w(v) < h - \alpha \cdot m$, whereas for any $s \in C_1$, we have $w(v) \geq h$.
(2) **Security**. Any less than $k$ participants have no information about the secret image. More precisely, for any $i_1 < i_2 < \cdots < i_t$ in $\{1, 2, \ldots, n\}$ with $t < k$, the two collections of $t \times m$ matrices $D_j$, $j = \{0, 1\}$, obtained by restricting each $n \times m$ matrix in $C_j$, $j = \{0, 1\}$ to rows $i_1, i_2, \ldots, i_t$ are indistinguishable in the sense that they contain the same matrices with the same frequencies.

In Definition 1.1, $h$ is called the blackness bound and $l$ is called the whiteness bound under the dot operation (·). The possible numbers of black sub-pixels to represent a black or white pixel in the recovered secret image are called the darkness levels, i.e., $h$ is the lower bound of the darkness levels for encrypting a black pixel in the recovered secret image, and $l$ is the upper bound of the darkness levels for encrypting a white pixel in the recovered secret image, and $m$ is the pixel expansion of the scheme.

The basis matrices are a pair of $n \times m$ binary matrices $(M_0, M_1)$, which generate the collections $C_0$ and $C_1$ by permuting all the columns in all possible ways. This approach of VCS construction will have small memory requirement (it keeps only the basis matrices) and it is efficient (to choose a matrix in $C_0$ (resp. $C_1$) as it only needs to generate a permutation of the basis matrix, there are at most $m!$ permutations at most) [26].

The most two important parameters in VCS are the contrast and the pixel expansion, where the contrast reflects clearness of the recovered secret image, since the contrast is relevant only in the recovered secret image, so the contrast should be a function with parameters $m$, $h$ and $l$. There are three definitions of the contrast:

$$\alpha_{NS} = \frac{h - l}{m} \tag{1.1}$$

$$\alpha_{VV} = \frac{h - l}{m(h + l)} \tag{1.2}$$

$$\alpha_{ES} = \frac{h - l}{m + l} \tag{1.3}$$

After observations, we find the best definition of VCS contrast should be:

$$\alpha_{(m,h,l)} = \frac{(h - l) \cdot m}{h \cdot (m - h) + l \cdot (m - l) + m^2} \tag{1.4}$$

where the parameters $m$, $h$, and $l$ are the pixel expansion, blackness and whiteness bound respectively. This equation is suitable for both OR and XOR based schemes.

To make them clearer, we give the following experimental results to show the above observations, where in Fig. 1.3, the images are the recovered secret image with parameters (a) $m = 9, h = 9, l = 8$; (b) $m = 9, h = 8, l = 7$; (c) $m = 9, h = 7, l = 6$; (d) $m = 9, h = 6, l = 5$; (e) $m = 9, h = 5, l = 4$; (f) $m = 9, h = 1, l = 0$; (g) $m = 9, h = 2, l = 1$; (h) $m = 9, h = 3, l = 2$; and (i) $m = 9, h = 4, l = 3$ respectively.

From Fig. 1.3 we observe that the recovered secret image becomes less clear when the value $|h + l - m|$ decreases. More precisely, in Fig. 1.3, for the sequence of the value of $(h, l)$ being $(a)(9, 8)$, $(b)(8, 7)$, $(c)(7, 6)$, $(d)(6, 5)$, $(e)(5, 4)$, $(f)(4, 3)$, $(g)(3, 2)$, $(h)(2, 1)$ and $(i)(1, 0)$, the recovered secret image first becomes less clear, and then becomes clearer by the watershed $(e)(5, 4)$. And we also observe that clearness of the recovered secret images $(a)$ and $(i)$ (resp. $(b)$ and $(h)$, $(c)$ and $(g)$, and $(d)$ and $(f)$) looks quite similar.

In order to show that our definition of contrast is more appropriate than some of the known ones on the well-known constructions of VCS, we take the $(2, 4)$-VCS as an example. The parameters of Droste's $(2, 4)$-VCS [6] are $m = 4, h = 2$ and $l = 1$, and that of Blundo et al.'s are $m = 4, h = 4$, and $l = 3$. Hence, we have Table 1.1.

Overall, the clearness of the recovered secret image of Blundo's $(2, 4)$-VCS is better than that of Droste's. Table 1.1 shows that only $\alpha_{(m,h,l)}$ appropriately reflects the contrast of these two $(2, 4)$-VCS.

The pixel expansion reflects the size of the recovered secret image. Pixel expansion represents the expansion ratio of the sizes that the recovered secret image is over the original image.

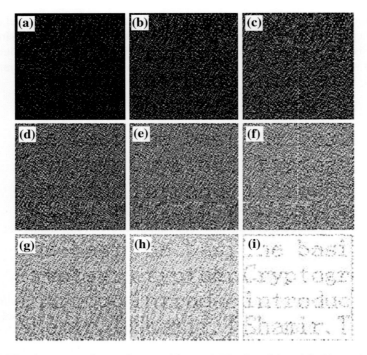

**Fig. 1.3** The nine recovered secret images with $m = 9$. The size of the original image is reduced by 50 %

**Table 1.1** Comparisons of the contrast of various VCS

|                | Droste's (2,4)-VCS | Blundo's (2,4)-VCS |
|----------------|--------------------|--------------------|
| $\alpha_{NS}$      | 1/4                | 1/4                |
| $\alpha_{VV}$      | 1/12               | 1/28               |
| $\alpha_{ES}$      | 1/5                | 1/7                |
| $\alpha_{(m,h,l)}$ | 4/23               | 4/19               |

In the above definition $\alpha_{(m,h,l)}$, $m$ is called the *pixel expansion* of the scheme, and each secret pixel is represented by $m$ sub-pixels in the recovered secret image. We denote $m_{OR}$ and $m_{XOR}$ as the pixel expansions under the operation OR and XOR, respectively.

The $\alpha$ in $\alpha_{(m,h,l)}$ is called the *contrast* and is related to the visual quality of the recovered secret image. For different operations OR and XOR, we use the notations $\alpha_{OR}$ and $\alpha_{XOR}$, respectively.

The implementation of VCS has two phases: the distribution phase and the reconstruction phase. In the distribution phase, the dealer generates all the share images and distributes them to the participants; in the reconstruction phase, the participants reconstruct the secret image by stacking a qualified set of share images.

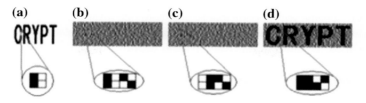

**Fig. 1.4**  An example of (2, 2)-VCS

*Example 1.1*  The $(2, 2)$-$VCS_{OR}$:

$$C_0 = \left\{ \begin{bmatrix} 1 & 0 \\ 1 & 0 \end{bmatrix}, \begin{bmatrix} 0 & 1 \\ 0 & 1 \end{bmatrix} \right\} \tag{1.5}$$

and

$$C_1 = \left\{ \begin{bmatrix} 1 & 0 \\ 0 & 1 \end{bmatrix}, \begin{bmatrix} 0 & 1 \\ 1 & 0 \end{bmatrix} \right\} \tag{1.6}$$

The $(2, 2)$-$VCS_{XOR}$:

$$C_0 = \left\{ \begin{bmatrix} 1 \\ 1 \end{bmatrix}, \begin{bmatrix} 0 \\ 0 \end{bmatrix} \right\} \tag{1.7}$$

and

$$C_1 = \left\{ \begin{bmatrix} 1 \\ 0 \end{bmatrix}, \begin{bmatrix} 0 \\ 1 \end{bmatrix} \right\} \tag{1.8}$$

For the $(2,2)$-$VCS_{OR}$, the pixel expansion and contrast are $m_{OR} = 2$ and $\alpha_{OR} = \frac{1}{2}$, respectively, i.e., size of the recovered secret image and share images will be twice that of the original secret image, contrast of the recovered secret image will be half of that of the original secret image. For $(2, 2)$-$VCS_{XOR}$, we have that $m_{XOR} = 1$ and $\alpha_{XOR} = 1$, i.e., the recovered secret image is identical to the original secret image and the share images have no pixel expansion.

Figure 1.4 is an example of (2, 2)-VCS. (a) is the original image, (b) and (c) are VC shares, (d) is the restored secret. We zoom the corresponding pixels in the VC to demonstrate the mechanism of VC.

## 1.4  Equivalence of VCS Definitions

There are two different definitions of basis matrix $(k, n)$-VCS. The definition of unconditional secure basis matrix $(k, n)$-VCS is the generally accepted one, and has been widely used since the pioneer work of Naor and Shamir in 1994, while the definition of stacking secure basis matrix $(k, n)$−VCS is relatively new, and has been used in a myriad of studies in recent years. The above two definitions are actually equivalent.

In a VC scheme with $n$ participants, we share one pixel at a time. The pixel is either white or black. If the pixel to be shared is white (resp. black), we randomly permutated the columns of $S_0$ (resp. $S_1$) and distribute the $j$th ($0 \leq j \leq n$) row to share $j$, in which 0 denotes a white pixel and 1 denotes a black pixel. Formally, unconditional secure basis matrix $(k, n)$-VCS is defined as follows:

**Definition 1.2** (*Unconditional Secure Basis Matrix $(k, n)$-VCS*) The two $n \times m$ Boolean matrices $(S_0, S_1)$ constitute an unconditional secure basis matrix $(k, n)$-VCS if the following conditions hold:
(1) **Contrast**. For any participant set $X$ with $|X| \geq k$, we denote $l = H(S_0[X])$, and denote $h = H(S_1[X])$. It holds that $0 \leq l < h \leq m$.
(2) **Security**. For any participant set $Y$ with $|Y| \leq k - 1$, $S_0[Y]$ and $S_1[Y]$ are equal up to a column permutation.

**Definition 1.3** (*Stacking secure basis matrix $(k, n)$-VCS*) The two $n \times m$ Boolean matrices $(S_0, S_1)$ constitute a stacking secure basis matrix $(k, n)$-VCS if the following conditions hold:
(1) **Contrast**. For any participant set $X$ with $|X| \geq k$, we denote $l = H(S_0[X])$, and denote $h = H(S_1[X])$. It holds that $0 \leq l < h \leq m$.
(2) **Security**. For any participant set $Y$ with $|Y| \leq k - 1$, it holds that $H(S_0[Y]) = H(S_1[Y])$.

The Definitions 1.2 and 1.3 of basis matrix $(k, n)$-VCS are actually equivalent. The equivalence relationship could be extended to general access structure basis matrix VCS and general access structure SIVCS, however, the equivalence relationship cannot be extended to non-basis matrix $(k, n)$-VCS.

### 1.4.1 The Equivalence of Two Definitions of Threshold Basis Matrix VCS

We first illustrate the terminologies we will use. Numbers $0, 1, 2, \ldots, 2^m - 1$ are represented as $m$-tuple Boolean row vectors $(\underbrace{00 \cdots 0}_{m})$, $(\underbrace{00 \cdots 0}_{m-1} 1)$, $(\underbrace{00 \cdots 0}_{m-2} 11)$, $(\underbrace{11 \cdots 1}_{m} 11)$. To get $m$-tuple Boolean column vectors, we transpose the above $m$-tuple Boolean row vectors. Now we have a 1-1 mapping between the set of all $m$-tuple Boolean column vectors and the set of numbers $0, 1, 2, \ldots, 2^m - 1$. The above 1-1 mapping is also referred to as the coding rule.

Given two numbers $a, b \in \{0, 1, 2, \ldots, 2^m - 1\}$, if the $m$-tuple Boolean column vector of $b$ is obtained by turning some (possibly 0) '1' bits of the $m$-tuple Boolean column vector of $a$ into '0' bits, then we say that $a$ covers $b$ or that $b$ is covered by $a$, which is denoted as $a \diamond b$.

According to the coding rule, the column vectors of the $n \times m$ Boolean matrix are mapped to numbers in $\{0, 1, 2, \ldots, 2^m - 1\}$. Thus the $n \times m$ Boolean matrix is also viewed as a multi-set of cardinality $m$, with its column vectors as elements. Given two $n \times m$ Boolean matrices $S_0$ and $S_1$, which is also viewed as two multi-sets, the following two propositions about them are equivalent: (1) $S_0$ and $S_1$ are equal up to a column permutation; (2) the two multi-sets $S_0$ and $S_1$ are equal. Since the OR result of a column vector is 0 if and only if it is a zero vector, the Hamming weight of the OR result of the rows of $S_0$ (resp. $S_1$) is equal to the number of nonzero column vectors in the multi-set $S_0$ (resp. $S_1$). From another viewpoint, it is equal to $m$ minus the number of zero vector in the multi-set $S_0$ (resp. $S_1$).

**Lemma 1.1** *Given two $n \times m$ Boolean matrices $(S_0, S_1)$ and a participant set $X$ with $|X| \geq 1$, if it holds that $H(S_0[Y]) = H(S_1[Y])$ for any participant set $Y$ with $Y \subseteq X$, then $S_0[Y]$ and $S_1[Y]$ are equal up to a column permutation for any participant set $Y$ with $Y \subseteq X$.*

**Theorem 1.1** *The definition of stacking secure basis matrix $(k, n)$-VCS and the definition of unconditional secure basis matrix $(k, n)$-VCS are equivalent.*

## 1.4.2 The Equivalence of Two Definitions of General Access Structure Basis Matrix VCS

First we give some preliminaries of general access structure [1]. Suppose the participant set is denoted as $P = \{1, 2, \ldots, m\}$. A general access structure is a specification of qualified participant sets $\Gamma_{Qual} \in 2^P$ and forbidden participant sets $\Gamma_{Forb} \in 2^P$. Any participant set $X \in \Gamma_{Qual}$ reveals the secret by stacking their share images, but any participant set $Y \in \Gamma_{Forb}$ cannot obtain any information of the secret image, except the size of it. All the minimal qualified sets are defined as $\Gamma_0 = \{A \in \Gamma_{Qual} : \forall A' \widetilde{\subseteq} A, A' \widetilde{\in} \Gamma_{Qual}\}$. If for any $A \in \Gamma_{Qual}$, any superset of $A$ is also in $\Gamma_{Qual}$, then $\Gamma_{Qual}$ is said to be monotone increasing. If for any $B \in \Gamma_{Forb}$, any subset of $B$ is also in $\Gamma_{Forb}$, then $\Gamma_{Forb}$ is said to be monotone decreasing. If $\Gamma_{Qual}$ is monotone increasing and $\Gamma_{Forb}$ is monotone decreasing and $\Gamma_{Qual} \bigcup \Gamma_{Forb} = 2^P$, then the access structure is said to be strong.

In a strong access structure, $\Gamma_{Qual} = \{A \subseteq P : \exists B \in \Gamma_0, A \supseteq B\}$, and we say that $\Gamma_{Qual}$ is the closure of $\Gamma_0$. If $\Gamma_{Qual} = \Gamma_0$, then the access structure is said to be weak. In $(k, n)$ threshold access structure, $\Gamma_0 = \{B \subseteq P : |B| = k\}$ and $\Gamma_{Qual} = \{B \subseteq P : |B| \leq k - 1\}$. If the $(k, n)$ threshold access structure is strong, $\Gamma_{Forb} = \{B \subseteq P : |B| \geq k\}$. On the other hand, if the $(k, n)$ threshold access structure is weak, $\Gamma_{Qual} = \Gamma_0 = \{B \subseteq P : |B| = k\}$. Hence, in a strong $(k, n)$-VCS, it is required that the stacking of more than or equal to $k$ shares should reveal the secret, while in a weak $(k, n)$-VCS, it is only required that the stacking of $k$ shares reveal the secret. All the maximal forbidden sets are defined as $\Gamma_M = \{A \subseteq \Gamma_{Qual} : \forall a \in P \backslash A, A' = A \bigcup \{a\}, A' \in \Gamma_{Qual}\}$. In $(k, n)$ threshold access structure, $\Gamma_M = \{B \subseteq P : |B| = k - 1\}$.

**Definition 1.4** (*Unconditional Secure Basis Matrix* $\{\Gamma_{Qual}, \Gamma_{Forb}\}$-*VCS*) The two $n \times m$ Boolean matrices $(S_0, S_1)$ constitute an unconditional secure basis matrix $\{\Gamma_{Qual}, \Gamma_{Forb}\}$-VCS if the following conditions hold:
(1) **Contrast**. For any participant set $X \in \Gamma_{Qual}$, we denote $l = H(S_0[X])$, and denote $h = H(S_1[X])$. It holds that $0 \le l < h \le m$.
(2) **Security**. For any participant set $Y \in \Gamma_{Forb}$, $S_0[Y]$ and $S_1[Y]$ are equal up to a column permutation.

**Theorem 1.2** *The definition of stacking secure basis matrix* $\{\Gamma_{Qual}, \Gamma_{Forb}\}$-*VCS and the definition of unconditional secure basis matrix* $\{\Gamma_{Qual}, \Gamma_{Forb}\}$-*VCS are equivalent.*

### 1.4.3 The Equivalence of Two Definitions of General Access Structure SIVCS

The two definitions of general access structure SIVCS are the same as the two definitions of general access structure basis matrix VCS. However, their encoding processes are different. In SIVCS, to share a black (resp. white) pixel, we randomly choose a column from the black (resp. white) basis matrix, and then distribute the $i$th row of the column to participant $i$, while in VCS, to share a black (resp. white) pixel, we randomly permutated the columns of the black (resp. white) basis matrix, and then distribute the $i$th row of the permuted matrix to participant $i$. From Theorem 1.2, we know that the following Theorem 1.3 also holds.

**Theorem 1.3** *The definition of stacking secure* $\{\Gamma_{Qual}, \Gamma_{Forb}\}$-*SIVCS and the definition of unconditional secure* $\{\Gamma_{Qual}, \Gamma_{Forb}\}$-*SIVCS are equivalent.*

### 1.4.4 The Inequivalence of Two Definitions of Non-basis Matrix VCS

A more general definition of $(k, n)$-VCS is given by two collections of $n \times m$ Boolean matrices $C_0$ and $C_1$. To share a white pixel, we randomly choose a share matrix from $C_0$ and distribute the $j$th $(0 \le j \le n)$ row to share $j$. $(k, n)$-VCS is also classified as unconditional secure and stacking secure. Similarly, the contrast conditions are the same, both require that, for any participant set $X$ with $|X| \ge k$, if we denote $l_X = \max_{M \in C_0(X)} H(M)$ and denote $h_X = \min_{M \in C_1(X)} H(M)$, then it must hold that $0 \le l_X < h_X \le m$. On the other hand, the security conditions are different. The unconditional secure condition requires that $C_0[Y]$ and $C_1[Y]$ should contain the same matrices with the same frequencies for any participant set $Y$ with $|Y| \le k - 1$, while the stacking secure condition requires that the two multi-set of numbers $H(C_0[X])$ and $H(C_1[X])$ be the same for any participant set $Y$ with $|Y| \le k - 1$.

Formally, unconditional secure $(k, n)$-VCS is defined as follows:

**Definition 1.5** (*Unconditional Secure $(k, n)$-VCS*) The two collections of $n \times m$ Boolean matrices $(C_0, C_1)$ constitute an unconditional secure $(k, n)$-VCS if the following conditions hold:
(1) **Contrast**. For any participant set $X$ with $|X| \geq k$, we denote $l_X = max_{M \in C_0(X)} H(M)$ and denote $h_X = min_{M \in C_1(X)} H(M)$. It holds that $0 \leq l_X < h_X \leq m$.
(2) **Security**. For any participant set $Y$ with $|Y| \leq k - 1$, $C_0[Y]$ and $C_1[Y]$ contain the same matrices with the same frequencies.

Now, we formally give the definition of stacking secure $(k, n)$-VCS as follows:

**Definition 1.6** (*Stacking Secure $(k, n)$-VCS*) The two collections of $n \times m$ Boolean matrices $(C_0, C_1)$ constitute a stacking secure $(k, n)$-VCS if the following conditions hold:
(1) **Contrast**. For any participant set $X$ with $|X| \geq k$, we denote $l_X = max_{M \in C_0(X)} H(M)$ and denote $h_X = min_{M \in C_1(X)} H(M)$. It holds that $0 \leq l_X < h_X \leq m$.
(2) **Security**. For any participant set $Y$ with $|Y| \leq k - 1$, it holds that $H(C_0[Y]) = H(C_1[Y])$.

For $(k, n)$-VCS, the unconditional secure condition trivially implies the stacking secure condition. However, the following Lemma 1.2 shows that the converse does not hold.

**Lemma 1.2** *For $(k, n)$-VCS, the stacking secure condition does not imply the unconditional secure condition.*

Although the above two definitions of $(k, n)$-VCS have the same contrast condition, however, from the Lemma 1.2, we know that their security conditions are inequivalent. Hence we have the following Theorem 1.4.

**Theorem 1.4** *The Definition 1.5 of stacking secure $(k, n)$-VCS and the Definition 1.6 of unconditional secure $(k, n)$-VCS are inequivalent.*

*Example 1.2* The following two share matrix collections define a $(2, 2)$-VCS.

$$C_0 = \left\{ \begin{bmatrix} 0 & 0 & 1 & 0 \\ 0 & 0 & 1 & 0 \end{bmatrix}, \begin{bmatrix} 0 & 0 & 0 & 1 \\ 0 & 0 & 0 & 1 \end{bmatrix} \right\} \tag{1.9}$$

and

$$C_1 = \left\{ \begin{bmatrix} 1 & 0 & 0 & 0 \\ 0 & 1 & 0 & 0 \end{bmatrix}, \begin{bmatrix} 0 & 1 & 0 & 0 \\ 1 & 0 & 0 & 0 \end{bmatrix} \right\} \tag{1.10}$$

The above two collections satisfy the stacking secure condition, yet violate the unconditional secure condition.

In this section, we have examined the intuitive differences between the stacking secure condition and the unconditional secure condition. The generalizations to general access structure basis matrix VCS and general access structure SIVCS are given. At last, it is proved that the equivalence relationship does not hold for non-basis matrix $(k, n)$-VCS.

## 1.5  Step Construction of VCS

In this section, we present a step construction to construct $VCS_{OR}$ and $VCS_{XOR}$ for general access structure by applying $(2, 2)$-VCS recursively, where a participant may receive multiple share images [21, 27]. The step construction generates $VCS_{OR}$ and $VCS_{XOR}$ which have optimal pixel expansion and contrast for each qualified set in the general access structure in most cases [4]. Our scheme applies a technique to simplify the access structure, which reduces the average pixel expansion (APE) in most cases compared with many of the results in the literature.

### 1.5.1  Definition of Step Construction and Step Construction of $(n, n)$-VCS

Recall that $\Gamma_m$ and $\Gamma_M$ are the minimal qualified access structure and the maximal forbidden access structure of $(\Gamma_{Qual}, \Gamma_{Forb})$, respectively. The formal definition of step construction VCS is as follows:

**Definition 1.7** (*Step Construction*) Denote $\Gamma_m$ as an access structure on the participant set $V = \{1, 2, \ldots, n\}$. The step construction $\Gamma_m$-VCS exists if there exist values satisfying:
**Contrast**. Any qualified set of participants recovers the secret image by stacking (the "·" operation) their share images. More precisely, for any share images in a qualified set $Q = \{s_1, s_2, \ldots, s_p\} \in \Gamma_m$ with pixel expansion $m_1, m_2, \ldots, m_p$, respectively, let $m = \{m_1, m_2, \ldots, m_p\}$, then the adjusting stack (the "·" operation) of the share images $s_1, s_2, \ldots, s_p$ can recover the secret image. If the secret pixel is black, the adjusting stack (the "·" operation) of $\{s_1, s_2, \ldots, s_p\}$ is a vector $v$ that satisfies $w(v) \geq h_Q$, whereas for a white secret pixel, we have $w(v) < h_Q - \alpha_Q \cdot m$.
**Security**. Any forbidden set of participants has no information about the secret image. More precisely, for any forbidden set $F \subset M$, there exists a participant $i$, then the share images of set $F \bigcup \{i\}$, after being adjusted, form a VCS, where $F$ is a forbidden set of the VCS.

In Definition 1.7, because a qualified set of share images may have different pixel expansion when they are stacked, they should first be adjusted to the same size, i.e., the share images $s_1, s_2, \ldots, s_p$ should be expanded by replicating their sub-pixels for $(m/m_1, m/m_2, \ldots, m/m_p)$ times, respectively. The adjusting stack makes sense because the share images need to be stored, and only need to be expanded when used to recover the secret image. Apparently a smaller share image is more convenient to preserve. Furthermore, the VCS often carries important secret information, however, it does not provide authentication ability. Hence, the participants should authenticate other participants by using other authentication means. Therefore, it is reasonable to assume that the participants have authenticated each other before stacking their share images, i.e., they can know, in advance, the exact set of participants who are going to stack their shares. According to the step constructions (Constructions 1.1, 1.2, and 1.3), any participant can know, in advance, the size of other participants share images. This also implies the reasonableness of the adjusting stack.

In a traditional VCS, each participant takes one share image and all the share images have the same pixel expansion. However, each of the participants may take multiple share images with different pixel expansions. So, in the following part, we list the pixel expansions of all the share images for each participant. We compute the average pixel expansion (APE) as well, where the APE is defined as the average value of the total pixel expansions of the share images that each participant holds.

Particularly, for a set of participants $A$, we define the pixel expansion of $A$ as the largest pixel expansion of the share images of $A$. If $A$ is a qualified set, then define the contrast of $A$ as the contrast of the recovered secret image after adjusting stack.

The participants may have multiple share images, and different qualified sets of share images may result in different contrasts. So, in the following, we will list all the possible contrasts of the proposed VCS. For step construction of $(n, n)$-VCS, we start with a $(2, 2)$-VCS, and by taking one of its share images as the secret image of another $(2, 2)$-VCS, we get a $(3, 3)$-VCS; then we take one of the newly generated share images as the secret image of another $(2, 2)$-VCS, and so on, repeat the process $n-1$ times, and then get an $(n, n)$-VCS (Construction 1.1). The procedure is described by using the binary tree. We call such a binary tree the construction tree, and we call this kind of construction the step construction.

In a construction tree, once a $(2, 2)$-VCS is applied, we generate two new share images out of a "secret image" we call such a generation of share images the dividing generation. For example, the "secret image" $s_1^R$ is divided into two new share images $s_2^R$ and $s_2^{RR}$.

Because the construction tree depicts how to generate the share images precisely, hence in the Constructions 1.1, 1.2, and 1.3, we only provide the construction trees instead of the detailed text descriptions for explicit access structures.

Formally, we give the following step construction of $(n, n)$-VCS.

**Construction 1.1**   As the construction tree, we apply the traditional $(2, 2)$-VCS for $n - 1$ times which takes $s_1, s_1^R, s_2^{RR}, \ldots, s_{n-2}^{RR}$ as the secret images in turn, and distributes the $n$ share images $s_1^R, s_2^{RR}, \ldots, s_{n-1}^{R}, s_{n-2}^{RR}$ to the $n$ participants, respectively.

For the step construction of VCS, the share images of the $(n, n)$-VCS may not have the same pixel expansions. So, in the distribution phase, the dealer distributes the primary share images to the participants, and in the reconstruction phase, the participants adjust the smaller share images to the size of the largest share image before

**Fig. 1.5** An example of
(2, 2)-VCS

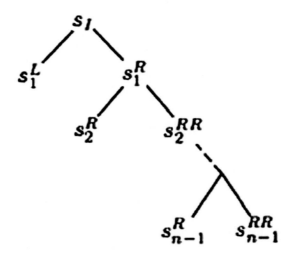

stacking. More precisely, the share images $s_1^R, s_2^R, \ldots, s_{n-2}^R$ should be expanded by times $2^{n-2}, \ldots, 2$, respectively (Fig. 1.5).

For the step construction of $\mathrm{VCS}_{XOR}$, because all the share images have the same pixel expansion, the participants do not need to adjust their share images.

It should be pointed out that the construction trees all satisfy that at most one of the two share images of a dividing generation is divided by other dividing generation, i.e., there does not exist the case that both of the share images of a dividing generation are divided by another dividing generation.

The reason why we do not divide both the share images of a dividing generation is to avoid the bad visual quality of the recovered secret image. In fact, if both the share images of a dividing generation are divided, then the newly generated share images will not satisfy the contrast condition of Definition 1.7 (or equivalently that of Definition 1.6) anymore, and the newly generated share images will form a probabilistic VC scheme (PVCS) [8, 14, 31]. However, the PVCS has bad visual quality of the recovered secret image, and Yang et al. has pointed out the phenomenon and given some simulations about the visual quality of PVCS.

**Theorem 1.5** *Construction 1.1 is a step construction of $(n, n)$-VCS which is realized by applying traditional (2, 2)-VCS recursively for several times. For $\mathrm{VCS}_{XOR}$, the pixel expansion for each share image is $m_{XOR} = 1$, and the APE of the $\mathrm{VCS}_{OR}$ is $\mathrm{APE}_{OR} = (3 \cdot 2^{n-1} - 2)/n$, and the contrast is $\alpha_{OR} = 2^{-(n-1)}$.*

From the theorem of step construction, for the $(n, n)$-$\mathrm{VCS}_{OR}$, it is easy to see that, the largest pixel expansion of the share images is $m_{OR} = 2^{n-1}$. The pixel expansion grows exponentially on the number of the participants $n$. However, it is still the optimal value [4].

**Theorem 1.6** *In any* $(n, n)$-*VCS*$_{OR}$ *and* $\alpha_{OR} \leq 1/2^{n-1}$ *and* $m_{OR} \geq 2^{n-1}$.

The Theorem 1.5 confirms the Theorem 1.6 after adjusting the size of the share images of Construction 1.1. For the $(n, n)$-VCS$_{XOR}$, according to the definition, it is obvious that $0 \leq \alpha_{XOR} \leq 1$ and $m_{XOR} \leq 1$. Hence, the step construction for the $(n, n)$-VCS also generates the VCS with optimal pixel expansion and optimal contrast [4, 18]. The above discussions are summarized as the following theorem:

**Theorem 1.7** *The step construction generates the* $(n, n)$-*VCS*$_{OR}$ *and* $(n, n)$-*VCS* $_{XOR}$ *with optimal pixel expansion and contrast.*

## *1.5.2 Simplifying the Access Structure by Using Equivalent Participants*

Now, we introduce the concept of equivalent participants (equivalent participants are viewed as the participants who have the same rights). Participant $i$ is equivalent to $j$ in a secret sharing scheme means that they are assigned to identical shares without affecting the access structure of the secret sharing scheme. Formally, we define the equivalent participants as follows:

**Definition 1.8** (*Equivalent Participants*) Denote $m$ as an access structure on participant set $V = \{1, 2, \ldots, m\}$. If participants $i$ and $j$ satisfy that, for $\forall B \in \Gamma_m, i \in B$ hold *iff* $j \in B$ hold, then participants $i$ and $j$ are called to be equivalent participants on $\Gamma_m$, denoted by $i \sim j$.

It is easy to verify that '$\sim$' is an equivalence relationship on $V$. Then we simplify the access structure based on the equivalent participants as follows:

**Definition 1.9** (*Simplified Access Structure*) Denote $m$ as an access structure on participant set $V = \{1, 2, \ldots, n\}$. Let $V$ be the quotient set of the equivalence relationship $\sim$. We call $\Gamma'_m = \{p \in V' : p \in A, A \in \Gamma_m\}$ the simplified access structure on $V'$, where $p'$ is the equivalence class of $p$ (simply we call $p'$ the corresponding participant of $p$, and the set $A'$ is called the corresponding set of $A$). When $\Gamma'_m = \Gamma_m$, we call $\Gamma_m$ the most simplified access structure.

Based on this point, we construct VCS for the most simplified access structure instead of the original access structure. To demonstrate how to simplify an access structure, we give the following example.

**Theorem 1.8** *Let* $\Gamma_m$ *be an access structure with equivalent participants on the participant set* $V$, *denote* $V'$ *as the quotient set* $V$ *of the equivalent relationship* $\sim$. *Let* $\tilde{\Gamma}'_m = \{\tilde{p} \in \tilde{V}' : p \in A, A \in \Gamma_m\}$, *we have that by distributing the share images of corresponding participants to the equivalent participants, a construction* $\tilde{\Gamma}_m$ *of VCS is also a construction of VCS for* $\Gamma_m$.

### 1.5.3 Step Construction of VCS for Access Structure $\Gamma_m = \{A_1, A_2, \ldots, A_r\}$ such that $A_1 \bigcap A_2 \bigcap \cdots \bigcap A_r = \{a_1, a_2, \ldots, a_r\} \neq \emptyset$

In this section, we give Construction 1.2 for the particular access structure $\Gamma_m = \{A_1, A_2, \ldots, A_r\}$ such that $A_1 \bigcap A_2 \bigcap \cdots \bigcap A_r = \{a_1, a_2, \ldots, a_r\} \neq \emptyset$, and then discuss its contrast and pixel expansion properties [27].

**Construction 1.2** For the access structure $\Gamma_m = \{A_1, A_2, \ldots, A_r\}$, where $A_1 \bigcap A_2 \bigcap \cdots \bigcap A_r = \{a_1, a_2, \ldots, a_r\} \neq \emptyset$, let $\Gamma' = \{A \backslash \{a_1, a_2, \ldots, a_r\}\}$ and denote $d_{max}$ as the maximum value of $|B|$ for all $B \in \Gamma'$, i.e., two methods (Methods 1.1 and 1.2) of step construction for the $\Gamma_m$ are depicted by the construction trees.

**Method 1.1** In the construction tree, the dealer distributes the share images $s_1^L, s_2^R, \ldots, s_t^R$ to the participants $a_1, a_2, \ldots, a_t$. For all $B \in \Gamma'$, if $|B| = 1$, distributes $s_t^{RR}$ to the participant in $B$, else for every $B$, let $d = |B|$, takes $s_t^{RR}$ as the secret image and generates the share images for $B$ (i.e., the sub-tree in the dashed box is changeable for the sets in $\Gamma'$), and distributes the share images of $s_{t+1}^L, s_{t+2}^R, \ldots, s_{t+d-1}^R$ and $s_{t+d-1}^{RR}$ to the participants in $B$.

**Method 1.2** In the construction tree, for the step construction based on the OR operation, in the left branch of the construction tree, the share image $s_{i+1}^L$ is obtained by expanding the share image $s_i^L$ to its double pixel expansion. For the XOR operation, the share image $s_{i+1}^L$ is identical to the share image $s_i^L$.

For all $B \in \Gamma'$, if $|B| = 1$, the dealer distributes $s_1^R$ to the participant in $B$, else for every $B$, let $d = |B|$, the dealer takes $s_1^R$ as the secret image and generates the share images for $B$ (i.e., the sub-tree in the dashed box is changeable for the sets in $\Gamma$), and distributes the share images of $s_2^R, \ldots, s_d^R$, and $s_d^{RR}$ to the participants in $B$. If $t = 1$, then it distributes share image $s_1^L$ to the participant $a_1$, else distributes the share images $s_{d_{max}+1}^L, \ldots, s_{d_{max}+t-1}^L$ and $s_{d_{max}+t-1}^{LL}$ to the participants $a_1, a_2, \ldots, a_t$.

It is clear that the step construction of $(n, n)$-VCS is just a special case of Construction 1.1.

Note that the participants $a_1, a_2, \ldots, a_t$ are distributed with only one share image, and the participants that appear in access structure $\Gamma'$ may be distributed with more than one share images. We will use the indexes of the participants, directly, in the construction trees. In such a case, it is easy to obtain the number of share images that are distributed to each participant by counting the number of times that each participant appears in the construction trees.

According to the two methods of step construction, we know that the pixel expansion of each share image is at most $2^{d_{max}+t-1}$. The difference between the two construction trees of Methods 1.1 and 1.2 is that, the construction tree of Method 1.1 first generates the share images for participants $a_1, a_2, \ldots, a_t$, whereas the construction tree of the Method 1.2 first generates the share images for the participants in $\Gamma'$.

Generally, a construction tree for a qualified set $A$ is a binary tree that contains all the share images that distributed to the participants in $A$. A construction tree for an access structure is a binary tree with several changeable sub-trees.

According to the construction tree of Method 1.2, we define another way of generating share images, called the transmitting generation, where the information of a share image is duplicated to another share image with or without pixel expansion.

Together with the dividing generation, we have two ways of generating share images in the construction trees. Note that the dividing generation generates at least one share image that will be distributed to the participants, and the transmitting generation does not generate share images that will be distributed to the participants.

In light of the above discussions, we have the following Theorem 1.9.

**Theorem 1.9** *Construction 1.2 is a step construction of VCS for the access structure* $m = \{A_1, A_2, \ldots, A_r\}$ *such that* $A_1 \cap A_2 \cap \cdots \cap A_r = \{a_1, a_2, \ldots, a_r\} \neq \emptyset$, *which is implemented by applying traditional (2, 2)-VCS recursively.*

We then discuss the pixel expansion and contrast properties of the $\text{VCS}_{XOR}$ and $\text{VCS}_{OR}$ that constructed by the step construction of Methods 1.1 and 1.2.

For the $\text{VCS}_{OR}$, for any qualified set $A \in \Gamma_m$, there is a corresponding construction tree. Note that the share images that are distributed to the participants of $A$ are all the leaves of the construction tree. Because both the transmitting generation and dividing generation expand the share image to twice its original size, denote $h$ as the height of the construction tree, then the pixel expansion of $A$ is $m_{OR} = 2^{h-1}$. Because the dividing generation applies the (2, 2)-VCS which reduces the contrast of the recovered image to the half of its original value, and the transmitting generation does not affect the contrast of the recovered image, when we denote the number of dividing generations in the construction tree of $A$ as $n_d$, we have that the value of contrast of the recovered secret image by adjusting stack the share images $A$ of is $\alpha_{OR} = 2^{-n_d}$. For the $\text{VCS}_{XOR}$, similar to the above discussion, the pixel expansion of all the share images is equal to $m_{XOR} = 1$, and the contrast is $\alpha_{XOR} = 1$.

In light of the above discussion, we get the following Theorem 1.10.

**Theorem 1.10** *The step construction of Construction 1.2 generates VCS with the following pixel expansion and contrast.*

For the step construction of Method 1.1, the values of pixel expansion and contrast are optimal for each qualified set of both for the $\text{VCS}_{XOR}$ and $\text{VCS}_{OR}$; i.e., for any qualified set $A \in \Gamma_m$, the pixel expansion and contrast of $A$ satisfy that $m_{XOR} = 1$, $\alpha_{XOR} = 1$ and $m_{OR} = 2^{|A|-1}$, $\alpha_{OR} = 2^{-(|A|-1)}$ [7].

For the step construction of Method 1.2, we have the following:

(1) The values of pixel expansion and contrast are optimal for each qualified set in $\Gamma_m$ for the $\text{VCS}_{XOR}$, i.e., for any qualified set $A \in \Gamma_m$, the pixel expansion and contrast of $A$ satisfy $m_{XOR} = 1$ and $\alpha_{XOR} = 1$.
(2) The value of contrast is optimal for each qualified set in $\Gamma_m$ for the $\text{VCS}_{OR}$, i.e., for any qualified set $A \in \Gamma_m$, the contrast of $A$ satisfies $\alpha_{OR} = 2^{-(|A|-1)}$.

(3) The value of pixel expansion is optimal for the maximum qualified set of $\Gamma_m$ for the VCS$_{OR}$, i.e., let $A$ be a maximum qualified set of $\Gamma_m$, the pixel expansion of $A$ satisfies $m_{OR} = 2^{|A|-1}$.

From Theorem 1.10 it is noted that, Method 1.2 may not always generate optimal pixel expansion for each qualified set in $\Gamma_m$-VCS$_{OR}$. However, Method 1.2 is still useful, because Method 1.2 generated VCS with smaller APE in some cases.

Recall that the APE of VCS$_{OR}$ is defined as the average value of the total pixel expansions of the share images each participant holds. Define the multi-set $D = \{|B| : B \in \Gamma'\}$; denoting $APE_1$ and $APE_2$ as the $APE$ of Methods 1.1 and 1.2 respectively, we have,

$$APE_1 = \frac{1}{n}\left[\sum_{n=1}^{t} 2^i + \sum_{d\in D} 2^{t+d-1} + \sum_{i=t+1}^{t+d-1} 2^i\right] \tag{1.11}$$

and

$$APE_2 = \frac{1}{n}\left[2^{d_{max}+t-1} + 2^{d_{max}}\sum_{i=1}^{t-1} 2^i + \sum_{d\in D}\left(2^d + \sum_{i=2}^{d} 2^i\right)\right] \tag{1.12}$$

The above values of $APE_1$ and $APE_2$ are easily verified since they are the sum of the pixel expansion of the leaves in the construction trees.

Hence, for different $t$, $d_{max}$ and $D$, the dealer chooses the method with APE$_{OR}$ = $min$ (APE$_1$, APE$_2$) according to different requirements.

### 1.5.4 Step Construction of VCS for General Access Structure

In this section, we give the step construction of VCS for general access structure based on the access structure simplifying technique and Construction 1.2.

Note that a general access structure $\Gamma_m$ is divided into several parts where each part has the form $\Gamma_i = \{A_1, A_2, \ldots, A_{r_i}\}$ such that $A_1 \cap A_2 \cap \cdots \cap A_{r_i} = \{a_1, a_2, \ldots, a_t\} \neq \emptyset$, i.e., each part satisfies the condition of Construction 1.2. Hence, each part is constructed by applying Construction 1.2. However, in order to construct a step construction of VCS with smaller APE, we also need to apply the access structure simplifying technique.

**Construction 1.3** For a general access structure $\Gamma_m$, the dealer generates the construction trees of the step construction of $m$-VCS by executing the following steps:

**Step 1.** Simplify $\Gamma_m$ to $\Gamma'_m$ according to Theorem 1.4;
**Step 2.** Divide $\Gamma'_m$ into several parts with each part being in the form $\Gamma_i = \{A_1, A_2, \ldots, A_{r_i}\}$ such that $A_1 \cap A_2 \cap \cdots \cap A_{r_i} = \{a_1, a_2, \ldots, a_t\} \neq \emptyset$;
**Step 3.** For each part, let $\Gamma_i = \{A\backslash\{a_1, a_2, \ldots, a_t\} : A \in \Gamma_i\}$ and $\Gamma''_i = \{B \in \Gamma'_i : |B| \neq 1\}$. If $\Gamma''_i \neq \emptyset$, then apply Construction 1.2 directly on $\Gamma_i$, and the construction

is done, else treat $\Gamma_i''$ as a participant $i'$ in $\Gamma_i$, by applying Construction 1.2, we have two cases:

**Case 1.** If Method 1.1 of Construction 1.2 is used, denote the share image that distributed to $i'$ as $s_i'$, go to step 1 for a new step construction of VCS, which takes $s_i'$ as the secret image, for the access structure $\Gamma_i''$.

**Case 2.** If Method 1.2 of Construction 1.2 is used, denote the share image that distributed to $i'$ as $s_i'$, and denote $d_{max}$ as the cardinality of the maximum set of $\Gamma_i''$, i.e., $d_{max} = max\{|A| : A \in \Gamma_i''\}$. We insert $d_{max} - 1$ transmitting generations between the secret image and the sub-tree corresponding to the participant set $\{a_1, a_2, \ldots, a_t\}$, and go to step 1 for a new step construction of VCS, which takes $s_i'$ as the secret image, for the access structure $\Gamma_i''$.

**Step 4.** Repeat Steps 1, 2, and 3 until all the participants receive their share images for all the qualified sets in $\Gamma_m$.

*Remark 1.1* In Construction 1.3, we call the participant $i'$ and the share image $s_i'$ the virtual participant and virtual share image, respectively.

Because Theorem 1.10 simplifies the access structure $\Gamma_m$, step 1 reduces the number of qualified sets in $\Gamma_m$, and hence reduces the number of dividing generations in the construction trees of Construction 1.3.

In Step 2, since each part of $\Gamma_m'$ satisfies the condition of Constructions 1.2 and 1.3 seems to terminate at Step 2. However, in order to obtain a smaller APE, the dealer needs to further divide each $\Gamma_i''$, i.e., Construction 1.3 needs to be recursively applied until all the participants receive their share images for all the qualified sets in $\Gamma_m$.

As a summary, we give the following Theorem 1.11.

**Theorem 1.11** *Construction 1.3 is a step construction of VCS for general access structure $\Gamma_m$, which is implemented by applying traditional (2, 2)-VCS recursively.*

Then we consider the pixel expansion and contrast properties of the $\Gamma_m$-VCS generated by applying Construction 1.3; we give the following Theorem 1.12:

**Theorem 1.12** *The step construction of Construction 1.3 generates VCS with pixel expansion and contrast as follows.*

If only Method 1.1 of Construction 1.2 is used in Construction 1.3, then the values of pixel expansion and contrast are optimal for each qualified set of $\Gamma_m$ both for the $VCS_{XOR}$ and $VCS_{OR}$, i.e., for any qualified set $A \in \Gamma_m$, the pixel expansion and contrast of $A$ satisfy $m_{XOR} = 1$, $\alpha_{XOR} = 1$ and $m_{OR} = 2^{|A|-1}$, $\alpha_{XOR} = 2^{-(|A|-1)}$.

Once Method 1.1 of Construction 1.2 is used in Construction 1.3, then:

(1) The values of pixel expansion and contrast are optimal for each qualified set in $\Gamma_m$ for the $VCS_{XOR}$, i.e., for any qualified set $A \in \Gamma_m$, the pixel expansion and contrast of $A$ satisfy $m_{XOR} = 1$, $\alpha_{XOR} = 1$.

(2) The value of contrast is optimal for each qualified set in $\Gamma_m$ for the $VCS_{OR}$, i.e., for any qualified set $A \in \Gamma_m$, the contrast of $A$ satisfies $\alpha_{OR} = 2^{-(|A|-1)}$.

(3) The value of pixel expansion is optimal for the maximum qualified set of $\Gamma_m$ for the VCS$_{OR}$, i.e., let $A$ be a maximum qualified set of $\Gamma_m$, the pixel expansion of $A$ satisfies $m_{OR} = 2^{|A|-1}$.

According to the step construction, the VCS with general access structure [1] is constructed by only applying (2, 2)-VCS recursively, regardless of whether the underlying operation is OR or XOR, where a participant may receive multiple share images. This result is most interesting, because the construction of VCS for general access structure has never been claimed to be possible before. The presented construction generates optimal VCS [5] and VCS for each qualified set in $\Gamma_m$, and our schemes also reduce the APE in most cases compared with the known results in the literature. However, how to efficiently partition the access structure to reduce the APE to the minimum remains as an open problem.

## 1.6 Exercises

(1) Give an example to show that the equivalence of unconditional secure basis matrix $(k, n)$-VCS and stacking secure basis matrix $(k, n)$-VCS.
(2) Prove the Theorem 1.1.
(3) Explain the physical meaning of the NS contrast and compare it with other definitions.
(4) Please make use of the step construction method in this chapter to get $(k, n)$-VCS and use an algorithm to describe the steps.

## References

1. Ateniese G, Blundo C, Santis AD, Stinson DR (1996) Visual cryptography for general access structures. Inf Comput 129:86–106
2. Blundo C, Santis AD, Stinson DR (1999) On the contrast in visual cryptography schemes. J Cryptol 12(4):261–289
3. Blundo C, Bonis AD, Santis AD (2001) Improved schemes for visual cryptography. Des Codes Cryptogr 24:255–278
4. Blundo C, D'Arco P, Santis AD, Stinson DR (2003) Contrast optimal threshold visual cryptography schemes. SIAM J Discret Math 16(2):224–261
5. Bose M, Mukerjee R (2006) Optimal (2, $n$) visual cryptographic schemes. Des Codes Cryptogr 40:55–267
6. Bose M, Mukerjee R (2010) Optimal $(k, n)$ visual cryptographic schemes for general $k$. Des Codes Cryptogr 55:19–35
7. Cimato S, Santis AD, Ferrara AL, Masucci B (2005) Ideal contrast visual cryptography schemes with reversing. Inf Process Lett 93:199–206
8. Cimato S, Prisco RD, Santis AD (2006) Probabilistic visual cryptography schemes. Comput J 49(1):97–107
9. Ciou CB, Yang CN (2010) Image secret sharing method with two-decoding-options: lossless recovery and previewing capability. Image Vis Comput 28(12):1600–1610

10. Droste S (1996) New results on visual cryptography. In: CRYPTO '96. LNCS, vol 1109. Springer, Berlin, pp 401–415
11. Eisen PA, Stinson DR (2002) Threshold visual cryptography schemes with specified whiteness levels of reconstructed pixels. Des Codes Cryptogr 25:15–61
12. Horng GB, Chen TH, Tsai DS (2006) Cheating in visual cryptography. Des Codes Cryptogr 38:219–236
13. Hou YC, Tu CF (2004) Visual cryptography techniques for colour images without pixel expansion. J Inf Technol Soc 1:95–110
14. Hou YC, Xu CS (2003) A probability-based optimization model for sharing multiple secret images without pixel expansion. J Inf Technol Soc 2:19–38
15. Hu CM, Tzeng WG (2007) Cheating prevention in visual cryptography. IEEE Trans Image Process 16(1):36–45
16. Ito R, Kuwakado H, Tanaka H (1999) Image size invariant visual cryptography. IEICE Trans Fundam Electron Commun Comput Sci E82-A(10):2172–2177
17. Koga H (2002) A general formula of the $(t, n)$-threshold visual secret sharing scheme. In: ASIACRYPT '2002. LNCS vol 2501. Springer, Berlin, pp 328–345
18. Krause M, Simon HU (2003) Determining the optimal contrast for secret sharing schemes in visual cryptography. Comb Probab Comput 12(3):285–299
19. Liu F (2009) Designs of visual cryptography schemes (Ph.D. thesis). Chinese Academy of Sciences, Beijing
20. Liu F, Wu CK, Lin XJ (2009) The alignment problem of visual cryptography schemes. Des Codes Cryptogr 50:215–227
21. Liu F, Wu CK, Lin XJ (2010) Step construction of visual cryptography schemes. IEEE Trans Inf Forensics Secur 5(1):27–38
22. Naor M, Shamir A (1995) Visual cryptography. In: EUROCRYPT '94. LNCS, vol 950. Springer, Berlin, pp 1–12
23. Prisco RD, Santis AD (2006) Cheating immune $(2, n)$-threshold visual secret sharing. LNCS. Springer, Berlin 4116:216–228
24. Tsai DS, Chen TH, Horng GB (2007) A cheating prevention scheme for binary visual cryptography with homogeneous secret images. Pattern Recognit 40:2356–2366
25. Tuyls P, Hollmann HDL, Lint JH, Tolhuizen L (2005) XOR-based visual cryptography schemes. Des Codes Cryptogr 37:169–186
26. Tzeng WG, Hu CM (2002) A new approach for visual cryptography. Des Codes Cryptogr 27:207–227
27. Verheul E, Tilborg HV (1997) Constructions and properties of $k$ out of $n$ visual secret sharing schemes. Des Codes Cryptogr 11(2):179–196
28. Wang ZM, Arce GR, Crescenzo GD (2009) Halftone visual cryptography via error diffusion. IEEE Trans Inf Forensics Secur 4(3):383–396
29. Yang CN, Chen TS (2006) New size-reduced visual secret sharing schemes with half reduction of shadow size. IEICE Trans Fundam E89-A(2):620–625
30. Yang CN, Chen TS (2007) Visual secret sharing scheme: prioritizing the secret pixels with different pixel expansions to enhance the image contrast. Opt Eng 46(9):097005
31. Yang CN, Chen TS (2008) Colored visual cryptography scheme based on additive colour mixing. Pattern Recognit 41:3114–3129
32. Yang CN, Chung TH (2010) A general multi-secret visual cryptography scheme. Opt Commun 283(24):4949–4962

# Chapter 2
# Various Problems in Visual Cryptography

## 2.1 Alignment Problems

Pixel expansion is an important parameter for Visual Cryptography Schemes (VCS) [11, 25, 32, 33]. However, most research in the literature is dedicated to reduce pixel expansion at pixel level [34], i.e., to reduce number of subpixels that represent a pixel in original secret image. It is quite insufficient since final size of the transparencies of the VCS is affected not only by number of the subpixels, but also by size of the subpixels in the transparencies. However, reducing the size of the subpixels in transparencies is due to difficulties of the transparencies alignment [29, 34].

We notice that, final goal of reducing the pixel expansion is to reduce size of the transparencies that are distributed to the participants [34], because smaller transparencies are easier to be transported. However, the subpixels that are printed on the transparencies affect the final size of the transparencies, in fact, size of the transparencies is the product of size of the subpixels and number of the subpixels in each transparency. Unfortunately, there is a dilemma when one tries to determine the size of the subpixels: when the subpixel size is large, it is easy to align the shares (most publications in the literature require alignment of the shares precisely in the decrypting phase), but large subpixel size will lead to large transparencies. On the other hand, when the subpixel size is small, it is relatively hard to align the shares. From the viewpoint of VCS participants, the goal is to align the shares easily and have small transparencies as well. Table 2.1 shows the relationship between size of the subpixels of the transparencies and the ease to align them from experiential viewpoint.

In this chapter, we take the alignment problem of VCS into consideration [29], and prove that in order to visually recover the original secret image, it is not necessary to align the transparencies precisely. This study is restricted to the case when only one transparency is shifted.

© Springer International Publishing Switzerland 2015
F. Liu and W.Q. Yan, *Visual Cryptography for Image
Processing and Security*, DOI 10.1007/978-3-319-23473-1_2

**Table 2.1** The advantages and disadvantages of different sizes of the subpixels printed on the transparencies

| Size of subpixels | Advantages | Disadvantages |
| --- | --- | --- |
| Larger | Easier to align | Larger transparencies size |
| Smaller | Smaller transparencies size | Hard to align |

## 2.1.1 Precise Alignment of VCS

The shares of visual cryptography are printed on transparencies which need to be superimposed [12, 21, 23, 25, 31, 39, 40]. However, it is not very easy to do precise superposition due to the fine resolution as well as printing noise [39]. Furthermore, many visual cryptography applications need to print shares on paper in which case scanning of the share is necessary [40]. The print and scan process can introduce noise as well which can make the alignment difficult [22, 34]. In this section, we consider the problem of precise alignment printed and scanned visual cryptography shares. Due to the vulnerabilities in the spatial domain [13], we have developed a frequency domain alignment scheme. We employ the Walsh transform [1] to embed marks in both of the shares so as to find the alignment position of these shares.

Visual cryptography possesses these characteristics:

- Perfect security.
- Decryption (secret restoration) without the aid of a computing device.
- Robustness against lossy compression and distortion due to its binary attribute.

However, the shortcomings of visual cryptography are as salient as its merits. There are three main drawbacks in visual cryptography:

- It results in a loss of resolution [39]. The restored secret image has a resolution lower than that of the original secret image.
- Its original formulation is restricted to binary images [3–8, 24, 27, 36–38]. For color images, some additional processing such as halftoning and color separation are required [6, 14–16, 18, 19, 36].
- The superposition of two shares is not easy to perform unless some special alignment marks are provided. The manual alignment procedure can be tedious especially for high resolution images [39].

We will focus on the third problem in this section. The shares of VC printed on transparencies are very difficult to be overlapped with proper alignment even if we ignore the printing errors. A wide variety of applications of visual cryptography would require the printing of the shares on paper like that of documents, checks, tickets or cards. In such cases, scanning of the printed shares is inevitable for restoring the secret. The scanned shares (with printing, handling, and scanning errors) have to be superimposed in order to reconstruct the secret image which could be a photo, code or other such important information.

**Fig. 2.1** Cross alignment for
basic visual cryptography

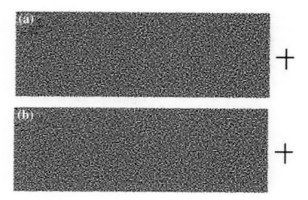

In this section, we concentrate on the print and scan applications of visual cryptography, i.e., to obtain the precise position of scanned shares which requires rotation
and alignment correction. Putting alignment marks in the spatial domain is extremely
vulnerable to cropping and editing. Therefore, we use the Walsh transform [1] domain
to embed perceptually invisible alignment marks. We show that the Walsh transform
helps in recovering the marks in spite of noise and we can precisely align the scanned
shares to recover the secret.

In order to carry out the superposition, initially a spatial tag is marked beside
the shares. In Fig. 2.1, we put a cross beside each share. For restoring the secret,
the two crosses need to be precisely overlapped. If this is done, the secret image
will be revealed. Another solution to this problem is by utilizing the extended visual
cryptography scheme [2, 21]. This scheme shares a secret by using two protection
images $B$ and $C$. The procedure of visual cryptography is performed as: $A = B' \bigoplus C'$
where the secret $A$ is divided into two shares $B'$ and $C'$ using VCS scheme. On these
shares $B'$ and $C'$, images $B$, and $C$ are also visible. During restoration, images $B$
and $C$ are aligned to make them disappear (by cancelling) revealing the secret in
the process. An example of this technique is shown in Fig. 2.2, the cross beside the
shares is the marks in Fig. 2.1.

Actually, Figs. 2.1 and 2.2 belong to the same class of techniques since they both
work in the spatial domain. The problem with this class is that the alignment marks are
visible to an attacker and thus can be easily removed by cropping or localized image
alteration. We therefore explore the alternative idea of using marks in the frequency
domain. In particular, we consider the use of the discrete Walsh transform [1], which
is useful for pulse signals and is distinct from the discrete fourier transform (DFT),
discrete cosine transform (DCT) and discrete wavelet transform (DWT) [1]. Walsh
functions are a complete set of orthogonal functions with the value being only $-1$
and 1. We use the 2D discrete Walsh transform:

$$\omega_{xy}(u, v) = \frac{1}{N_x} \frac{1}{N_y} \sum_{x=0}^{N_x-1} \sum_{y=0}^{N_y-1} f(x, y) \cdot (-1)^\alpha \qquad (2.1)$$

**Fig. 2.2** Cross alignment by
using extended visual
cryptography

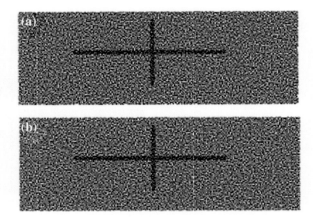

$$f(x, y) = \sum_{u=0}^{N_x-1} \sum_{v=0}^{N_y-1} \omega_{xy}(u, v) \cdot (-1)^\alpha \tag{2.2}$$

$$\alpha = \sum_{r=0}^{P_s-1} x_r \cdot u_r + \sum_{s=0}^{P_t-1} y_s \cdot v_s \tag{2.3}$$

where $f(x, y)$ is a pixel value of the image, $(x, y)$ is its position, $\omega_{xy}(u, v)$ represents the transform coefficients, $N_x = 2^{P_x}$, $N_y = 2^{P_y}$, ($P_x$ and $P_y$ are positive integers), $x_r$, $u_r$, $y_s$ and $v_s$ are either 0 or 1 (i.e., one bit of $x$, $u$, $y$, and $v$, respectively).

Unlike the Walsh transform [1], transforms [1] like DFT, DCT, and DWT are mainly used for continuous tone color images [15, 16, 18]. The results of applying these three transformations to a VC share is shown Fig. 2.3. In Fig. 2.3, the left image is a VC share. The subsequent images show the result of applying the Walsh, DCT and the DFT transforms. The differences are quite apparent. Note that the bottom-left rectangle of the image for the Walsh transform is totally dark. This information can be exploited in removing noises by filtering the coefficients in this quadrant.

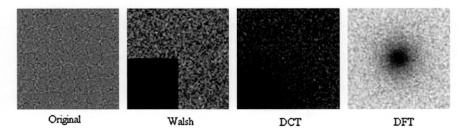

Original              Walsh                DCT                 DFT

**Fig. 2.3** The original shares and their transformations

**Fig. 2.4** Adjustment of
visual cryptography shares

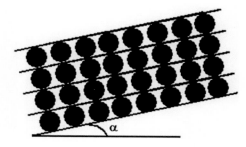

**Fig. 2.5** The shift operation
to the overlapping shares

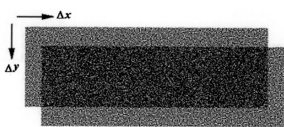

In this section, we will describe our contributions. During encryption, we apply the Walsh transform on the shares. Then we embed marks in the high frequency coefficients of the transform. Then the inverse transform is applied to obtain the new shares with hidden marks that are printed on paper to be transmitted via public channels.

During the process of decryption, we scan the paper image and extract the marks by performing the Walsh transform to obtain the approximate alignment for shares superimposition. We then fine-tune the alignment by performing rotation and translation. The rotation is done by using Figs. 2.4 and 2.5.

The rotation adjustment in increments of angle $\alpha$ is done as shown in Fig. 2.4. The translation adjustment by $x$ and $y$ is done as shown in Fig. 2.5. The criteria for finding the best alignment position are that the superimposed image should have the least number of black pixels if we perform the XOR operation between them. This is because the XOR operation allows for perfect restoration of the secret image.

Figure 2.6 shows a share and the mark in the Walsh transform domain. The mark is in the form of a cross. Figure 2.7 is an example of a scanned marked share. Figure 2.8 shows the minimization of black pixels when the correct alignment is obtained.

## 2.1.2 Visual Alignment of VCS

We found that, the precise alignment of small subpixels is not critical [29]. The secret image can still be recovered visually even if the participants do not align

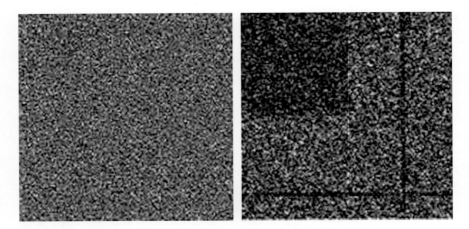

**Fig. 2.6**  Marked VC share in Walsh transform domain

**Fig. 2.7**  The scanned
watermarked VC shares

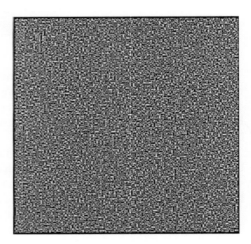

the transparencies precisely. This phenomenon helps to determine the size of the
subpixels printed on the transparencies.

The usual way of tackling the alignment problem of the VCS is by adding frames
to the shares [29]. To align the shares one just needs to align the frames. Another
study employs the Walsh transform to embed marks in both of the shares so as to find
the alignment position of these shares. However, both the two methods need to align
the transparencies precisely. Besides, Kobara and Imai calculated the visible space
when viewing the transparencies. The results are somehow related to the alignment
problem, but not exactly.

According to the traditional view, the subpixels of the transparencies should be
aligned precisely, however, in this study, we point out that, to recover the secret image
visually, it is not necessary to align the subpixels precisely. We will show that, by

**Fig. 2.8** Number of black
pixels at various alignments

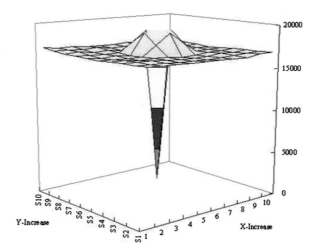

shifting one of the shares by a number (at most $m - 1$) of subpixels to the right (resp.
left), one can still recover the secret image visually, for the reason that the average
contrast $\tilde{\alpha} \neq 0$ [3, 22]. This result can naturally be extended to the case when more
than one share is shifted. However we leave the numerical analysis of this case as an
open problem. So, in this chapter, we will only consider the case with only one share
(transparency) being shifted by some number of subpixels. And we call the scheme
with a share being shifted the shifted scheme, the basis matrices and share matrices
of the shifted scheme are called the shifted basis matrices and shifted share matrices.

Generally, we aim at proving the conclusion that, the shifted scheme can visually
recover the original secret image based on the $(k, n)$-VCS. However, it is noticed
that this proof can be reduced to the proof based on the $(2, 2)$-VCS in the case that
only one share is shifted. The reason is as follows:

First, a $(k, n)$-DVCS consists of $\binom{n}{k}$ $(k, k)$-VCS. For a set of $k$ shares, if no share
is shifted, then the $k$ shares can recover the secret image obviously. And because
we only consider the case when only one of the $n$ shares is shifted, we only need to
consider the $k$ shares that contain the shifted share, i.e., we only need to prove our
conclusion based on a $(k, k)$-VCS.

Second, denote the $k$ shares of a $(k, k)$-VCS as $s_1, s_2, \ldots, s_k$, without loss of
generality, let $s_k$ be the share that is shifted, and let $s_k$ be the resulting image of
stacking the remaining $k - 1$ shares $s_1, s_2, \ldots, s_{k-1}$ together. Then, the scheme
becomes a $(2, 2)$-VCS, where the two shares are $s_k'$ and $s_k$. Note that the stacking
result of this $(2, 2)$-VCS is the same as that of the previous $(k, k)$-DVCS. The previous
$(k, k)$-VCS can visually recover the secret image if and only if $s_k'$ and $s_k$ can do so.
Hence, it is sufficient to prove the conclusion based on a $(2, 2)$-VCS.

We analyze the structure of the basis matrix of the (2, 2)-VCS. Denote $M_0$ and $M_1$ as the basis matrices of the (2, 2)-VCS, then the $M_0$ and $M_1$, without loss of generality, are in the following form:

$$M_0 = \begin{pmatrix} \underbrace{1 \cdots 1}_{a} \underbrace{0 \cdots 0}_{b} \underbrace{1 \cdots 1}_{c} \underbrace{0 \cdots 0}_{d} \\ \underbrace{1 \cdots 1}_{} \underbrace{0 \cdots 0}_{} \underbrace{0 \cdots 0}_{} \underbrace{1 \cdots 1}_{} \end{pmatrix} \qquad (2.4)$$

and

$$M_1 = \begin{pmatrix} \underbrace{1 \cdots 1}_{a'} \underbrace{0 \cdots 0}_{b'} \underbrace{1 \cdots 1}_{c'} \underbrace{0 \cdots 0}_{d'} \\ \underbrace{1 \cdots 1}_{} \underbrace{0 \cdots 0}_{} \underbrace{0 \cdots 0}_{} \underbrace{1 \cdots 1}_{} \end{pmatrix} \qquad (2.5)$$

where $a, b, c, d, a', b', c'$ and $d'$ are nonnegative integers satisfying $a + c + d = l$ and $a' + c' + d' = h$. According to the contrast and security property of Definition 1 [3], we have,

$$\begin{cases} a + b + c + d = a' + b' + c' + d' \\ a + c = a' + c' \\ a + d = a' + d' \\ b > b' \end{cases} \qquad (2.6)$$

solving the above system, we get $a - a' = b - b' = c - c' = d - d'$. Let $e = b - b'$, hence by deleting identical columns of $M_0$ and $M_1$, we get,

$$M_0' = \begin{pmatrix} \underbrace{1 \cdots 1}_{e} \underbrace{0 \cdots 0}_{e} \\ \underbrace{1 \cdots 1}_{} \underbrace{0 \cdots 0}_{} \end{pmatrix} \qquad (2.7)$$

$$M_1' = \begin{pmatrix} \underbrace{1 \cdots 1}_{e} \underbrace{0 \cdots 0}_{e} \\ \underbrace{0 \cdots 0}_{} \underbrace{1 \cdots 1}_{} \end{pmatrix} \qquad (2.8)$$

where the number of columns in $M_0$ and $M_1$ is $2e$.

Now we know that the basis matrices of an arbitrary (2, 2)-VCS $M_0$ and $M_1$ contain the same number of identical columns $\binom{1}{1}$, $\binom{1}{0}$, $\binom{0}{1}$, $\binom{0}{0}$ apart from the submatrices $M_0'$ and $M_1'$, Hence, without loss of generality, they can be represented as the following form:

$$M_0 = \begin{pmatrix} \underbrace{1 \cdots 1}_{a'} \underbrace{0 \cdots 0}_{b'} \underbrace{1 \cdots 1}_{c} \underbrace{0 \cdots 0}_{d} \underbrace{1 \cdots 1}_{e} \underbrace{0 \cdots 0}_{e} \\ \underbrace{1 \cdots 1}_{} \underbrace{0 \cdots 0}_{} \underbrace{0 \cdots 0}_{} \underbrace{1 \cdots 1}_{} \underbrace{1 \cdots 1}_{} \underbrace{0 \cdots 0}_{} \end{pmatrix} \qquad (2.9)$$

and

$$M_1 = \begin{pmatrix} \underbrace{1 \cdots 1}_{a'} & \underbrace{0 \cdots 0}_{b'} & \underbrace{1 \cdots 1}_{c} & \underbrace{0 \cdots 0}_{d} & \underbrace{1 \cdots 1}_{e} & \underbrace{0 \cdots 0}_{e} \\ \underbrace{1 \cdots 1}_{a'} & \underbrace{0 \cdots 0}_{b'} & \underbrace{0 \cdots 0}_{c} & \underbrace{1 \cdots 1}_{d} & \underbrace{0 \cdots 0}_{e} & \underbrace{1 \cdots 1}_{e} \end{pmatrix} \qquad (2.10)$$

Let $m$ be the pixel expansion, then it is obvious that $m = a' + b' + c + d + 2e$. The collections $C_0$ and $C_1$ contain all the permutations of the basis matrices $M_0$ and $M_1$, and hence each has $m!$ share matrices.

The shifted scheme is generated as follows.

Shift the second row of the $m!$ share matrices in $C_0$ (resp. $C_1$) to the left (resp. right) by $r$ subpixels, and let $c_1, c_2, \ldots, c_r$ be the $r$-bit string that is shifted in, where each $c_i \in \{0, 1\}$ represents a subpixel. By the above discussion, we get $m!$ shifted share matrices for $C_0$ (resp. $C_1$). Take the share matrix $M_0 \in C_0$ as an example, then the shifted share matrix, denoted by $M_0^{(r)}$, is as follows:

$$M_0^{(r)} = \begin{pmatrix} * \cdots * & \underbrace{1 \cdots 1}_{a'} & \underbrace{0 \cdots 0}_{b'} & \underbrace{1 \cdots 1}_{c} & \underbrace{0 \cdots 0}_{d} & \underbrace{1 \cdots 1}_{e} & 0 \cdots 0 \\ \underbrace{1 \cdots 1}_{a'} & \underbrace{0 \cdots 0}_{b'} & \underbrace{0 \cdots 0}_{c} & \underbrace{1 \cdots 1}_{d} & \underbrace{1 \cdots 1}_{e} & \underbrace{0 \cdots 0}_{e} & \underbrace{c_1 \cdots c_r}_{r} \end{pmatrix} \qquad (2.11)$$

where $c_1, c_2, \ldots, c_r$ of share 2 are the adjacent subpixels of the right pixel that are shifted in. By going through all $m!$ share matrices of $C_0$ and $C_1$ and all the possible string of subpixels $c_1, c_2, \ldots, c_r \in \{0, 1\}^r$, where $\{0, 1\}^r$ is the set of all the binary strings of length $r$, the shifted scheme is generated. Hence, we have:

**Theorem 2.1** *The shifted scheme of a VCS is a PVCS, where the average contrast of the shifted scheme is $\bar{\alpha} = \frac{-(m-r)e}{m^2(m-1)}$, $1 \leq r \leq m - 1$ is the number of subpixels by which the share 2 (the second share) is shifted.*

Note that after a shift, the value of the average contrast is negative $\bar{\alpha} < 0$, which means that the recovered secret image is the complementary image of the original one, and the absolute value of $\bar{\alpha}$ reflects how clear the image can be viewed visually.

The above theorem shows that in order to align the transparencies when decrypting the VCS, one does not need to align the transparencies precisely. So, when the participants of a VCS want to align the transparencies, for example, the transparencies in the Example 3.1, they can first align the transparencies precisely in the vertical direction, and then move the second transparencies to the right then to the left in the horizontal direction. Then, they will get the recovered secret image for three times. Furthermore, this phenomenon also helps to determine the size of the subpixels printed on the transparencies.

In order to reduce the size of transparencies, one needs to reduce not only the pixel expansion, but also the size of each subpixel in the transparencies [7]. However, smaller size of subpixels results in more difficulties when aligning the transparencies together. We study the alignment problem of the VCS [29], and proved that, the original secret image can be recovered visually when one of the transparencies is

shifted by at most $m - 1$ subpixels, and the average contrast becomes a $\bar{\alpha} = \frac{-(m-r)e}{m^2(m-1)}$.
Our study is based on a DVCS, and the shifted scheme is a PVCS with less contrast
but still visible. This result helps to determine the size of the subpixel printed on the
transparencies.

Our result is able to be extended to the case when $l$ transparencies are shifted all
together. In this case, we only need to consider the resulting transparency of stacking
all these shifted transparencies together, which is also equivalent to a (2, 2)-VCS.
Further generalization when the $l$ transparencies are shifted differently is possible,
but numerical analysis becomes more complicated. We leave this as an open problem.

## 2.2 Flipping Issues in VCS

Plane transformation visual cryptography takes a unique approach to some of the
shortcomings of current visual cryptography techniques. Typically, the direction and
placement of the encrypted shares are critical when attempting to recover the secret.
Many schemes are highly dependant on this stacking order. Within this section, the
scheme presented illustrates a technique, whereby, this restriction is loosened such
that the number of acceptable alignment points is increased by performing a simple
plane transform on one of the shares [29]. This results in the same secret being
recovered when the shares correctly aligned. The technique has also been extended
to encompass multiple secrets [17, 27, 38], each of which can be recovered depending
on the type of transformation performed on the shares.

Many schemes within visual cryptography suffer from alignment issues and are
dependant on how the shares are stacked together [29]. Loosening or removing this
restriction would be a very desirable advance, as it enables an end user to recover the
secret without having to work out how he must stack the shares. Figure 2.9 provides
an example of this stacking and alignment problem. It can be observed that successful
recovery is achieved when the shares are superimposed correctly. However, if the
second share is transformed about its center point in the $x$-axis direction, then the
secret cannot be recovered. Removing this limitation would improve the end users
experience when it comes to recovering the hidden secret.

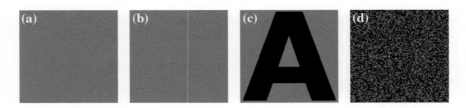

**Fig. 2.9** Traditional visual cryptography decryption process. **a** Share one. **b** Share two. **c** Secret
recovered by superimposing share two on share one. **d** Attempted secret recovery after flipping
share two vertically and superimposing it on share one

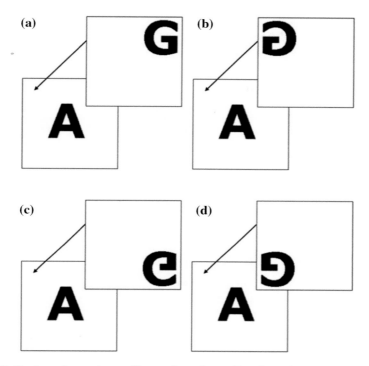

**Fig. 2.10** Configurations under specific transformations. **a** Transformation one. No specific transformation. **b** Transformation two. Vertical transform. **c** Transformation three. Horizontal transform. **d** Transformation four. Vertical + horizontal transform

Creating shares in such a way that allows for secret recovery when the shares are superimposed after having been transformed was a valid line of research as it removes these specific types of restrictions which are demonstrated in Fig. 2.9.

The main idea is that one share is printed onto a normal white page, but the second is printed onto a transparency. This transparency is then transformed as previously mentioned. Figure 2.10 illustrates each of the transformations that each share undergoes in order to recover each of the secrets. Share one is marked with an 'A', share two is marked with a 'G'. The arrow denotes superimposing the shares in their specific configurations. After each of the transformation, the same or unique secrets can be recovered.

The term 'plane' used within this chapter refers to a flat two-dimensional surface. We used this term when describing the shares in order to illustrate the type of movement that they undergo using geometric expressions. Therefore, the whole space is used when working in a two-dimensional Euclidean space.

When compared to the plethora of visual cryptography schemes [11] in use today, this scheme attempts to improve upon them by allowing the shares to be stacked in a variety of ways, after having been transformed about the horizontal, vertical,

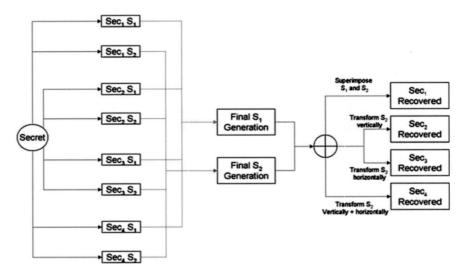

**Fig. 2.11** Plane transform visual cryptography flowchart

and a combination of both axes. This is a much more intuitive way to manipulate a quadrilateral in order to recover each of the secrets. Especially, when dealing with two shares.

Removing the specific stacking order required by the majority of the previous schemes is a great advantage, as it allows for easier secret recovery. Illustrated within this section is one main idea which accomplishes two goals, the same secret recovery based on different transforms and unique secret recovery based on the same set of transformations. Ideally, the same secret is used, this means that no matter how the shares are stacked, the same results are obtained. The unique secrets are illustrated to prove that it is possible for unique secrets to be shares as well.

The steps involved in order to create the resulting two shares can be examined in Fig. 2.11. Figure 2.11 provides a flowchart of the proposed system which details each of the corresponding actions required. Each of these steps is detailed below.

It can be observed from Fig. 2.11 that a secret is input and four sets of shares are generated accordingly, $Sec_1S_1 \rightarrow Sec_4S_1$ for the set of secrets belonging to share one and $Sec_1S_2 \rightarrow Sec_4S_2$ for the set of secrets belong to share two. Where $Sec_1S_1$ refers to share one from secret and $Sec_1S_2$ refers to share two from the corresponding set of secrets.

Whether one secret is input (recovering the same secret for each transform: $Sec_1 = Sec_2 = Sec_3 = Sec_4$) or four secrets (unique secret recovery for each transform), four sets of shares are generated. Based on these sets of shares, the final set of two shares is generated which allows for the recovery. When, the final $S_1$ and the final $S_2$ are superimposed, $Sec_1$ is recovered. When final $S_2$ is transformed vertically about its center point on the $x$-axis, $Sec_2$ can be recovered. $Sec_3$ can be observed when final

$S_2$ is transformed about its center point along the $y$-axis in a horizontal direction. Finally, $Sec_4$ is revealed after final $S_2$ is transformed both center points of each axis.

The algorithm required is presented within Algorithm 2.1, which provides a pseudocode implementation of the plane transformation visual cryptography process. Further details are presented in the following sections. They provide more insight into what happens during each of the steps.

This transformation requires a lot of thought when creating a suitable scheme that can recover black-and-white pixels accordingly. Some pixel configurations may be representing white pixels, while, after a vertical transformation the pixel representation required is black.

---

**Algorithm 2.1**: Pseudo code for generating two shares of plan transform VCS

**Input**  : One secret four times or four secrets $Sec_i$, $i = \overline{1,4}$.
**Output**: Final two shares $S_1$ and $S_2$.

for $i = \overline{1,4}$ do
    $(Sec_i S_1, Sec_i S_2) = GenVCShares(Sec_i)$ ;
end
for $i = \overline{1,4}$ do
    $ExpVCShares(Sec_i S_1, Sec_i S_2)$ ;
end
for $i = \overline{1,4}$ do
    $ProcVCShares(Sec_i S_1, Sec_i S_2)$;
end
$S_1 = \oplus_i^4 Sec_i S_1$;
$S_2 = \oplus_i^4 Sec_i S_2$;
Return $S_1, S_2$;

---

## 2.2.1  Share Generating

The shares are generated using a combination of processes. A size invariant scheme is used initially and then using these size invariant shares [20], it is then expanded into a more traditional scheme where one pixel from the invariant shares is represented by a $2 \times 2$ block. This is the general process used to create the final share. Each of the invariant shares patterns is used to create a new suitable pattern capable of recovering each of the secrets.

The structure of this scheme is described by a Boolean $n$-vector $V = [v_0, v_1]^T$, where $v_i$ represents the color of the pixel in the $i$th shared image. If $v_i = 1$ then the pixel is black, otherwise, if $v_i = 0$ then the pixel is white. To reconstruct the secret, traditional $OR$ing is applied to the pixels in $V$. The recovered secret can be viewed as the difference of probabilities with which a black pixel in the reconstructed image is generated from a white and black pixel in the secret image. As with traditional visual cryptography [2, 11], $n \times m$ sets of matrices need to be defined for the scheme (in this case $2 \times 2$):

$$C_0 = \left\{ \text{All the matrices obtained by permuting the columns of } \begin{pmatrix} 1 & 0 \\ 1 & 0 \end{pmatrix} \right\}$$

$$C_1 = \left\{ \text{All the matrices obtained by permuting the columns of } \begin{pmatrix} 1 & 0 \\ 0 & 1 \end{pmatrix} \right\}$$

Because this scheme uses no pixel expansion [34], $m$ is always equal to one and $n$ is based on the type of scheme being used, for example a (2, 2) scheme, $n = 2$. Using the defined sets of matrices $C_0$ and $C_1$, $n \times m$ Boolean matrices $S_0$ and $S_1$ are chosen at random from $C_0$ and $C_1$, respectively: $S_0 = \begin{pmatrix} 1 & 0 \\ 1 & 0 \end{pmatrix}$ and $S_1 = \begin{pmatrix} 1 & 0 \\ 0 & 1 \end{pmatrix}$

To share a white pixel, one of the columns in $S_0$ is chosen and to share a black pixel, one of the columns in $S_1$ is chosen. This chosen column vector $V = [v_0, v_1]^T$ defines the color of each pixel in the corresponding shared image. Each $v_i$ is interpreted as black if $v_i = 1$ and as white if $v_i = 0$. Sharing a black pixel for example [9], one column is chosen at random in $S_1$, resulting in the vector: $V = [0, 1]^T$. Therefore, the $i$th element determines the color of the pixels in the $i$th shared image, thus in this (2, 2) example, $v_1$ is white in the first shared image, $v_2$ is black in the second shared image.

## 2.2.2 Share Expansion

After the shares for each identical or unique secret have been generated, each set of shares for each secret is expanded into a $2 \times 2$ block and inserted into the final set of shares by the *processShare*($\cdot$) function from Algorithm 2.1. The following steps are involved when *processShare*($\cdot$) is executing. This function generates the final set of shares required in order to successfully recover the secrets.

Generating the final $S_1$ is a relatively simple procedure where each of the corresponding expanded shares is placed into the following coordinates on the share:

- $Sec_1 S_1$ has not change, leaves its current pixel locations intact.
- $Sec_2 S_1$ shifts its pixel locations one pixel to the right, in order to fill in the space to the right of $Sec_1 S_1$'s pixels.
- $Sec_3 S_1$ shifts its pixel locations down one pixel, this fills in the space beneath $Sec_1 S_1$'s pixels.
- $Sec_4 S_1$ shifts its pixel locations down one and right one, this fills in the final space remaining on the final share.

**Generating the final $S_2$ is more challenging**. The reason is that the transformations that this share undergoes need to be taken into consideration so that the correct black and white pixels can be represented. Accurate reconstruction is very difficult because four different situations arise due to the transforms.

Final $S_2$ is generated according to the following scheme:

- $Sec_1 S_2$ has not change, leaves its current pixel locations intact.
- $Sec_2 S_2$ places its pixels in the same locations as those which belong to $Sec_2 S_1$, but its vertical inverse must be placed at those locations.
- $Sec_3 S_2$ places its pixels in the same locations as those which belong to $Sec_3 S_1$, but its horizontal inverse must be placed at those locations.
- $Sec_4 S_2$ places its corresponding vertical and horizontal inverse pixels at the same coordinates as those of $Sec_4 S_1$.

No change is made to the placement of the first set of secret shares, this corresponds to simply superimposing each of the shares in the traditional way. The inverse of the pixel locations is required in order to reconstruct each of the secrets after a specific transformation occurs. Determining the inverse pixel patterns required for each of the specific transformed patterns proved to be rather difficult in terms of alignment [29].

After a transform on a pixel block was performed, simply supplying the inverse at a pixels transformed location was not possible. This is down to the fact that other pixels may be required at that location in order to provide a white pixel representation at one instance, but a black pixel at another.

This resulted in a compromise between full secret recovery and a probabilistic secret recovery which would be closer to a "best effort" style of recovery. This best effort is mostly a trade-off between visual representation and resulting contrast [3]. The results from this process are good when the same secret is to be recovered after each transformation. The recovered quality would be similar in terms of contrast of the extended visual cryptography scheme which employ halftoning [2, 36]. The contrast ratio is typically around 1/4. The contrast suffers, when different secrets are added. The recovered secrets remain readable, but a much lower contrast is available. This is due to the nature of the scheme, completely new patterns have to be generated which must represent a unique letter each time. Using the same letter as the secret, the same patterns can be selected, therefore giving a higher contrast. This is not possible when using unique secrets.

Another important aspect of the scheme that must be mentioned and analyzed is the security. Traditional VC schemes exhibit good security due to the nature of the patterns that are chosen to represent pixels from the original. If a white pixel is to be represented then each pattern used to represent the white pixel is placed in each share. Similarly, corresponding patterns are placed in each share when a black pixel is to be represented. This results in a potential attacker (who has obtained one of the shares) having to make a 50/50 choice for each pixel pattern in order to guess the correct corresponding share. It can be observed that this is not feasible at all.

Based on each of the individual shares that are created for each of the secrets, a new pattern is created which is capable of revealing the secret while being transformed invariant. These new patterns work in the same way as the traditional patterns. An attacker would have to generate identical or corresponding patterns for each of the pixel representations. Correctly guessing those patterns to reveal one of the secrets is extremely unlikely, guessing the correct patterns that four secrets are revealed is even

**(a)**                  **(b)**                  **(c)**

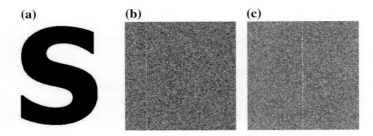

**Fig. 2.12**   The corresponding shares where all the secrets are identical. **a** Original secret. **b** Final $S_1$. **c** Final $S_2$

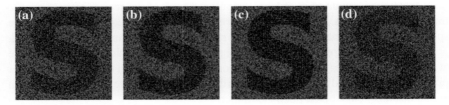

**Fig. 2.13**   The same secret recovered after different plane transformations. **a** Share two no transformation. **b** Share two transformed about the horizontal axis. **c** Share two transformed about the vertical axis. **d** Share two transformed about the horizontal and vertical axis

more unlikely again. The probabilities drop even further when four unique secrets are examined.

Randomness of the generated shares can also be examined in a security context. Visually, the shares do not leak any information about the secrets that are hidden within. On further inspection of the shares, the distribution of the pixels is uniform. This makes it much harder for an attacker to concentrate on a specific area on the share in order to force information to leak out regarding the secret.

A number of results are presented within this chapter which show the capability of the scheme discussed. The two shares that are generated using this scheme are depicted in Fig. 2.12. These shares look like normal visual cryptography shares and do not give away any information about the secret or secrets concealed within.

When superimposed, these shares can recover the secret 'S'. Figure 2.13 provides the results of each of the transformations which the share can be made to go through in order to recover the same secret. Figure 2.13a is simply share one superimposed upon share two. Figure 2.13b shows the secret recovery after the share two has been transformed about the horizontal axis. Figure 2.13c highlights the secret recovery after the share two has been transformed about the vertical axis and Fig. 2.13d provides the final secret recovery after the share two has been transformed in both the horizontal and vertical axis.

In the following results, multiple and unique secrets have been embedded within a set of shares [17, 38]. Using the same technique as previously described, each of the secrets can be recovered. Figure 2.14 provides each of the secrets along with their

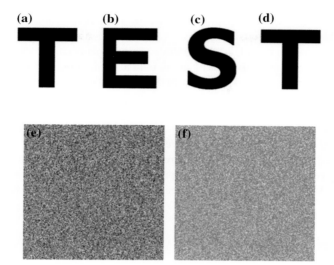

**Fig. 2.14** The corresponding shares when all the secrets are unique. **a** Original secret one. **b** Original secret two. **c** Original secret three. **d** Original secret four. **e** Final $S_1$. **f** Final $S_2$

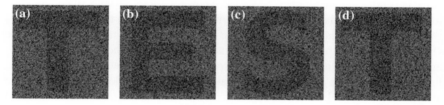

**Fig. 2.15** The same secret recovered at different plane transformations. **a** Share two no transformation. **b** Share two transformed about the horizontal axis. **c** Share two transformed about the vertical axis. **d** Share two transformed about the horizontal and vertical axis

corresponding shares. Each secret has its own set of decryption blocks embedded within the shares so that each of the secrets is recovered, no information leaks out with regard to the other secrets. This is vital in any multi-secret sharing visual cryptography scheme [7, 26, 30, 35].

The recovered results are presented within Fig. 2.15. Figure 2.15a shows the first 'T' from the secret 'TEST'. Figure 2.15b–d provide the remaining results after specific transformations have been performed on the second share as it is superimposed.

Using a simple transform, accurate and effective secret recovery can be achieved. No rotation is required, what is needed is a simple geometric transformation. This helps users to recover secrets almost immediately without having to determine the correct angle and stacking order of the shares.

Testing these shares can be done very easily and quickly using the very simple microsoft paint program. The final $S_1$ can be loaded into the application, the final $S_2$ can be pasted on top and set to have a transparent background. Using the flip/rotate option [21], final $S_2$ can be manipulated vertically, horizontally, and both in order to test the validity of the results.

From these results it is clear that contrast improvements can be made in particular, when transforming share two twice, in both axial directions. The secret is still readable but the contrast does suffer. From the results and discussion presented, it is easy to see the advantages of a scheme like this have existing schemes. Reducing the alignment problem to a simple transform while being able to recover four identical or unique secrets is a great advantage to the end user [29]. This scheme removes the onus on the user when aligning and recovering the secrets.

This type of invariant placement of shares should be considered in the future when new cutting-edge VC schemes are being proposed. Making secret recovery easy for the end user is highly valuable and may help to push VC into the mainstream.

## 2.3 Distortion Problems

For visual cryptography scheme (VCS) [2], normally, the size of the recovered secret image will be expanded by $m(\geq 1)$ times of the original secret image. In most of the cases, $m$ is not a square number, hence the recovered secret image will be distorted. Sometimes, $m$ is too large that will bring much inconvenience to the participants to carry the share images. In this section, we introduce a visual cryptography scheme which simulated the principle of fountains. The proposed scheme has two advantages: non-distortion and flexible (with respect to the pixel expansion). Furthermore, the presented scheme can be applied to any VCS that is under the pixel by pixel encryption model [10], such as VCS for general access structure [1], color VCS and extended VCS [2, 21], the VCS does not restrict to any specific underlying operation. Compared with other non-distortion schemes, the scheme discussed in this chapter is more general and simpler, real flexible, it has competitive visual quality for the recovered secret image.

In general, the recovered secret image of VCS will be expanded by $(\geq 1)$ times over the size of the original secret image, i.e., the pixel expansion is $m$. However, in most of cases, $m$ is not a square number, hence, the recovered secret image will be distorted. An example of distorted VCS can be found in Fig. 2.16.

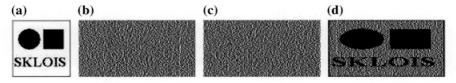

**Fig. 2.16** An example of traditional VCS with pixel expansion 2, **a** is the original secret image with image size $100 \times 100$, **b** and **c** are the share images with image size $200 \times 100$, **d** is the recovered secret image with image size $200 \times 100$

In Fig. 2.16, the circle and square are compromised to an oval and a rectangle, respectively and hence lead to the loss of information. This will not be allowed, especially, when the aspect ratio is viewed as important information of the secret image [32]. To avoid distortion, many methods have been proposed. Naor and Shamir recommended adding extra subpixels to retain the value of $m$ as a square number. In such a case, the pixel expansion of the scheme will increase significantly for some $m$ and meanwhile may degrade the visual quality of the scheme [37]. Yang et al. proposed some aspect ratio invariant VCS's which relied on adding dummy subpixels to the shares, such methods also increase the overall pixel expansion [32]. Beside, their method is complicated, how to design a mapping pattern that reduces the number of dummy subpixels to the minimum is [34], as they said, a huge challenge, especially for some pixel expansions and secret image sizes [7, 27, 28].

Sometimes, $m$ is so large that will bring much inconvenience to the participants to carry them. Some other studies, hence, consider size invariant VCS [20], i.e., VCS with no pixel expansion [12, 34]. For such schemes, the recovered secret image will have no distortion. The size invariant VCS's are usually called probabilistic visual cryptography scheme (PVCS) [8, 31] for the reason that a secret pixel can only be recovered with a certain probability. In contrast to PVCS, the traditional VCS's are called deterministic visual cryptography schemes (DVCS), which means that a secret pixel can be recovered deterministically. Because of PVCS's probabilistic nature, the recovered secret images of PVCS often have bad visual quality. Usually, better visual quality of the recovered secret image requires larger pixel expansion.

**Definition 2.1** (*Probabilistic VCS*) Let $k$, $n$ and $m'$ be nonnegative integers, $\bar{l}$ and $\bar{h}$ be positive numbers, satisfying $2 \le k \le n$ and $0 \le \bar{l} < \bar{h} \le m$. The two collections of $n \times m'$ binary matrices $(C_0, C_1)$ constitute a probabilistic visual cryptography Scheme, $(k, n)$-PVCS, if the following properties are satisfied:

**Contrast**. For the collection $C_0$ and a share matrix $s \in C_0$, by $v$ a vector resulting from the $OR$ of any $k$ out of the $n$ rows of $s$. If $\overline{w(v)}$ denotes the average of the Hamming weights of $v$, over all the share matrices in $C_0$, then $\overline{w(v)} \le \bar{l}$.
**Contrast**. For the collection $C_1$, the value of $\overline{w(v)}$ satisfies $\overline{w(v)} \ge \bar{h}$.
**Security**. For any $i_1 < i_2 < \cdots < i_t$ in $1, 2, \ldots, n$ with $t < k$, the two collections of $t \times m'$ matrices $D_j$, $j = 0, 1$, obtained by restricting each $n \times m'$ matrix in $C_j$, $j = 0, 1$, to rows $i_1, i_2, \ldots, i_t$, are indistinguishable in the sense that they contain the same matrices with the same frequencies.

The definition of PVCS only considers the case with $n \times 1$ share matrices, we extend this definition to the $n \times m'$ case. And the definition of PVCS used the factor $\beta$ to reflect the contrast, we use the values $\bar{l}$ and $\bar{h}$ to reflect the contrast. The common point of the three definitions of PVCS is that, for a particular pixel in the original secret image, the qualified participants can only correctly represent it in the recovered secret image with a certain probability. Because human eyes always average the high frequency black-and-white dots into gray areas, so the average value of the Hamming weight of the black dots in the area reflects the grayness of the area. The PVCS does not require the satisfaction of the difference in grayness for each pixel in the recovered secret image as the DVCS does. It only reflects the difference in grayness in the overall view.

The contrast [3] of the DVCS is fulfilled for each pixel (consisting of $m$ subpixels) in the recovered secret image, however, this is quite different in the PVCS. The application of the average contrast, denoted by $\bar{\alpha}$. This term is often used in the PVCS, where the traditional contrast of the PVCS does not exist. Here, we define the average contrast to be the average value of the overall contrast of the recovered secret image, i.e., the mean value of the contrast of all the pixels in the recovered secret image. According to our definition of the contrast $\alpha = (h - l)/m$, the average contrast can be calculated by the formula $\bar{\alpha} = (\bar{h} - \bar{l})/m'$ where $\bar{l}$ and $\bar{h}$ are the mean values of $w(v)$ for the black and white pixels in the overall recovered secret image respectively [23], and $m$ is the pixel expansion of the PVCS. Because the number of pixels is large in the recovered secret image, the values $\bar{l}$ and $\bar{h}$ are equivalent to the mean values of the $w(v)$ in the collections $C_1$ and $C_0$, respectively. Note that, the DVCS also has the average contrast, and many proposed DVCS in the literature have $\bar{\alpha} = \alpha$.

When comparing DVCS that has $\bar{\alpha} = \alpha$, in the overall view, the visual quality of the recovered secret image of the PVCS is the same as the visual quality of the recovered secret image of a DVCS. However, because of the probabilistic nature, a PVCS is disadvantaged in displaying the details of the original secret image, especially for the white background areas in the recovered secret image. A simple construction of PVCS based on a given DVCS (we will call it the original DVCS hereafter) can be as follows:

**Construction 2.2** (*PVCS*) Denote $(C_0, C_1)$ as the share matrix collections of a $(k, n)$-DVCS with pixel expansion $m$. The $n \times m$ share matrix collections of a $(k, n)$-PVCS, denoted by $(C_0, C_1)$, can be generated by restricting each share matrix in $C_0$ and $C_1$ to its first $m$ columns, respectively.

According to the Construction 2.2 of PVCS, we have the following lemma:

**Lemma 2.1** *The Construction (PVCS) generates a $(k, n)$-PVCS based on an original $(k, n)$-DVCS, where the average contrast of $(k, n)$-PVCS equals to the contrast of $(k, n)$-DVCS, i.e., $\bar{\alpha} = \alpha$.*

## 2.3.1 The Fountain Algorithm

The main idea of our scheme is reflected by Fig. 2.17. Imagine a pool with several water nozzles as depicted in Fig. 2.17. The nozzles spray water with the same speed. In such a case, the water will fill up the pool. Think of a blank image as a pool which has no distortion to the shape of original secret image (only differs in the size), think of the secret pixels of the original secret image as water injection nozzles that are evenly distributed in the pool, think of the subpixels of each secret pixel as water drops. As a result, the pool will be filled up by subpixels of secret pixels, and hence

**Fig. 2.17** A pool with 36 water injection nozzles

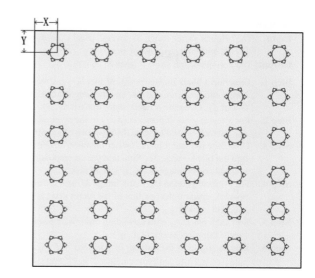

becomes a share image. Note that, each water nozzle sprays water with the same speed, and hence, each nozzle will spray almost the same number of subpixels into the pool. We do the same process to all the share images, we get a VCS with no distortion. Certainly, the stacking of the share images will recover the secret image visually.

For the case of Fig. 2.17, the size of the secret image is $6 \times 6$, where each secret pixel is a water nozzle. The size of the share image can be flexible and its size equals to the size of the pool. The water nozzles (secret pixels) spray water (subpixels) and fill up the pool (secret image). Clearly, the generated share images will have no distortion with the secret image.

Formally, we give the following Algorithm 2.2.

In the above Algorithm 2.2, the new position $(p', q')$ of a pixel at position $(p, q)$ in the original secret image can be calculated as follows: $p' = p\sqrt{m_N} + X$ and $q' = q\sqrt{m_N} + Y$, $X$ and $Y$ are shown in Fig. 2.17.

Denote the length (resp. width) of the secret image as $e$ (resp. $f$), then the length (resp. width) of the pool will be $e\sqrt{m_N}$ (resp. $f\sqrt{m_N}$), if $e\sqrt{m_N}$ (resp. $f\sqrt{m_N}$) is not an integer, then, we will use $e\sqrt{m_N}$ (resp. $f\sqrt{m_N}$) instead.

By saying "applying the original DVCS in order", we mean applying the DVCS by several times and concatenating the output shares (subpixels) in order, for each participants, respectively.

Note that the overall pixel expansion $m_N$ of our scheme is not necessarily equal to the pixel expansion of the original DVCS $m_0$, and it can be any value larger than 0.

---

**Algorithm 2.2**: The fountain algorithm.

---

**Input**  : The original secret image $S_I$, overall pixel expansion (pool expansion) $m_N$, an original
DVCS with pixel expansion $m_o$.

**Output**: The non-distortion share images $S_1, S_2, \ldots, S_n$.

**Step 1.**  Generate a blank image (pool), $M$ that is $m_N$ times of the size of the original secret
image and has no distortion, i.e., the length (resp. width) of $M$ is $\sqrt{m_N}$ times of
that of $S_I$. Generate $n$ blank share images $S_1, S_2, \ldots, S_n$, which have the same size of $M$.

**Step 2.**  For a secret pixel at position $(p, q)$ in the original secret image, initialize an empty list
$L_{p,q}$ which is used to store the positions of subpixels in $M$ (or $S_1, S_2, \ldots, S_n$).

**Step 3.**  Distribute the secret pixels (water injection nozzles) of the original secret image evenly
into the blank image $M$. Note that the corresponding coordinates of a pixel $(p, q)$ of the
original secret image is $(p', q')$ in $M$ now.

**Step 4.**  For each subpixel in the blank image $M$, and the nearest secret pixel (water injection
nozzle), suppose the position of the secret pixel is $(p', q')$. Add the position of the
subpixel to list $L_{p,q}$.

**Step 5.**  Sort each list $L_{p,q}$ with ascending order with respect to the distance to the secret pixel
(water injection nozzle) $(p', q')$.

**Step 6.**  Denote $|L_{p,q}|$ as the number of positions in $L_{p,q}$. Encrypt the secret pixel $(p, q)$ by
applying the original DVCS in order, by $\lceil \frac{|L_{p,q}|}{m_0} \rceil$ times and distribute the subpixels of the
shares in order, to the positions of $L_{p,q}$ in $S_1, S_2, \ldots, S_n$, respectively, while discarding
the redundant subpixels.

---

In order to make things clear, we give the Example 2.1 for the (2, 2)-VCS, where
the share matrix collections are as follows.

$$C_0 = \left\{ \begin{bmatrix} 1 & 0 \\ 1 & 0 \end{bmatrix}, \begin{bmatrix} 0 & 1 \\ 0 & 1 \end{bmatrix} \right\} \text{ and } C_1 = \left\{ \begin{bmatrix} 1 & 0 \\ 0 & 1 \end{bmatrix}, \begin{bmatrix} 0 & 1 \\ 1 & 0 \end{bmatrix} \right\}$$

*Example 2.1*  The recovered secret images of the presented scheme can be found in
Fig. 2.18.

As depicted in Fig. 2.18, by comparing the three recovered secret images (b),
(c), and (d), we can observe that, larger pixel expansion will result in better visual
quality, and smaller pixel expansion will compromise poorer visual quality. Our
scheme is flexible with respect to the compromise between the visual quality and
overall pixel expansion of the recovered secret image. Formally, we give the following
Theorem 2.2.

**Theorem 2.2**  *The fountain Algorithm 2.2 generates a PVCS with no distortion and
the size of its share images and recovered secret image can be flexible.*

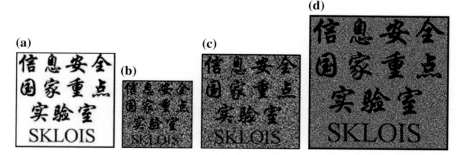

**Fig. 2.18** **a** is the original secret image with size $300 \times 300$, **b** is the recovered secret image with overall pixel expansion $m_N = 0.5$ and image size $213 \times 213$, **c** is the recovered secret image with overall pixel expansion $m_N = 1$ and image size $300 \times 300$, **d** is the recovered secret image with overall pixel expansion $m_N = 2$ and image size $425 \times 425$

### 2.3.2 Improving VC Quality

Suppose that the pixel expansion of the original DVCS is $m_0$ and the pool expansion is $m_N$. When the pool expansion $m_N$ is not a multiple of the pixel expansion $m_o$, the pool expansion subpixels is divided into two parts: the multiple part and the remaining part. Denote $d = \lceil \frac{m_N}{m_0} \rceil$, $m_N = d \cdot m_0 + t$, $0 < t < m_0$, the multiple part contains $d \times m_0$ subpixels and the remaining part contains $t$ (*resp.* $0 < t < m_0$) subpixels. The multiple part is filled by repeating the original DVCS for $d$ times. The remaining part is filled by choosing $t$ columns from the basis matrices (respectively the remaining part is filled by a PVCS with pixel expansion $t$). So when $m_N$ is not a multiple of $m_0$, pool expansion subpixels will be filled by $d \times m_0$ subpixels from the original DVCS and $t$ subpixels from a PVCS. The probabilistic subpixels will add some visual-noise to the recovered image, which will blur the details in the recovered image. Thus, the visual quality of the recovered image will be degraded. So we would like to remove the PVCS part. Our strategy is: the remaining part is assigned by $m_0$ subpixels with probability $t/m_0$ or assigned by no subpixels with probability $(m_0 - t)/m_0$. On average, the remaining part is assigned by $t$ subpixels. From an overall view, a pixel of the original secret image (a water nozzle) is assigned by $\lceil \frac{m_N}{m_0} \rceil \cdot m_0$ subpixels with probability $(m_0 - t)/m_0$, and is assigned $\lceil \frac{m_N}{m_0} \rceil \cdot m_0$ subpixels with probability $t/m_0$. Suppose there is a Boolean matrix the same size as the original secret image, then there is a one-to-one mapping between a secret pixel and an entry in the Boolean matrix. If the secret pixel is assigned by $\lfloor \frac{m_N}{m_0} \rfloor \cdot m_0$ subpixels, we denote the corresponding entry as 0, else if the secret pixel is assigned by $\lceil \frac{m_N}{m_0} \rceil \cdot m_o$ subpixels, we denote the corresponding entry as 1. Then we will get a Boolean matrix for which $t \times m_0$ proportion of its entries are 1, and the entries of 1 are evenly distributed. Meanwhile the entries of 0 are evenly distributed in the Boolean matrix too. For example, for a (2, 2)-DVCS with pixel expansion 2. Suppose the pool is three times as large as the original secret image. We distribute two subpixels for 50 % water nozzles and four subpixels for the remaining 50 % water nozzles, where there will be three subpixels for each water nozzle on average. And the two cases (two subpixels for a water nozzle, four subpixels for a water nozzle) are evenly distributed in the pool.

---

**Algorithm 2.3**: The fountain algorithm.

| | |
|---|---|
| **Input** : | The original secret image $S_I$, overall pixel expansion $m_N$, an original DVCS with pixel expansion $m_0$. |
| **Output**: | The non-distortion shares $S_1, S_2, \ldots, S_n$. |
| **Preprocess** | Let $s = \lfloor \frac{m_N}{m_0} \rfloor \cdot m_0, t = \lceil \frac{m_N}{m_0} \rceil \cdot m_0$ where $s$ and $t$ satisfy $s \times m_0 \leq m_N \leq t \times m_0$. Let $a$ and $b$ be two non-negative real numbers satisfying $a + b = 1$ and $a \times (s \times m_0) + b \times (t \times m_0) = m_N$. Suppose the size of $S_I$ is $m \times n$. Then we generate an $m \times n$ random Boolean matrix $D$, in which 0 appears with probability $a$ and 1 appears with probability $b$. Then, there is a one-to-one mapping between the pixels of the original secret image and the entries of $D$. |
| **Step 1-3.** | Step 1–3 are as the same as that of Algorithm 2.2. |
| **Step 4.** | Step 4 For each secret pixel (water injection nozzle) in the blank image $M$, if the entry of $D$ is 0, and $s/m_0$ nearest and undistributed subpixels, else if the entry of D is 1, and $t \times m_0$ nearest and undistributed subpixels. Suppose the position of the secret pixel is $(p', q')$. Add the positions of the subpixels to list $L_{p,q}$. |
| **Step 5.** | Encrypt the secret pixel $(p, q)$ by applying the original DVCS in order, by $s$ or $t$ times and distribute the subpixels of the shares in order, to the positions of $L_{p,q}$ in $S_1, S_2, \ldots, S_n$, respectively. The undistributed subpixels in the pool are simply set to black. If the entry in $D$ is 0, we distribute $s \times m_0$ subpixels for the corresponding pixel of the original secret image. If the entry in $D$ is 1, we distribute $t \times m_0$ subpixels for the corresponding pixel of the original secret image. |

---

In the above construction, if the pool expansion $m_N$ is a multiple of the pixel expansion $m_0$, hence every water nozzle will be assigned by $m_N$ subpixels. If the pool expansion $m_N$ is smaller than the pixel expansion of the original DVCS $m_0$, then each water nozzle will be assigned by $m_0$ subpixels with probability $m_N/m_0$ or assigned by no subpixels with probability $(m_0 - m_N)/m_0$, which implies that $(m_0 - m_N)/m_0$ of the secret pixels in the original secret image are lost in the recovered secret image on average.

In the following, we give a comparison for Algorithms 2.2 and 2.3 for (2, 2)-VCS, where the original DVCS is the same as that of Example 3.1.

*Example 2.2* Suppose that the pool is 1.37311 (this value can be arbitrarily chosen) times as large as that of the original secret image. Thus the length (resp. width) of the pool is 1.1718 times the length (resp. width) of the original secret image. The parameters in the stage of preprocess of Algorithm 2.3 are $m_N = 1.37311$, $m_0 = 2$, $s = 0$ and $t = 1$. In Algorithm 2.3, we assign one or two subpixels for each secret pixel (water injection nozzle), for which about 37.311 % secret pixels are assigned with two subpixels (filled by a (2, 2)-DVCS) and about 62.689 % secret pixels are assigned with one subpixel (filled by a (2, 2)-PVCS with pixel expansion 1). In

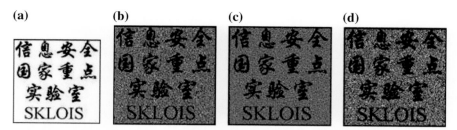

**Fig. 2.19  a** is the original secret image characters with image size $300 \times 300$. **b** and **c** are the recovered secret images of Algorithms 2.2 and 2.3 with image size $352 \times 352$, respectively. **d** is the recovered secret image of Yang's VCS with image size $352 \times 352$

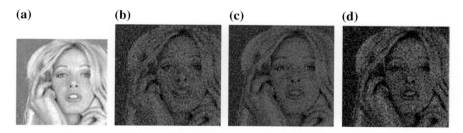

**Fig. 2.20  a** is the original secret image Human face with image size $512 \times 512$. **b** and **c** are the recovered secret images of Fig. 2.18 and Algorithm 2.3 with image size $600 \times 600$, respectively. **d** is the recovered secret image of Yang's VCS with image size $600 \times 600$

Algorithm 2.3, we assign two subpixels for $68.6555\%$ secret pixels (water injection nozzles) and assign no subpixel for $31.3445\%$ secret pixels (water injection nozzles).

We make use of two types of secret images: characters and human face. The original secret images are in the first column. The visual quality of Algorithm 2.3 can be found in the second column of Figs. 2.19 and 2.20. The visual quality of Construction 3.1 can be found in the third column of Figs. 2.19 and 2.20.

As depicted in Figs. 2.19 and 2.20, by comparing the recovered secret images (generated by Algorithm 2.3 and that of Algorithm 2.3, we can observe that, the recovered secret images for both constructions are clear and one can easily identify the contents of the original secret image. One also can observe that Construction 2.2 results in better visual quality than Construction 2.2 with respect to the evenness. Particularly, the recovered secret image is much more even at the white background areas.

## 2.4  Thin Line Problems (TLP)

Traditionally, the SIVCS is only suitable to encrypt coarse secret images that do not contain much detail information. The reason is that, SIVCS can only recover the secret image from an overall view point, each secret pixel can only be correctly

**(a)**                          **(b)**                          **(c)**

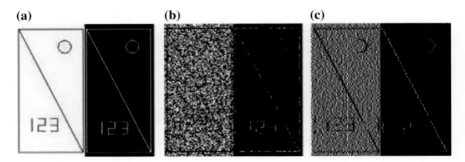

**Fig. 2.21** The visual quality for secret images with *thin lines*, the image size is: $200 \times 200$. **a** Secret image **b** TLP share 1 **c** TLP share 2

represented with a certain probability in the recovered secret image. In such a case the thin lines, in the secret image, are usually unclear and misrepresented in the recovered secret image of SIVCS, where we call such phenomena the thin line problem (TLP). In this section, we classify the TLP into three types.

According to the recovered secret image (b) of Fig. 2.21, for P-SIVCS, the visual quality of the recovered secret image is seriously degraded. One can observe that, there are many chaotic pixels appear in the recovered secret image, especially for the white background areas. It is hard to identify the thin lines from the white background. We call this type of thin line problem as the first type thin line problem (TLP-1).

According to the recovered secret image (c) of Fig. 2.21, it is clear that the thin lines can be seen more clearly especially the horizon lines, diagonal lines and the right part of the circle, i.e., the TLP-1 is avoided in the Construction 2.2. The reason is that, it has smaller variance of the darkness level of each block of two secret pixels. However, according to Construction 2.2, because every $m$ of $B_{m,b}$ blocks are encrypted by $b$ of $M_1$ and $m - b$ of $M_0$ alternatively, it is possible that the patterns in the secret image can be falsely recovered, especially for images only consisting of thin lines, where the blocks on a thin line may be always encrypted by $M_0$ (resp. $M_1$), which means the thin line may be missing if it is a black (resp. white) thin line on the white (resp. black) background. This problem can be clearly observed in (c) of the Fig. 2.21, where the vertical lines and the left part of the circle are missing. We call this type of thin line problem as the second type thin line problem (TLP-2).

One way to solve the TLP-1 and TLP-2 is to replace thin lines by thick lines in the secret images. They also calculated the reference thickness of the lines which can be found in Table 2.1. However, if secret information in the secret image is characters, maps or geometry shapes etc., then after replace the thin lines by thick lines. One needs to enlarge the secret image, put down the given amount of secret information. This process will result in larger share images. Recall that the main advantage of SIVCS is the ability to generate smaller share images. Hence, for Yang's solution for TLP-1 and TLP-2, the advantage of SIVCS on the pixel expansion is no more.

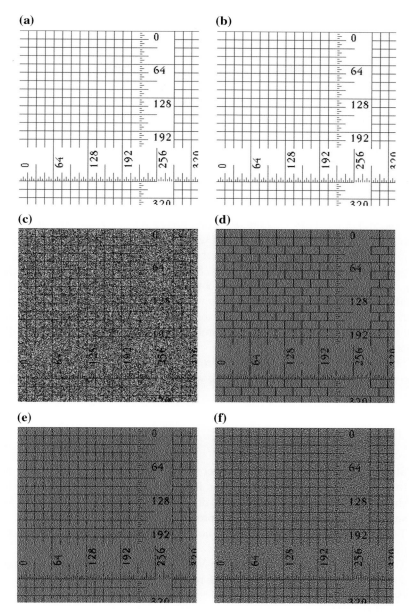

**Fig. 2.22** Experimental results for image Ruler, the image size is: 500 × 500. **a** and **b** are secret images; **c** and **d** TLP are image shares; **e** and **f** TLP has been successfully removed

Another problem of the recovered secret image (c) of Fig. 2.21 is that, a thin line in the secret image may be represented by a thicker line. Particularly, the vertical and diagonal thin lines that are with width 1, are represented by lines with width 2. The reason of this problem is that, a $B_{m,b}$ block may be encrypted by $M_1$ (resp. $M_0$), and in the recovered secret image, the $B_{m,b}$ block is represented by $m$ pixels which contains $h$ (resp. $l$) black pixels, and these black pixels spread evenly in the $m$ positions of the $B_{m,b}$ block, hence, the human eyes will view the block as a uniform area, i.e., the thin lines become as thick as the size of the block. We call this problem the third thin line problem (TLP-3).

One also can observe the thin line problems TLP-1, TLP-2, and TLP-3 in the images (c) and (d) of Fig. 2.22, where we use the fine image Ruler as the original secret image.

In Fig. 2.22 shows, all the three thin line problems TLP-1, TLP-2, and TLP-3 are avoided. For the TLP-3, taking the encryption of $b$ black pixels in a block $B_{r_s,b}$ as example, because the black pixels and white pixels are encrypted separately, the $b \cdot h / m$ black pixels in the recovered secret image only spread evenly in the original $b$ positions of the $b$ black pixels in $B_{r_s,b}$. Similarly, for the $r_s - b$ white pixels in $B_{r_s,b}$, the $(r_s - b) \cdot l / m$ black pixels in recovered secret image only spread evenly in the original $r_s \times b$ positions of the $r_s \times b$ white pixels in $B_{r_s,b}$. Hence, the average darkness level for the white and black pixels are different, and the human eyes can identify the difference, i.e., the TLP-3 problem is avoided in the recovered secret image of Construction 2.2.

The TLP is, more or less, a common problem for all kinds of SIVCS. There may be no perfect solution for the secret image which is a simple and regular line image.

## 2.5 Exercises

(1) Shifting one of the shares by a number (at most $m - 1$) of subpixels to the right (resp. left) is presented in this chapter. Please think another alignment problem: shifting one of the shares up (resp. down) by a number (at most $m - 1$) of subpixels, and give the analysis and proof.

(2) Take (2, 3)-TVCS as an example to show how two participants collude to cheat the victim.

(3) The Fountain algorithm is utilized in VCS to resolve the distortion problem of conventional VCS, please analyze the reason of flexibility of this scheme.

(4) How are the thin line problems generated in SIVCS? How to resolve the relevant thin line problems?

# References

1. Akansu AN, Haddad RA (1992) Multiresolution signal decomposition: transforms, subbands, and wavelets. Academic Press, Boston
2. Ateniese G, Blundo C, Santis AD, Stinson DR (1996) Visual cryptography for general access structures. Inf Comput 129:86–106
3. Biham E, Itzkovitz A (1997) Visual cryptography with polarization. In: CRYPTO'98
4. Blundo C, Bonis A, Santis A (2001) Improved schemes for visual cryptography. Des Codes Cryptogr 24:255–278
5. Blundo C, D'Arco P, Santis A, Stinson DR (2003) Contrast optimal threshold visual cryptography schemes. SIAM J Discret Math 16(2):224–261
6. Bose M, Mukerjee R (2010) Optimal $(k, n)$ visual cryptographic schemes for general $k$. Des Codes Cryptogr 55:19–35
7. Chen TH, Tsao KH, Wei KC (2008) Multiple-image encryption by rotating random grids. Int Conf Intell Syst Des Appl 3:252–256
8. Cimato S, Prisco R, Santis A (2005) Optimal colored threshold visual cryptography schemes. Des Codes Cryptogr 35:311–335
9. Cimato S, Prisco RD, Santis AD (2006) Probabilistic visual cryptography schemes. Comput J 49(1):97–107
10. Cimato S, Yang CN (2011) Visual cryptography and secret image sharing. CRC Press, Taylor & Francis, Boca Raton
11. Degara-Quintela N, Perez-Gonzalez F (2003) Visible encryption: using paper as a secure channel, security and watermarking of multimedia contents. In: Proceedings of SPIE'03, vol 5020
12. Droste S (1996) New results on visual cryptography. In: CRYPTO'96, vol 1109. Springer, Berlin, pp 401–415
13. Fang WP (2009) Non-expansion visual secret sharing in reversible style. Int J Comput Sci Netw Secur 9(2):204–208
14. Floyd RW, Steinberg L (1976) An adaptive algorithm for spatial grey scale. In: Proceedings of the society of information display, vol 17, pp 75–77
15. Goldberg L, Swan L (2011) A biosemiotic analysis of Braille. Biosemiotics 4:25–38
16. Horng G, Chen T, Tsai D-S (2006) Cheating in visual cryptography. Des Codes Cryptogr 38:219–236
17. Hou YC, Chang CY, Lin F (1999) Visual cryptography for colour images based on colour decomposition. In: Proceedings of 5th conference on information management, pp 584–591
18. Hou YC, Chang CY, Tu SF (2001) Visual cryptography for color images based on halftone technology. In: Proceedings of international conference on information systems, analysis and synthesis (World Multiconference on Systemics, Cybernetics and Informatics)
19. Hou YC (2003) Visual cryptography for color images. Pattern Recognit 36:1619–1629
20. Hou YC, Tu CF (2004) Visual cryptography techniques for colour images without pixel expansion. J Inf Technol Soc 1:95–110
21. Hsu HC, Chen TS, Lin YH (2004) The ringed shadow image technology of visual cryptography by applying diverse rotating angles to hide the secret sharing. Netw Sens Control 2:996–1001
22. Ito R, Kuwakado H, Tanaka H (1999) Image size invariant visual cryptography. IEICE Trans Fundam Electron Commun Comput Sci E82-A(10):2172–2177
23. Jin D (2003) Progressive color visual cryptography. Masters thesis. National University of Singapore, Singapore
24. Katoh T, Imai H (1996) An extended construction method for visual secret sharing schemes. IEICE Trans J79-A(8):1344–1351
25. Koga H (2002) A general formula of the $(t, n)$-threshold visual secret sharing scheme. In: (ASIACRYPT'02). LNCS, vol 2501. Springer, Heidelberg, pp 328–345
26. Krause M, Simon HU (2003) Determining the optimal contrast for secret sharing schemes in visual cryptography. Comb Probab Comput 12(3):285–299
27. Kuwakado H, Tanaka H (2004) Size-reduced visual secret sharing scheme. IEICE Trans Fundam E87-A(5):1193–1197

28. Lin CH (2002) Visual cryptography for color images with image size invariable shares. Masters thesis. National Central University, Taiwan
29. Liu F, Wu CK (2011) Embedded meaningful share visual cryptography schemes. IEEE Trans Inf Forensics Secur 6(2):307–322
30. Liu F, Wu CK, Lin XJ (2010) A new definition of the contrast of visual cryptography scheme. Inf Process Lett 110:241–246
31. Monoth T, Anto B (2010) Tamperproof transmission of fingerprints using visual cryptography schemes. Procedia Comput Sci 2:143–148
32. Naor M, Shamir A (1995) Visual cryptography. In: (EUROCRYPT'94). LNCS, vol 950. Springer, Berlin, pp 1–12
33. Shamir A (1979) How to share a secret. Commun ACM 22(11):612–613
34. Shyu SJ (2006) Efficient visual secret sharing scheme for color images. Pattern Recognit 39(5):866–880
35. Shyu SJ, Huang SY, Lee YK, Wang RZ, Chen K (2007) Sharing multiple secrets in visual cryptography. Pattern Recognit 40(12):3633–3651
36. Surekha B, Swamy G, Rao KS (2010) A multiple watermarking technique for images based on visual cryptography. Comput Appl 1:77–81
37. Viet DQ, Kurosawa K (2004) Almost ideal contrast visual cryptography with reversing. In: Topics in cryptology—CT-RSA, pp 353–365
38. Weir J, Yan W (2009) Sharing multiple secrets using visual cryptography. In: IEEE international symposium on circuits and systems (ISCAS'09), pp 509–512
39. Weir J, Yan W (2010) Resolution variant visual cryptography for street view of Google maps. In: IEEE international symposium on circuits and systems (ISCAS'10)
40. Yan W, Duo J, Kankanhalli MS (2004) Visual cryptography for print and scan applications. In: Proceedings of IEEE international symposium on circuits and systems (ISCAS'04), Canada, pp 572–575

# Chapter 3
# Cheating Prevention of Visual Cryptography

Most cheating immune visual cryptography schemes (CIVCS) are based on a traditional visual cryptography scheme (VCS) and are designed to avoid cheating when the secret image of the original VCS is to be recovered. However, all the known *CIVCS* have some drawbacks. Most usual drawbacks include the following: the scheme needs an online trusted authority, or it requires additional shares for the purpose of verification, or it has to sacrifice the properties by means of pixel expansion and contrast reduction of the original VCS or it can only be based on such VCS with specific access structures. In this chapter, we introduce a new *CIVCS* that can be based on any VCS, including those with a general access structure [1], and show that their *CIVCS* can avoid all the above drawbacks. Moreover, their *CIVCS* does not care about whether the underlying operation is OR or XOR.

The cheating problem in VCS is quite interesting. The possibility of cheating activity in VCS has been studied. For cheating, the cheaters present some fake shares so that the stacking of fake and genuine shares together reveals a fake image, and the victims who cannot detect the cheating activities will be fooled to believe that the recovered fake image is the genuine secret image. This is terrible because the secret image is usually important to the victims.

Many studies focused on the cheating problems in VCS, and consequently many cheating immune visual cryptography schemes (CIVCS) have been proposed. We classify the techniques in these CIVCSs as follows:

- Make use of an online trusted authority who can verify the validity of the stacked shares.
- Generate extra verification shares to verify the validity of the stacked shares.
- Expand the pixel expansion of the scheme to embed extra authentication information [13].
- Generate more than $n$ shares to reduce the possibility that the cheaters can correctly guess the distribution of the victims' shares.
- Make use of the genetic algorithm to encrypt homogeneous secret images.

© Springer International Publishing Switzerland 2015
F. Liu and W.Q. Yan, *Visual Cryptography for Image Processing and Security*, DOI 10.1007/978-3-319-23473-1_3

By examining the above techniques, we found that the first technique is not practical in real applications, because the beauty of VCS is its simplicity, which is meant to be useful even when no computer networks is available. The second technique requires the extra verification shares, which inevitably increases the burden of the participants. The third and forth techniques increase the pixel expansion and reduce the contrast of the original VCS [2]. The fifth technique requires strong computational overhead and degrades the quality of the recovered secret image, where the secret image can only be a password. It is also noted that most CIVCS can only be based on a VCS with specific access structure, for example, the $(2, n)$ threshold access structure.

## 3.1 Definitions

We give some definitions about cheating:

**Definition 3.1**  A shareholder of a *VCS* is called a cheater if, during the reconstruction phase, he presents a fake share, which results in the recovered image to be different from the original secret image. A participant is called a victim if he cannot tell whether a recovered image is the original image, and hence has to believe that the recovered image is the original one.

**Definition 3.2**  A successful cheating on $e$ victims is that a fake image is recovered in the reconstruction phase owing to the cheaters presenting fake shares, and $e$ victims cannot tell whether the recovered image is the original one, that is, the victims cannot tell whether the cheaters presented fake shares or genuine ones.

**Definition 3.3**  A pe-secure CIVCS is a VCS such that the probability of cheating $e$ victims successfully is no more than $p_e$.

**Definition 3.4**  A successful cheating method (SCM) is a cheating against a VCS that can succeed with probability 1.

In the practical sense of VCS, when we assume that a powerful cheater knows the basis matrices, it is reasonable to assume that all the other participants know such information as well. It is noted that the basis matrices require little memory to hold. It is also reasonable to assume that every participant knows the qualified sets where he belongs to. More precisely, we give the following assumption.

**Assumption 3.1**  For any participant $i \in V$ of a VCS, (s)he should know the following information:

- All the qualified sets in which $i$ is a member.
- The basis matrices $M_0$ and $M_1$.

Knowing the assumed information about the VCS helps the cheaters to cheat; it also helps other genuine participants make use of the extra information to detect the existence of cheaters. Hence, in the rest of this chapter, an SCM under the Assumption 3.1 means that the fake share can pass the victim's verification.

## 3.2 Attacks

In this section, we show that a forbidden set of participants can also recover the original secret image. We also show that all the cheating attacks can be detected. However, successful cheating does exist in the CIVCS, and this can be done by modifying an SCM for VCS, and we show that the SCM can be applied to general access structure [1] under Assumption 3.1 for the case of cheaters colluding.

### *3.2.1 Attack on Horng's CIVCS*

Two CIVCSs are proposed by Horng et al., where the schemes only tackle the $(2, n)$-VCS. We found that the first CIVCS is not secure, that is, the confidentiality of the secret image cannot be guaranteed and any single participant (which forms a forbidden subset) can almost recover the secret image. This is not acceptable and even the recovered image has low visual quality than the original, as in many cases the content of the hidden image is more important.

First, we recall the CIVCS of Horng et al. as follows. Horng's CIVCS: assume the set of participants is $V = \{1, \ldots, n\}$. In the distribution phase, each participant is assigned a share $S_i$ and a verification share $V_i$. The verification share $V_i$ is divided into $n - 1$ regions $R_{i,j}$ where $1 \leq i, j \leq n, j \neq i$. Then the verification shares are generated by a $(2, 2)$-VCS with the secret image being the logos $L_i$ which are chosen by the participants and sent to the dealer securely. So, the logo $L_i$ will appear in $R_{i,j}$ when stacking the $V_i$ and $S_i$.

In the reconstruction phase, the participant $i$ first stacks the shares $V_i$ and $S_i$ to check whether $S_j$ is a fake share or not. If the authentication is passed, the participants stack their shares to decrypt the secret image (Fig. 3.1).

Our attack is given as follows.

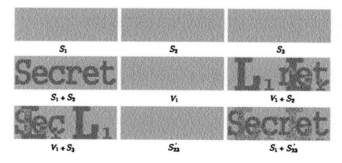

**Fig. 3.1** Experimental results of the attack on Horng's CIVCS

**Attack 2.2** According to the above construction, we get to know that a participant $i$ owns the share $S_i$, the verification share $V_i$ and the logo $L_i$. Since the region $R_{i,j}$ and the $S_j$ constitute a $(2, 2)$-VCS with the secret image being $L_i$, and the participant $i$ owns $R_{i,j}$ and $L_i$, it is clear that (s)he can restore part of the share $S_j$ (the part corresponding to the region $R_{i,j}$), denoted by $S'_j$. By stacking $S_i$ and $S'_j$ in the region $R_{i,j}$, the participant $i$ recovers the secret image in the region $R_{i,j}$. Repeat the above process for the remaining $n \geq 2$ regions in $V_i$, the participant $i$ can eventually recover the whole secret image by himself.

It is noted that $S'_j$ is not necessarily the same as $S_j$ in the region $R_{i,j}$; this is because a $(2,2)$-VCS is not unique. However, the recovered images are very close, and hence, the secret image can almost be recovered with a good visual effect.

We give the experimental results for the scenario with three participants Alice, Bob and Carol, where the secret image is the word 'secret', and the logo of Alice is '$L_1$', the image $S'_{23}$ is the concatenation of the images $S'_2$ (left) and $S'_3$ (right).

From the experimental results, we can observe that the secret image can be recovered by stacking the images $S_1$ and $S'_{23}$, although the result is not so clear. This is not acceptable when the content of the secret image is what is meant to hide [6]. Here $S'_{23}$ can be generated by $V_1$ and $L_1$ using a $(2, 2)$-VCS. This shows that the first CIVCS is not secure.

Cheating detection method:

- Check if any participant takes more than one share in the reconstruction phase; only cheaters could take more than one share (a cheater is assumed to take $r + 1$, 2, and $r + 3$ shares in the first, second, and third attacks respectively).
- Check if the shares used to recover the original image form a qualified subset in $G_m$. It is apparent that there must exist cheaters if a forbidden set of participants attempts to recover the original image.
- Check if every share is necessary to recover a visual image. This can be done by seeing if the rest of shares (excluding the participant's genuine share) give a meaningful visual image (the fake image can be recovered only by the cheater's shares in the three attacks) [11].
- Check whether there exists a column permutation of the basis matrices $M_0$ and $M_1$ that correspond to the distribution of the stacked shares for each pixel in the recovered secret image (the distribution of the stacking shares for each black pixel may not agree with any permutation of the basis matrices $M_0$ and $M_1$ for the three attacks).

The first three cheating detection methods are to verify the access structure according to the first item of Assumption 3.1 of the last section, and the fourth cheating detection method is to verify the basis matrices according to the second item of Assumption 3.1.

### 3.2.2 Detectable Attacks

Hu and Tzeng have the three attacks on the traditional VCS. However, all the three attacks can be detected under the Assumption 3.1. The main idea of the three attacks are that a cheater generates $r$ fake shares ($r = 2$ for the second attack), and the stacking of these fake shares together with the cheater's own genuine share recovers a fake image chosen by the cheater (if the cheater does not have a genuine share, then just stack the fake shares). Furthermore, by stacking the victims' shares and the cheater's genuine share, the fake image appears.

However, the drawbacks of those attacks are clear. First, one cheater needs to take more than one share in the reconstruction phase, which may not be allowed in many VCS. Second, the fake shares can recover the fake image without the victims' shares, which is also a way to detect the cheating. Third, the distributions of the stacked shares may not agree with any permutation of the basis matrices, and this is also a way to detect cheating. Fourth, the size of the subpixels and the size of the shares may not agree with the actual size of the subpixels and that of the victims' shares (the second attack). These drawbacks will incur the suspicion of the victims. Hence, the victims can detect these cheatings during the reconstruction phase.

### 3.2.3 Collaborating Cheaters

Given Assumption 3.1, it seems hard to find a SCM. Unfortunately, based on the detection methods, such an SCM does exist; in fact, the cheating example is indeed an SCM. However, Horng et al. only consider the cheating on $(2, n)$-VCS. Here we extended it to the general access structure [1].

**Theorem 3.1** *Denote $(C_0, C_1)$ as a VCS on access structure $\Gamma_m$ and participant set $V = \{1, 2, \ldots, n\}$. Denote $C = C_0 \bigcup C_1$. If a submatrix of $t$ participants (cheaters), $p_1, \ldots, p_t$ can uniquely determine a share matrix in the collection $C$, then there must exists a SCM under the Assumption 3.1 cheating the rest $n \geq t$ participants (victims), $p'_1, \ldots, p'_{n-t}$. More precisely, for any forbidden subset of $v$ participants $\{p'_{r_1}, p'_{r_2}, \ldots, p'_{r_v}\} \subseteq \{p'_{r_1}, p'_{r_2}, \ldots, p'_{r_{n-t}}\}$ satisfying $\{p'_{r_1}, p'_{r_2}, \ldots, p'_{r_v}\} \bigcup \{p_{r_1}, p_{r_2}, \ldots, p_{r_c}\} \subset \Gamma_m$ where $\{p_{r_1}, p_{r_2}, \ldots, p_{r_c}\} \subseteq \{p_1, p_2, \ldots, p_t\}$, then $\{p'_{r_1}, p'_{r_2}, \ldots, p'_{r_v}\}$ is successfully cheated by the collusion of cheaters $p_1, p_2, \ldots, p_t$.*

To make things clearer, we give the following experimental results.

*Example 3.1* For the access structure $\Gamma_m = \{\{1, 2, 3\}, \{1, 3, 4\}, \{1, 2, 4\}, \{1, 5\}\}$, assume that the basis matrices of the VCS are:

The collection $C_i$ is obtained by all the permutations of the basis matrix $M_i$, for $i = 0, 1$, and the collection $C = C_0 \bigcup C_1$. The dealer distributes the shares $S_1, S_2, S_3, S_4$, and $S_5$ to the participants 1, 2, 3, 4, and 5. It is easy to verify that the first three rows can uniquely determine a share matrix in the collection $C$. The cheaters can generate the fake shares $S_{f_1}$, $S_{f_2}$, and $S_{f_3}$ according to Theorem 3.1.

$$M_0 = \begin{pmatrix} 111000 \\ 100100 \\ 010100 \\ 001100 \\ 110100 \end{pmatrix} \tag{3.1}$$

and

$$M_0 = \begin{pmatrix} 111000 \\ 100100 \\ 100010 \\ 100001 \\ 100110 \end{pmatrix} \tag{3.2}$$

### 3.2.4 Cheater Colluding

Based on the SCM of Theorem 3.1, we found that the CIVCS is still vulnerable against collusion by cheaters. In this section, we construct an SCM based on Hu and Tzeng's CIVCS under Assumption 3.1 First, recall the CIVCS of Hu and Tzeng as follows.

Hu and Tzeng's CIVCS: Given the original VCS for an access structure $\Gamma_m$, and let the basis matrices be $M_0$ and $M_1$, denote the pixel expansion of the original VCS as $m$. In the distribution phase, the dealer generates $T_0$ and $T_1$ as follows:

$$M_0 = \begin{pmatrix} 10 \mid \\ \cdots \mid M_0 \\ 10 \mid \end{pmatrix} \tag{3.3}$$

and

$$M_1 = \begin{pmatrix} 10 \mid \\ \cdots \mid M_1 \\ 10 \mid \end{pmatrix} \tag{3.4}$$

The dealer will use $T_0$ and $T_1$ as the basis matrices for CIVCS to generate shares $S_1, \ldots, S_n$ with pixel expansion $m + 2$. The leading bits '10' of each row of $T_0$ and $T_1$ are treated as authentication subpixels for the CIVCS. Then for each participant $i(1 \leq i \leq n)$, choose a verification image and generate a verification share $V_i$ as follows:

- For each white pixel in the verification image, put the pixel of $(m+2)$-dimensional $[100...0]$ to $V_i$ (after corresponding permutation as for the share $S_i$).
- For each black pixel in the verification image, put the pixel of $(m+2)$-dimensional $[010...0]$ to $V_i$ (after corresponding permutation as for the share $S_i$).

In the reconstruction phase, the participant $i$ first stacks the shares $V_i$ with all the other $S_j$ to verify whether $S_j$ is a fake share. If all the verifications pass, then the participants can stack their shares to decrypt the secret image.

The colluding attack on the above scheme is given as follows.

**Attack 2.3.** Since $T_0$ and $T_1$ are generated by simply concatenating the authentication subpixels and the basis matrices of the original VCS, and the authentication subpixels are the same for all the shares, if the cheaters can locate the positions of the authentication subpixels, they can duplicate the authentication subpixels to the fake shares and make use of the SCM to generate the fake shares for the rest subpixels. In this way, the fake shares can pass the verification of the victim under Assumption 3.1, and hence, the colluding forms a new SCM for the above CIVCS.

The positions of the authentication subpixels can be located as follows:
For a qualified subset of participants $\{p'_{r_1}, \ldots, p'_{r_v}\} \bigcup \{p_{r_1}, \ldots, p_{r_c}\} \subseteq \Gamma_m$, where $p_{r_1}, \ldots, p_{r_c}$ are part of the cheaters $p_1, \ldots, p_t$. Recall that $p_1, \ldots, p_t$ are the cheaters that can uniquely determine a share matrix in the collection $C = C_0 \bigcup C_1$. Denote the shares of $p_1, p_2, \ldots, p_t$ as $S_1, S_2, \ldots, S_t$, the verification shares as $V_1, V_2, \ldots, V_t$ and the verification images as $L_1, L_2, \ldots, L_t$.

Because the positions of the two authentication subpixels are at the position of the 1 (black subpixel) of a white pixel in the verification share and the position of the 1 (black subpixel) of a black pixel in the verification share, and there is only one 1 in each pixel of the verification shares, the cheaters can obtain the positions of the authentication subpixels by choosing their verification images accordingly. More precisely, for the corresponding positions in the verification images $L_1, L_2, \ldots, L_t$, denote the pixels in these positions as $P_{e_1}, P_{e_2}, \ldots, P_{e_t}$; if there exist both black-and-white pixels in $P_{e_1}, P_{e_2}, \ldots, P_{e_t}$, then the cheaters can locate the positions of the authentication subpixels precisely by finding the 1's in their verification shares $V_1, V_2, \ldots, V_t$. Hence, the cheaters only need to choose verification images that have both black-and-white pixels in the same positions. A simple way to achieve this is by choosing complementary verification images for two out of the $t$ cheaters (Fig. 3.2). In fact there exist better methods to construct verification images $L_1, L_2, \ldots, L_t$ satisfying the above condition for arbitrary patterns.

Once the cheaters know the positions of the authentication subpixels, they can make use of the SCM to generate the fake shares for the remaining subpixels (other than the part used for authentication), while remaining the authentication subpixels intact. It is easy to verify that the above approach makes a new SCM for the above CIVCS.

To demonstrate how the above colluding attack works, we give some experimental results for the above SCM on the $(2, 3)$-CIVCS, where the participants $p_1$ and $p_2$ are the cheaters and $p_3$ is the victim.

**Fig. 3.2** Experimental results of the SCM on Hu and Tzeng's CIVCS under Assumption 3.1

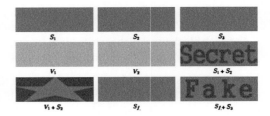

*Example 3.2* The secret image is the word 'secret', the fake image is the word 'fake', the logo of $p_1$ is a pentacle and the logo of $p_2$ is the complementary image of the pentacle. The size of these images is $120 \times 200$.

The basis matrices in this Example 3.2 are as follows:
From the experimental results, we can observe that the CIVCS is still cheatable, that is, a fake image appears when stacking the fake share $S_{f_1}$ and the victim's share $S_3$, while using the verification process proposed by Hu and Tzeng, the victim cannot identify that $S_{f_1}$ is a fake share.

$$M_0 = \begin{pmatrix} 10 \mid 100 \\ 10 \mid 100 \\ 10 \mid 100 \end{pmatrix} \tag{3.5}$$

and

$$M_1 = \begin{pmatrix} 10 \mid 100 \\ 10 \mid 010 \\ 10 \mid 001 \end{pmatrix} \tag{3.6}$$

### 3.2.5 New CIVCS

The results imply that the traditional VCS is not secure against cheater colluding under Assumption 3.1. We designed a new CIVCS to thwart against these SCMs for cheater colluding. A good CIVCS should satisfy the following properties to avoid some drawbacks of the known CIVCS:

- The CIVCS should not rely on the help of an online trusted authority.
- The CIVCS should not increase the pixel expansion of the original VCS.
- The CIVCS should not reduce the contrast of the original VCS.
- The CIVCS should be applicable to any VCS for general access structure $\Gamma_m$.
- The amount of the authentication information should be as small as possible, and the verification process does not have to rely on computing devices.
- The CIVCS should be able to detect the existence of cheaters, and it would be ideal if it is able to detect the actual cheaters.

In this section, we will discuss two methods to construct our CIVCS satisfying all the above required properties. However, because of the similarity of the two methods, we combine the main steps into the Construction 3.1, and we differentiate the steps of the two methods by using superscript *1 (for Method 1) and *2 (for Method 2).

**Construction 3.1** Given a VCS $(C_0, C_1)$ for the access structure $G_m$, denote its basis matrices as $M_0$ and $M_1$, then our construction of the CIVCS is as follows.
*Distribution phase:*

Step 1    Construct the $n$ shares by using the original VCS and record all the share matrices that chosen for each pixel from the original secret image.

Step 2    Randomly choose $t$ pixels from the original secret image as the authentication pixels (APs) for each participant $i$, and record the $t$ share matrices, $M_1^i, M_2^i, \ldots, M_t^i$ of the APs, where $i \in V$ (note that the $t$ APs are chosen separately for different participants).

Step 3*1  Distribute the $i$th share to the participant $i$ and mark the $t$ APs in the share of $i$ securely, where a black AP is marked by a green box and a white AP is marked by a red box.

Step 3*2  Distribute the $i$th share to the participant $i$ and tell the participant $i$ the $t$ share matrices $M_1^i, M_2^i, \ldots, M_t^i$ and mark the $t$ APs in the share of $i$ securely, where a black AP is marked by a green box and a white AP is marked by a red box.

*Reconstruction phase:*

Let $p_1, p_2, \ldots, p_r$ be members in a qualified subset, i.e., $\{p_1, p_2, \ldots, p_r\} \subseteq \Gamma_m$

Step 1*1  Each participant verifies whether the color of the recovered secret image at the positions of $t$ APs agrees with the color of the APs he received from the dealer.

Step 1*2  Each participant verifies whether the distribution of the stacked shares agree with the share matrices of the $t$ APs he received from the dealer.

Step 2*1  If the verification of Step 1*1 is passed, the participants stack their shares and recover the secret image, else reject the fake shares.

Step 2*2  If the verification of Step 1*2 is passed, the participants stack their shares and recover the secret image, else reject the fake shares and find out the cheaters whose shares do not agree with the distributions of the share matrices at the positions of the APs.

To demonstrate how Construction 3.1 works, we give the following Example 3.3.

*Example 3.3*  We give a simple example for a (2, 2)-CIVCS by using Method 1, where we let $t = 10$ for simplicity. The size of the secret image is $150 \times 120$; hence, we have $r = 1/1800$. We mark the shares by red and green boxes for white-and-black APs, respectively.

The following theorem shows the effectiveness of our CIVCS:

**Theorem 3.2** *Denote the size of the secret image as $l \times h$ and denote the participants set as $V = \{1, 2, \ldots, n\}$. Let $p = \frac{s_s}{s_t}$, where $s_s$ is the number of pixels in the fake image that have same color as the corresponding pixels (the pixels that at the same position) in the secret image, and $s_t$ is the total number of pixels in the fake image (secret image). Then Construction 3.1 is a $p_e$-secure CIVCS with $p_e = max\left(1/\binom{l \cdot h}{t \cdot e}, p^{te}\right)$, where $e$ is the number of target victims and $t$ is the number of APs for each share. The securer of each share is $r = \frac{t}{s_t}$.*

To show the effectiveness of our CIVCS, we compare the amount of the authentication information each participant carries in our CIVCS and that of the CIVCS proposed by Horng et al. and Hu and Tzeng for the $(k, n)$ access structure. Table 3.1 shows the comparison of the amount of information needed for authentication in our CIVCS.

In Table 3.1, $s_t$ is the number of pixels in the secret image. Note that $t$ should be far less than $s_t$; hence, it is obvious that the amount of the authentication information of the proposed CIVCS is far less than that of the CIVCS proposed by Horng et al. and Hu and Tzeng for the $(k, n)$ access structure. Hence, our CIVCSs do not bring a heavy burden to the participants. The following Example 3.4 shows the effectiveness of our CIVCS.

*Example 3.4* Suppose the fake image is shown as Fig. 3.3. As the CIVCS of Example 3.3 depicts, assume that there are a cheater and a target victim in the CIVCS. Let $t = 10$, then the probability $\binom{l \cdot h}{t \cdot e} \simeq 1.02 \times 10^{-36}$, which can be neglected.

**Table 3.1** Comparison of the amount of authentication information

| Method 1 | Method 2 | 1st CIVCS of Horng | 2nd CIVCS of Horng | CIVCS of Hu & Tzeng |
|---|---|---|---|---|
| Number $k$ | Number $k$ and indices of $t$ aPs the permutation of the basis matrices of $t$ aPs | Verification share with $s_t$ aPs | Enlarged share with $l \times s_t$ aPs | Enlarged share with $2 \times s_t$ aPs |

**Fig. 3.3** 'Fake' image with size $150 \times 120$

**Fig. 3.4** Examples of various barcode types (each of these barcodes has the same content). **a** QR code. **b** Aztec code. **c** Data matrix

**(a)**          **(b)**          **(c)**

The probability is even smaller when the value of $t$ is larger. Since the probability of being the same color at the same position in the secret image (Fig. 3.4) and the fake image in Fig. 3.3 is 0.5944 (which can easily be verified), the probability $p^{10} \simeq 0.0055$, which is very small. Note that, for different fake images, the values of $p$ can be different. All these values of $p$ satisfy $p < 1$, because if $p = 1$, then the secret image is identical to the fake image, and there will be no cheating at all.

In this section, we first discussed the drawbacks of some known CIVCSs, and then proposed a new CIVCS which avoids all the previous drawbacks. Our CIVCS is constructed based on a known VCS and can be applied to all VCSs for general access structure [1]. It is also noted that our CIVCS works when the underlying operation is XOR, although most discussions on CIVCS only consider the OR operation. Furthermore, our CIVCS can detect the cheaters or only detect the existence of cheaters depending on the amount of the authentication information provided. Our CIVCS achieves high security against the cheating attacks only with a small cost, only $r$ of the secret pixels are revealed to each of the participant, and in real applications, one can set $r$ to be a very small value, and hence, the confidentiality of the secret image can be ensured.

## 3.3  2D Barcode Authentication for Basic VC Shares

Even though VC schemes significantly support secret protection, participants who hold shares could not identify the authenticity of all shares and the secret, given cheaters the opportunity to create unauthorized shares which simulate the valid shares to obtain the hidden secret. Thus cheating prevention approaches are needed in association with VC to block devious practices. Nowadays, various cheating methods have been developed and each of the methods is capable of coaxing VC users. In VC, participants and outsiders are all able to provide counterfeit shares so as to deceive others in various circumstances. Collusive participants are also able to trick others by showing the fake overlaying results of their shares to other participants (victims). The forged shares from outsiders can be generated by encrypting fake secret into shares with different scales and pixel deployment methods.

The existing schemes of VC authentication are classified into two categories. The first is to employ an additional share to check authenticity of the revealed secret. This authentication method enables verification of the shares before the process of secret restoration. The other available authentication method is in use of a blind authentication technique which aims at preventing the prediction of genuine shares. However, as inconvenience of producing additional shares may have, the first type of authentication is hard to be implemented while the second one is always adopted.

Dissimilar to the basic VC scheme, in the extended VC scheme, more authentication processes were developed due to its nature of using meaningful pictures such as 2D barcodes. By applying the extended scheme of secret sharing, two shares were generated which have two selected barcodes visually on the entire shares. The original secret was revealed after superimposed the two VC shares. Authentication process exists in both methods, namely before and after the secret revealing in the extended VC.

One of authentication methods of VC shares is to seek the support from 2D barcodes [7–10]. There are four main benefits of using 2D barcodes in authentication. First, different from using another share for authentication, 2D barcodes are embedded into VC shares, therefore simplify the authentication process. In addition, cheaters are very hard to get information of the barcodes from secret prediction. Moreover, since the barcodes are able to present long character string using a small size of pattern with black dots, it is able to be applied as a tool to carry the secret. Furthermore, barcodes have the advantage of encoding a large scale of authentication information into a controllable set of shares. Lastly, as a vast majority of applications on mobile devices and personal computers have been developed for scanning barcode, it is convenient for a user to decode the barcodes by directly using the built-in cameras with a cellphone or laptop.

### 3.3.1 Barcode

Barcodes are very resilient to errors and changes in an acceptable extent. The threshold of visual angle for scanning a barcode is being increased with the rising resolution of a camera. This strengthens the robustness of barcode utilization when using cameras and software applications developed for cellphones. Especially in the case of embedding 2D barcodes into VC shares which requires high security and recognition ability, information verification needs to be fast and accurate in the process of authentication. As resolution of 2D barcodes could be adaptive to that of the VC shares, the scanning process therefore primarily relies on the information carried by those shares. Using VC shares embedded with 2D barcodes, the process is becoming easy for a dealer to check the correctness of VC authentication.

A barcode is defined as an optical machine-comprehensible representation of certain data, text, or other information which has been attached [5]. There are only black printable dots shown in a barcode, hereinafter it is easy to be detected by scanners but hard to be recognized by our human visual system (HVS) due to its encoding design. Conventionally, the data is stored in one-dimensional barcodes by utilizing parallel lines whose lengths and intervals are varying. With the development of barcode technologies, the adoption of regular 2D patterns, for example, rectangles, dots, and hexagons, has now been designed in the construction of 2D barcodes.

## 3.3.2  Barcode Embedding for Authentication of VC Shares

A scheme of embedding a 2D barcode into VC shares has been presented. The selection of VC schemes was recommended to choose XOR or OR operation. Subsequently, two shares were generated for embedding barcodes. The secret image was then decrypted by overlapping the shares. By embedded the 2D barcode into the secret image, the superimposed image was used for VC authentication by verifying the 2D barcode of the secret.

Apart from selecting embedding scheme, choosing barcodes is also crucial in authentication of VC shares since a suitable barcode not only decreases the observational difficulties of the secret, but also provides much sufficient and necessary information for VC authentication. The previous approach for using 2D barcode in VC authentication is to embed the barcode into the four corners of VC shares [10].

There exist contributions applied barcodes to VC authentication, the PDF417 barcode has been employed as an original secret which was divided into two VC shares using VCS earlier.

Barcodes are classified into two main types, namely linear barcodes (stacked barcode, one-dimensional barcode) and 2D barcodes (dot matrix barcode). Three examples of 2D barcodes are shown in Fig. 3.4.

Within the VC, using 2D barcodes has more advantages than that of other types in authentication. First, 2D barcodes can be applied to VC which tackles binary images that colors except black and white will not be taken into consideration. Even if binary attributes of 1D barcode can precisely represent the information based on specific protocols, the usages of 1D barcode are still restricted as its limited capacity of information to store. Therefore 2D barcodes, which have superior advantages such as large capacity with small size, ease to be carried, robustness as well as high security, etc. are more suitable to be applied to VC authentication than 1D barcodes [5]. Ordinarily in VC, participants expect the authentication information to be complicated enough for protecting the shares from being attacked by cheaters. Simultaneously, size of the authentication container is expected as small as that of a share within a controllable scale. Furthermore, VC shares are all depicted in 2D form which is similar to 2D barcodes. Therefore, 2D barcodes have the excellent advantage of being applied to VC shares for authentication.

According to different encoding designs, 2D barcodes also are grouped into stacked barcodes and dot matrix barcodes. Stacked barcodes present information by incorporating with height adapted 1D barcode. Typical stacked barcodes include Code 16K and PDF417. Aftermaths, a stacked barcode is not suitable for being embedded into VC shares as it has the similar attributes of 1D barcode. On the other hand, dot matrix barcodes are only organized by an array of printable dots in a regular flat place in order to conveniently deal with the information encoding, the recent developed coding schemes were based upon digital image processing, typical formats of dot matrix 2D barcodes include Aztec code, quick response code (QR Code), data matrix and maxi code. Among these barcodes, data matrix and QR Code are broadly used and supported by the scanner software installed in either personal computers or mobile devices.

A data matrix encapsulates three components, namely encoded data, four borders, and quite zone. Each of these components contains black solid squares which is called module. With being translated into mathematical expression, a black module in the barcode represents '1' and a white module is symbolized as '0', or vice versa. To locate the symbols, a data matrix code contains an L shape module to define its orientation, boarder and size. All the symbols are bordered by white modules marked as the quite zone. A Data Matrix symbol uses Reed-Solomon error correcting code (ECC) level 200 for error detection and correction.

In QR code, the encoded message is stored in both horizontal and vertical directions. The modules only represent dark or white elements by a digit '0' or '1'. QR code performs better in data capacity, size scale, and scanning speed than that of Aztec code and data matrix. Our goal of employing 2D barcodes is for authentication purpose since it is possible that an appropriate 2D barcode could find the most similar region from the given VC shares that minimizes visual differences in secret revealing. Therefore, on the basis of similar usability, 2D barcodes, like QR code, Aztec code, and data matrix all could be taken into consideration for authentication purpose in VC. We select the 2D barcodes, i.e., QR code, data matrix, and Aztec code for the authentication of VC shares.

### 3.3.3  VC Authentication Using 2D Barcodes

A 2D barcode has the advantage of only comprising of printable dots and provides security information for authentication, it is therefore reasonable to combine the VC shares and 2D barcodes together for VC authentication, as in traditional VC, the shares are also organized by arrays of only black and white dots.

Even though directly embedding 2D barcodes into the corners of VC shares possibly avoids any visual side effects of secret revealing when these shares are superimposed. In some cases, when VC secret is stored around corners of the VC shares, replacing the corner of shares using 2D barcodes will be harmful for the secret restoration. Much more severely, some useful information at the corners will be substituted by the 2D barcodes. As a result, it appears to be significant to develop other methods which can achieve both goals of authentication and revealing the entire secret.

There are commonly two approaches available to embed a 2D barcode into VC shares. First, searching for the regions which are not occupied by the secret data in the original picture, replacing these regions with 2D barcodes can be an ideal way to preserve the full data of secret and embed 2D barcodes for authentication. However, to achieve this approach which is to discriminate the meaningful regions from other regions of one image is still far from mature, cheaters can probably predict the regions having meaningful information which tends to facilitate their attack process. Furthermore, when the VC share is full of secret information, there will have not available space for barcode embedding.

The other effective method is to find a proper 2D barcode so as to replace certain regions of the VC shares which are similar. This approach is feasible to be applied

**Fig. 3.5**  Flowchart of
searching the similar regions
on a share

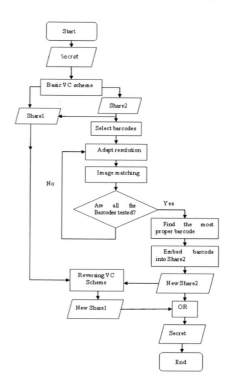

in practice as the image matching for finding similar regions of 2D barcodes can be easily implemented. Moreover, because of similarity between the 2D barcode and the found regions, the secret can still be revealed somehow even if using the shares embedded with 2D barcodes. The 2D barcodes are required to be similar to the replaced regions in an extent in order to make the superimposed VC shares present the secret, therefore, the 2D barcodes and embedded regions of VC shares both dramatically affect the result of secret revealing.

In order to compare the method of directly embedding a 2D barcode into the corners of shares and that of replacing similar regions of shares using the 2D barcode, we implement an algorithm and conduct experiments to verify the improvements. Figure 3.5 illustrates the proposed process for embedding a 2D barcode into VC shares, Fig. 3.6 presents an example which is used to explain how the VC region is replaced by the barcode.

In the Fig. 3.5, an image with secret is first divided into two VC shares Share1 and Share2. Then, a 2D barcode with the predefined content is constructed. The resolutions of 2D barcode and Share2 are adapted before similarity matching so as to find the most suitable regions on Share2 that could be replaced by the 2D barcode. The new Share2 will be reconstructed after replaced the similar regions with the barcode. Assisted by the new Share2, the secret image is then used to produce new Share1 by applying VC scheme again. Lastly, the new Share2 and newly generated Share1 are overlapped to restore the original secret.

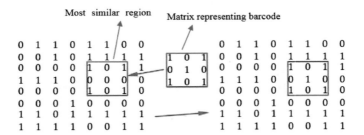

**Fig. 3.6** Replacing a region using a pixel array of the barcode

The resolution of a 2D barcode needs to be adjusted so as to match that of the target share for embedding 2D barcode. Specifically, there are three reasons for the necessity of this step. From the viewpoint of secret sharing, the employment of 2D barcodes is crucial for authentication of VC shares. Thus, we have to minimize the visual side effect of 2D barcode on the shares at an acceptable level that the barcodes could be read by a scanner. What is more, the necessity for tackling resolution adaption is to ensure the similarity between a 2D barcode and its similar regions on a share.

If the dots of 2D barcodes are bigger than those of the VC share in size, it will be more difficult to find the regions of the VC share which are similar to the barcode. Besides, a problem lies in visual side effect of secret revealing due to different sizes of those dots.

Figures 3.7 and 3.8 show an example of embedding 2D barcodes with different dot size into one VC share.

We assume the dot size of a VC share is uniform, typically is the size of one pixel, we take the dot size of a 2D barcode into consideration and resize it to match that of the given VC share, the Algorithm 3.1 is provided for this adaption. The dot size of a 2D barcode could be obtained by scanning the 2D image in both horizontal and vertical directions. If a 2D barcode has all dots size with that of $S2$ pixels, the dots will be replaced by pixels uniformly.

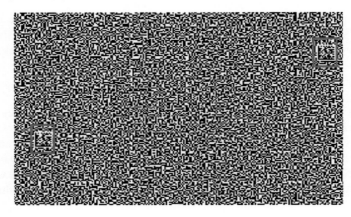

**Fig. 3.7** Embedding barcode (shown in *red rectangles*) whose resolution is $21 \times 21$

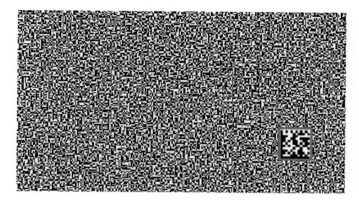

**Fig. 3.8** Embedding barcode (shown in *red rectangles*) whose resolution is $42 \times 42$

---

**Algorithm 3.1:** Image adaption

---

**Input**   : 2D barcode $B$
**Output**: 2D barcode $B'$

Set $Iw$ = the width of the barcode $B$ ;
Set $I_l$ = the height of $B$ ;
Set $I_W$ = the width of the VC share $D$ ;
Set $I_L$ = the height of $D$ ;
Set $s = 1000$ //initialization ;
$p = 1$;
**for** *all height of $B(j = 1, \cdots, I_l)$* **do**
  **for** *all width of $B(i = 1, \cdots, I_w - 1)$* **do**
    **if** $B(i, j) == B(i + 1, j)$ **then**
      $p = p + 1$;
    **else**
      **if** $s > p$ **then**
        $s = p, p = 1$;
      **end**
    **end**
  **end**
**end**
**for** *all width of $B(i = 1, \cdots, I_w)$* **do**
  **for** *all height of $B(j = 1, \cdots, I_l - 1)$* **do**
    **if** $B(i, j) == B(i, j + 1)$ **then**
      $p = p + 1$;
    **else**
      $s > p; s = p; p = 1$;
    **end**
  **end**
**end**
$C = s$;
$B$ = resized $B$ by shrinking its width and height to $I_l/C$ and $I_w/C$, respectively;
Return $B'$;

---

After adjusted dot size of the 2D barcode and that of the target VC share, it appears to be crucial to search for the similar regions on the share. Typically, an image can be treated as an array of pixels with various intensities. In both the VC share and the 2D barcode, pixels are clearly distinguished by black and white, thereafter this greatly facilitates the matching process.

In the case of VC, as there are only black-and-white pixels in the shares, the number of black-and white-colors will not be as diverse as that of various colors, thereby are less persuasive to determine the similarity of certain locations. As for the similarity measures of two images, a way of comparing two images by using the discrete metric is considered as the distance of a pair of pixels.

As the resolution of a barcode is usually uncertain before the embedding process starts, it is not easy to choose which matching method should be employed. For an example, the standard specification of the QR code resolution varies from $21 \times 21$ to $172 \times 172$. Moreover, as a VC share has no meaningful features to be extracted for analysis, this method is considered to be improper for VC. Searching every pixel of a 2D barcode and that of a VC share appears needing a long time when the resolutions are high, the searching workload will be much less when applied it to small pictures or blocks. More importantly, the accuracy of matching the barcode with a region of the VC share is another reason that should be taken into consideration. Therefore, the embedding procedure is to calculate the similarity distance between all pairs of corresponding regions on the share and the 2D barcode.

$$\delta(A, B) = \begin{cases} 0 & A \quad matches \quad B \\ 1 & Otherwise \end{cases} \qquad (3.7)$$

In the matching Algorithm 3.2, the 2D barcode as an image is compared to each same size region of a VC share one by one so as to calculate the similarity distances by using $\delta$-function Eq. (3.7). The pixel distance is 0 if these two compared pixels are same, meanwhile the region distance between the region of VC share and 2D barcode is calculated by simply summing up all the different pixels of two regions together. The most matching region is the region with the least distance.

Since different 2D barcodes have different coding designs, it is important to choose the most suitable one for replacing regions of the share with the least side effects on the revealed visual secret. Moreover, since different messages can be stored into these barcodes, these results in the various shapes, selecting proper type of 2D barcodes carrying an appropriate character string turns up to be an important step in embedding a 2D barcode into a basic VC share.

Nowadays, the source of free barcodes generating and downloading is easily to be obtained from public websites. It is not difficult to generate a 2D barcode at all. As a result, an optimized approach of selecting proper barcodes for a share is to find out the most suitable one. However, as it will cost a great deal of time to find out the best one from the given candidates so as to be treated as the embedded barcode.

From our observations, a little change of a barcode will lead to different matching results. Consequently it is important to keep the barcode in the share that can be identified clearly and accurately. Besides, different types of 2D barcodes have

---

**Algorithm 3.2:** Image matching and replacement

---

**Input**   : A VC share $D$ and a 2D barcode $B$
**Output**: New share with 2D barcode $D'$

Set $I_w$ = the width of barcode $B$;
Set $I_l$ = the length of $B$;
Set $I_W$ = the width of VC share $D$;
Set $I_L$ = the length of $D$;
Set $s$ = number of the similar pixels;
Set $p$ = number of the pixels in the region which is the most similar to barcode $B$;
**for** $a = 1, \cdots, (I_W - I_l + 1)$ **do**
   **for** $b = 1, \cdots, (I_L - I_w + 1)$ **do**
      **for** $i = a, \cdots, (I_l + a - 1)$ **do**
         Set $s = 0$;
         **for** $j = b, \cdots, (I_w + b - 1)$ **do**
            **if** $D(i,j) == B(i - a + 1, j - b + 1)$ **then**
               $s = s + 1$;
            **end**
         **end**
      **end**
      **if** $s > p$ **then**
         $p = s$;
      **end**
   **end**
**end**
**for** $a = 1, \cdots, (I_W - I_l + 1)$ **do**
   **for** $b = 1, \cdots, (I_L - I_w + 1)$ **do**
      **for** $i = a, \cdots, (I_l + a - 1)$ **do**
         Set $s = 0$;
         **for** $j = b, \cdots, (I_w + b - 1)$ **do**
            **if** $D(i,j) == B(i - a + 1, j - b + 1)$ **then**
               $s = s + 1$;
            **end**
         **end**
      **end**
      **if** $s == p$ **then**
         $o = a$;
         $r = b$;
         **for** $i = 1, \cdots, I_l$ **do**
            **for** $j = 1, \cdots, I_w$ **do**
               $D'(a + i - 1, b + j - 1) = B(i,j)$;
            **end**
         **end**
      **end**
   **end**
**end**

---

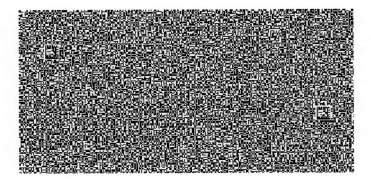

**Fig. 3.9**  Secret revealing using QR code

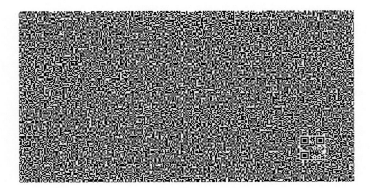

**Fig. 3.10**  Secret revealing using data matrix

obviously distinct shapes due to their encoding design. Thus the candidate barcodes are assumed to be different in both types and contents. Even though it is obvious that using data matrix has less side effect on the revealed secret than using QR code and Aztec code shown in Figs. 3.9, 3.10 and 3.11, respectively, the revealed secrets of using QR code and Aztec code, respectively, are acceptable since the superimposed regions embedded barcodes are visible to the secret. The results of using these three types of 2D barcodes to replace the regions of a VC share are compared in Table 3.2.

### 3.3.4 Secret Revealing

Even though the authentication problem of VC could be solved by embedding a 2D barcode into its most similar regions of a VC share, the visual side effects of the revealed secret still exist. Furthermore, the recovered secret using the new VC share

**Fig. 3.11**  Secret revealing using Aztec code

| Table 3.2 Comparison of similarities amongst three types of 2D barcodes | Samples | QR | Data matrix | Aztec |
|---|---|---|---|---|
| | Sample 1 | 19/400 | 22/144 | 5/400 |
| | Sample 2 | 15/400 | 13/144 | 7/400 |
| | Sample 3 | 14/400 | 14/144 | 6/400 |

will also be affected. Therefore, it appears crucially to make a change to the other VC share in order to reduce the visual side effect in secret revealing.

As illustrated in Fig. 3.5, the new Share1 is created by embedding a 2D barcode into proper locations at Share1 and the new Share2 is generated by modifying the corresponding pixels of Share2 corresponding to the regions of Share1. The superimposed result then is less affected by embedding the 2D barcodes.

In the final step of the 2D barcode embedding, we have the VC share embedded with 2D barcode (Share1) and the secret at our hand, then the new Share2 is generated by simply conducting VC operation between the corresponding pixels of new Share1 and that of the secret image as shown in Fig. 3.5. Consequently, we obtain the new Share2.

In the context of embedding 2D barcode into VC shares, messages carrying by 2D barcodes are texts, namely, words, sentences, and paragraphs which contain significant authentication messages. Another popular kind of 2D barcode is the URL of a website. Even though the script of web link itself has no meaningful information, the authentication texts can be easily retrieved on the website.

Furthermore, because all the kinds of 2D barcodes mentioned can be decoded and modified by cheaters without being noticed by VC shares holders, methods of one-way encryption in which the content is a cipher text that cannot be decoded are needed. Cryptographic Hash function has the premium merits of easily to calculate the Hash values for any input data which are hard to get data from a given Hash, difficult to modify a data without altering the Hash and tough to find two different data generated by the same Hash function, etc. Besides, as cryptographic Hash functions are used in a large range of areas like message authentication, message integrity, digital signatures, entity authentication and digital steganography, we decide to use a Hash function to encode a 2D barcode.

Another issue in authorization of VC shares is how to use a 2D barcode to differentiate the correct share from the unauthorized ones. As for the case of VC share, its recognizable features are size and pixel characteristics. The advantage of using the Hash code of these features is that modified shares can be prevented in the authentication process. Moreover, as modified shares can hardly be used to reveal the true secret, hints of secret can also be included as a significant content in a barcode. Thus, we decide to use the Hash code of VC shares such as width, length, the number of black-and-white pixels in the share as well as related information of secret. All the meta-data information of a 2D barcode can also be copied and kept by the dealer who is subsequently able to verify the correctness of authentication information stored in the 2D barcode of the VC shares by using a barcode scanner and a decoder. Figures 3.12, 3.13, and 3.14 illustrate the VC shares which are embedded by 2D barcodes with different types of messages.

The scheme of embedding 2D barcode is primarily for the security purpose. Embedding the 2D barcode into the most similar regions of VC share can effec-

**Fig. 3.12**  A VC share embedded with 2D Barcode having a textual string

**Fig. 3.13**  A VC share embedded with 2D Barcode having a URL

**Fig. 3.14** A VC share embedded with 2D Barcode having the Hash code of "Height: 432; Width: 886; Blackpixels: 18563; Hints of secret: ibm"

tively hide the 2D barcode. In this scenario, when a VC share holder attempts to cheat by modifying the share embedded with 2D barcodes, VC dealers are able to prevent this hoax promptly by verifying the information included in the 2D barcode. Similarly, it appears to be practical for the VC dealer to resist cheatings from attackers. The confidentiality, integrity, and availability (CIA) are commonly accepted security standards. As with the nature of information hiding, the security level of VC components is able to be evaluated by the standard of CIA.

Confidentiality prevents the security compromising by unauthorized individuals while ensuring that the real participants are able to acquire it. To make sure the authorized access, highly secure information of VC secret, such as significant account number and routing number of banking vault, is tremendously close to the stability of the society.

Ensuring the integrity means that only authorities might make changes to the assets. Integrity involves maintaining the consistency, accuracy, and trustworthiness of data over its entire life cycle. Data must not be changed in transit, and steps have to be taken to ensure that the data cannot be altered by authorities (e.g., in a breach of confidentiality). In addition, integrity also means responsively detecting any changes in data might cause a result of authentication failure. Thus, the cheating activities can be noticed and then prevented before the VC secret revealing.

Ensuring the availability refers that the assets are absolutely available to authorized users when required. By adding authentication process in VC, all the participants should have the chance to read the secret [12]. VC shares can distribute the secret while embedding 2D barcode can improve identifying the real shares from the unauthorized ones.

Another important security assess criterion is authentication, authorization, auditing and accounting (AAA). A 2D barcode can perform as a key of access to the VC shares and the authentication of VC shares thus should be ensured as the information stored in 2D barcodes only are read by a scanner. The AAA authentication of VC shares can compare a users authentication credentials (data in 2D barcodes) with others. The user is granted access to the VC secret revealing process only if the information is right. If the credentials are different, the request of access would be denied and the authentication fails.

Accounting offers the approaches for collecting information about the end users resource consumption, which can then be processed for billing, auditing, and capacity planning purposes. Auditing functionality permits to verify the correctness of procedures carried out based on accounting data. The information stored in 2D barcodes of VC shares needs to be verified and the process of secret recovery is conducted based on the result of data matching. We protect the security of the property from being obtained by cheaters.

Even though embedding 2D barcode into VC shares for the authentication can be evaluated by both CIA and AAA, there exist drawbacks of this approach of authenticating VC shares. First, despite the replaced regions of the VC share is the most similar one, cheaters are able to find the 2D barcode on VC share in some occasions. Therefore, it is expected to improve the barcode embedding so as to make the authentication process more effectively. Besides, our algorithm of embedding 2D barcode is only applied to $(2, 2)$-VCS. More cases of $(k, n)$-VCS are expected to be investigated.

On the basis of previous work of VC and advantages of various barcodes, we implemented a scheme of embedding a 2D barcode into a VC share by searching for the most similar region which is used to replace the corresponding regions of the share afterwards. Our contribution is to implement the VC authentication and minimize the side effects on the revealed secret by using the given 2D barcode.

## 3.4 Braille for Authentication of Basic VC Shares

Despite VC significantly assists secret protection, it appears to be difficult for participants to validate all shares and the secret, thereby given cheaters the opportunity to create unauthorized share. The role of cheater in VC as well as the authentication and successful cheat in VC are defined [4]. According to their definition, a cheater is someone who releases a fake share that is different from the one (s)he received from the dealer during the process of secret reconstruction. Thus cheating prevention approaches are necessary in association with VC to prevent those cheating practices. There are two authentication methods available for checking shares and secret. The first type is to use an additional share to check the authentication of the revealed secret. This authentication method enables verification of the shares before the process of secret restoration. The other available authentication method is to use a blind authentication technique which aims at preventing the prediction of genuine shares structure. As the inconvenience of producing and carrying additional shares, the first type of authentication is hard to be implemented. By contrast, using blind authentication methods such as cipher text is widely accepted in researches and applications. In this section, we will introduce Braille encoding and explain how it is applied to handle the authentication problem in VC. Our contribution is to use Braille for VC.

### 3.4.1 Braille

In 1824, a French visually impaired person Louis Blair invented Braille which is designed specifically for the visually impaired person to read by tactile perception [12]. In Braille, the alphabet is written in the form of blocks of the six dots which are also called Braille cells [3]. Braille cells are small, flat, rectangular objects of a standard size. The surface of each point can be either flat or salient. Each letter of the alphabet is uniquely represented in Braille cells by a pattern of six black dots.

While open circles indicate the flat positions in each cell, filled circles indicate salient dots in the cell. The American Library of Congress has published explicit unified standard for Braille print [3].

Visually impaired people read Braille articles by using their fingers padding over Braille cells and perceiving the characters by the dots arrangement in Braille cells. While Braille is very useful for visually impaired people, individuals can hardly understand the content on Braille passages if they have no experience in reading Braille [3]. Subsequently, Braille appears to be only unrecognizable signs for people who lack the knowledge of Braille. Therefore, Braille can be treated as a cipher text for normal people.

### 3.4.2 Braille Embedding in VC Shares

As for the embedding process, we firstly define how salient points on Braille are related to the pixels on VC shares. In order to facilitate the identification of Braille on images, each block of six pixels on VC shares represents a Braille cell and salient points are only embedded into black pixels.

The Braille also support for grayscale VC. Character a is able to represent the pixel with grayscale value of '1' and character b or c tends to be used for expressing pixels whose grayscale value is '2'. In a similar way, Braille of other alphabetic characters is utilized to represent pixels with certain grayscale values based on the number of their black dots. Furthermore, color images are separated into R, G, B channels and each of the RGB channels is able to be represented by Braille on the basis of depth of red, green, and blue in the picture.

As Braille cell has three rows, there is also a problem that the height of share may not be multiple of three. Two possible ways are presented. The first is to expand the resolution of VC shares to its triple size. The benefit of this operation is that the Braille can be used to occupy the whole space of VC shares. However, it would spend much time on recreating another share. Another way is to change the last one or two rows to be all white. This solution is more preferable than the former choice. The first reason is that a character of space is comprised by two columns of three dots, therefore, visually impaired people can easily differentiate this extra line from a character of space. Further, this method would not increase the size of VC shares, thereby keeping the consistency with the original shares and secret, it also saves

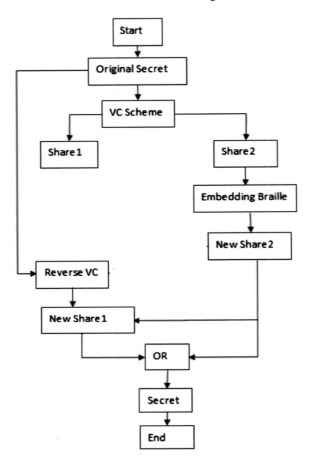

**Fig. 3.15** Flowchart of embedding Braille into VC shares

time than that of the first method. The flowchart of embedding Braille into a share is shown in Fig. 3.15.

The process of embedding Braille into VC is divided into two main subprocesses. First, using basic VC scheme separates the secret into two shares and one of the shares is replaced by Braille input. The second subprocess is to use the replaced share (New Share2) so as to determine the appearance of the other share. The whole process of embedding Braille focuses on input meaningful Braille information and the secret recovery result. Since VC secret is obtained by superimposing its shares together, it is possible to get one of the shares by reversing the operation on the other VC share and the original secret image (Figs. 3.16 and 3.17).

Algorithm 3.3 illustrates how Braille cells are embedded into VC shares. According to Braille rules, capital characters and numbers hold two Braille cells. Besides, every alphabetic character appears to have its own arrangement in the cell. Figure 3.18

**Fig. 3.16** Part of original share of visual cryptography

**Fig. 3.17** Replaced share (a) by Braille, the *red rectangles* are used to indicate Braille cells

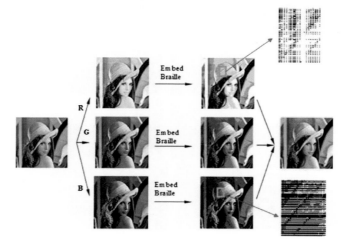

**Fig. 3.18** Color images presented by Braille

shows the color image which are presented by Braille. The tested images and their restored images as VC secrets using Braille are shown in Fig. 3.19.

In the process of embedding Braille, it is important to count the number of the Braille cells to be implanted in VC share since the scale of VC share is in a limited size. Current study of VC shows that it lacks of the strength of authentication process. Major benefits of embedding Braille into VC shares include helping visually impaired people understand the content on VC shares, enhancing decryption ability in dark environment and authentication information being coded as Braille and embedded into VC shares. And, Braille can be regarded as a cipher text. Authentication information can be coded as Braille and embedded into a VC share. At the same time, the other share also tends to have authentication.

Table 3.3 shows the degree how secret image is affected by embedding the Braille. This table indicates the similarity between the original secret and the recovered VC

**Fig. 3.19** The tested images embedding with Braille

---

**Algorithm 3.3:** Embedding Braille into a VC share

---

**Input**  : Braille string $A$, VC share $Img$
**Output**: A VC share embedded with Braille $Img'$

Set $i = 0$;
**while** $i < Length\ of\ A$ **do**

> Judge and find whether $A[i]$ is a capital letter or a number;
> If $A[i]$ is capital then $A[i]$ add one Braille cell in Img according to Braille rules of capital letter;
> If $A[i]$ is number then $A[i]$ add one Braille cell in Img according to Braille of number;
> Map $A[i]$ to Baille characters;
> If the lower case of $A[i]$ is from '$a$' to '$z$' then change the pixel order in every Braille cell-shaped region in Img complying to Braille coding rules ;
> If $A[i]$ is from '0' to '9' then change the pixels in Img according to the order of characters from '$a$' to '$j$';
> $i + +$;

**end**

---

**Table 3.3**  The accuracy of recovered secret image

| Samples | Sample size | Accuracy (%) |
|---------|-------------|--------------|
| 1 | 231 × 219 | 94 |
| 2 | 480 × 360 | 93 |
| 3 | 294 × 282 | 96 |
| 4 | 1024 × 946 | 96 |
| 5 | 1154 × 906 | 95 |
| 6 | 396 × 522 | 94 |

secret in the test bed. From the results in Table 3.3, it is obvious that secret revealing has only been affected slightly after embedding Braille into one of the VC shares.

Embedding Braille in VC shares effectively enhances the VC authentication process. While dealer is able to extract the authentication information from embedded shares, it is difficult for cheaters to realize how the shares are encrypted. This method of VC authentication by embedding Braille solely gives authorized participants the opportunity of accessing secret revealing. Modified and fake shares are able to be easily recognized by verifying the correctness of authentication information.

Even though the advantages of Braille in VC, there are drawbacks of Braille in VC needed to be paid attention to. As meaningful authentication information is embedded into one of the VC shares, the Braille on the other share is possibly meaningless and hard to be verified.

## 3.5  Exercises

(1)  What are the prominent features of 2D Barcode and Braille when they are applied to authentication of visual cryptography?
(2)  How to optimize the VC authentication schemes based on 2D Barcode and Braille?
(3)  2D Barcode and Braille are applied to the authentication of basic VC shares, please list the reasons why they are effective.

## References

1.  Charoenchaimonkon E, Janecek P, Hamratanaphon V (2009) Using advanced encryption standard to secure the content dissemination of electronic Braille books. In: Proceedings of the 3rd international convention on rehabilitation engineering and assistive technology
2.  Gao M, Sun B (2012) Blind watermark algorithm based on QR barcode. Found Intell Syst 122:457–462
3.  Goldberg L, Swan L (2011) A biosemiotic analysis of Braille. Biosemiotics 4:25–38
4.  Horng G, Chen T, Tsai D-S (2006) Cheating in visual cryptography. Des Codes Crypt 38:219–236

5. Kuo D,Wong D, Gao J, Chang L (2010) A 2D barcode validation systemformobile commerce. Adv Grid Pervasive Comput 6104:150–161
6. Van Boven RW, Hamilton RH, Kauffman T, Keenan JP, Pascual-Leone A (2000) Tactile spatial resolution in blind Braille readers. Neurology 54(12):2230–2236
7. Wang GY (2014) Content based authentication of visual cryptography. Masters Thesis, Auckland University of Technology (AUT), New Zealand
8. Wang GY, Liu F, Yan W (2014) 2D barcodes for visual cryptography. Multimedia tools and applications
9. Wang GY, Liu F, Yan W (2014) Braille For visual cryptography. In: IEEE international symposium on multimedia (ISM2014), Taiwan, pp 175–276
10. Weir J, Yan WA (2010) A comprehensive study of visual cryptography. Transactions on data hiding and multimedia security 5. Springer, Berlin
11. Weir J, Yan W (2012) Authenticating visual cryptography shares using 2D barcodes. In: Springer workshop on digital forensics and watermarking, pp 196–210
12. Yin J, Wang L, Li J (2010) The research on paper-mediated Braille automatic recognition method. In: Fifth international conference on frontier of computer science and technology (FCST), pp 619–624
13. Zhu BS, Wu JK, Kankanhalli MS (2003) Print signatures for document authentication. In: Proceedings of ACM conference on computer and communications security, pp 145–153

# Chapter 4
# Various Visual Cryptography Schemes

## 4.1 Embedded Extended VCS

### 4.1.1 Introduction

In this chapter, we present a construction of EVCS which is realized by embedding random shares into meaningful covering shares [23], and we call it as the embedded EVCS. In addition, it has many specific advantages against those well-known EVCSs, respectively [20, 28, 34, 35, 37].

The term of extended visual cryptography scheme (EVCS) was first introduced by Naor et al. [2, 25], where a simple example of (2, 2)-EVCS was presented. In this chapter, when we refer to a corresponding VCS of an EVCS, we mean a traditional VCS that has the same access structure with the EVCS. Generally, an EVCS takes a secret image and original share images as inputs, and output shares that satisfy the following three conditions: (1) any qualified subset of shares can recover the secret image; (2) any forbidden subset of shares cannot obtain any information of the secret image other than the size of the secret image; and (3) all the shares are meaningful images [23].

EVCS is also treated as a technique of steganography. One scenario of the applications of EVCS is to avoid the custom inspections, since the shares of EVCS are meaningful images [23], hence there are fewer chances for the shares to be suspected and detected.

There have been a breadth of EVCSs proposed in the literature. Droste, Ateniese et al. [2], and Wang et al. proposed three EVCSs, respectively, by manipulating the share matrices. Nakajima et al. proposed a (2, 2)-EVCS for natural images. Tsai et al. proposed a simple EVCS, where its shares were simply generated by replacing the white and black subpixels in a traditional VCS share with transparent pixels and pixels from the cover images, respectively. Furthermore, Zhou et al. presented an EVCS using halftoning techniques, which is used to treat grayscale input share

© Springer International Publishing Switzerland 2015
F. Liu and W.Q. Yan, *Visual Cryptography for Image
Processing and Security*, DOI 10.1007/978-3-319-23473-1_4

images. Their methods made use of the complementary images to cover the visual information of the share images. Recently, Wang et al. proposed three EVCSs using an error diffusion halftoning technique to obtain nice looking shares. Their first EVCS also made use of complementary shares to cover the visual information of the shares as the way proposed. Their second EVCS imported auxiliary black pixels to cover the visual information of the shares. In such a way, each qualified participants did not necessarily require a pair of complementary share images. Their third EVCS modified the halftoned share images and imported extra black pixels to cover the visual information of the shares [37, 38].

However, the limitations of these EVCSs mentioned above are obvious. The first limitation is that the pixel expansion is large. For example, the pixel expansion of the EVCS is $m + q$, where $m$ is the pixel expansion of the secret image and $q$ is the chromatic number of a hypergraph; in any case, the value $q$ of satisfies $q \geq 2$. The construction has the following pixel expansion: $\sum_{q=1}^{n} (2^{q-1} \cdot b_q)$ where $b_q$ is the number of elements of $S$ which contains exactly $q$ elements, and $S$ is the set of the qualified subsets. For example, for a $(3, 3)$-EVCS, the pixel expansion will be 13. The pixel expansion of the $(k, n)$ EVCS is $m + m_0$ where $m_0 \geq \lceil n/(k - 1) \rceil$. The second limitation is the bad visual quality of both the shares and the recovered secret images, this is confirmed by the comparisons.

Unfortunately, the EVCS has other limitations: first it is computation expensive; second, the void and cluster algorithm make the positions of the secret pixels dependent on the content of the share images, and hence decreases the visual quality of the recovered secret image; third and most importantly, a pair of complementary images are required for each qualified subset and the participants are required to take more than one shares for some access structures, which will inevitably cause the attentions of the watchdogs at the custom and increase the participants' burden. The same problems also exist in the first method proposed by Wang et al. For Wang's second method, each qualified subset does not require complementary images anymore; however, this method is only for threshold access structure, and the auxiliary black pixels of their EVCS also darkened the shares. For Wang's third method, the halftoned share images are modified and extra black pixels are imported to cover the visual information of the shares. The limitation of this method is that the visual effect of each share will be affected by the content of other shares, and the content of the input original share images should be chosen in a selected way.

Tsai's EVCS is simple, but it may not satisfy the contrast condition anymore [4], and the recovered secret image contains a mixture of the visual information of share images. Consider the essence of mixing gray-level pixels, the secret information may be hard recognize by our human eyes.

Lastly, the EVCS is only for $(2, 2)$ access structure; besides their limitations on the access structure, the scheme may have security issues when relaxing the constraint of the dynamic range.

## 4.1.2 Embedded EVCS

**Definition 4.1** Denote $M^0$ and $M^1$ as the basis matrices of a traditional VCS with access structure $(\Gamma_{Qual}, \Gamma_{Forb})$, and pixel expansion $m$. In order to encode a secret image $I$, the dealer takes $n$ grayscale original share images as inputs, and converts them into $n$ covering shares which are divided into blocks of $t$ subpixels ($t > m$). By embedding the rows of $M^0$ and $M^1$ (after randomly permuting their columns) into the blocks, the embedded EVCS outputs $n$ shares $e_0, e_1, \ldots, e_{n-1}$, and there exist values $\{h_X : for\ X \in \Gamma_{Qual}\}$, $\alpha$ and $\rho$ satisfying

(1) The stacking result of each block of a qualified subset of shares recovers a secret pixel. More precisely, if $X = \{i_1, i_2, \ldots, i_p\} \subset \Gamma_{Qual}$, denote $B_{i_1}, \ldots, B_{i_p}$ as the blocks at the same position of the shares $e_{i_1}, \ldots, e_{i_p}$, then for a white secret pixel, the OR of $B_{i_1}, \ldots, B_{i_p}$ is a vector $v$ that satisfies $w(v) \leq h_X - \alpha \cdot t$, and that for a black secret pixel, it satisfies $w(v) \geq h_X$.

(2) Part of the information of the original share images is preserved in the shares. Define $\rho = (t - m)/t$ be the ratio of the information of the original share images that preserved in the shares, and it satisfies $\rho > 0$ [33].

In Definition 4.1, the first condition ensures that the secret image is visually observed by stacking a qualified subset of shares. The second condition ensures that the shares are meaningful in the sense that parts of the information of the original share images are preserved. The value $\rho$ reflects the ratio of the information of the original share images preserved in the shares [33]. Explicitly, the value of $\alpha$ is between 0 and 1, where $\alpha = 0$ means that no information of the original share images is observed, and $\alpha = 1$ means that all the information of the original share images can be observed. Generally, when $\alpha = 0$, the shares can be considered as meaningful. The larger the value of $\alpha$ is the better visual quality the shares will have. At last, Definition 4.1 does not have the security condition. The secret image is, in fact, encrypted by the corresponding VCS, and then we embed its shares into the covering shares. Hence, the security of the embedded EVCS is guaranteed by the security of the corresponding VCS, i.e., the security condition of Definition 4.1.

Furthermore, we need to point out that, Ateniese et al. [2] proved the optimality of their scheme under their definition of EVCS. Under the definition of Ateniese et al. [2], all the information of the original share images is preserved in the shares. However, as the second condition of the above Definition 4.1 indicates, only parts of the information of the original share images are preserved in the shares, i.e., Definition 4.1 is a relaxed model of the EVCS model proposed. Hence our scheme has smaller pixel expansion by sacrificing part of the information of the original share images. We claim that our definition is reasonable, because the information of the original share images is not as important as that of the secret image for the participants.

The idea of embedded EVCS contains two main steps:

(1) Generate $n$ covering shares, denoted as $s_0, s_1, \ldots, s_{n-1}$;
(2) Generate the embedded shares by embedding the corresponding VCS into the $n$ covering shares, denoted as $e_0, e_1, \ldots, e_{n-1}$.

In step 1, we generate the covering shares for an access structure $\Gamma_m$. We take $n$ grayscale original share images, denoted as $I_0, I_1, \ldots, I_{n-1}$, as the inputs, and output $n$ binary meaningful shares $s_0, s_1, \ldots, s_{n-1}$, where the stacking results of the qualified shares are black images, i.e., the information of the original share images are covered. We call the $n$ output meaningful shares the covering shares. The covering shares have the advantage when the qualified subsets are stacked, all the information of the patterns in the original share images are covered. Hence, the visual quality of the recovered secret image is not affected. Otherwise, the information of the original share images may appear in the recovered secret image, and hence results in bad visual quality.

In step 2, we first make use of the corresponding VCS to encode a secret image, and then embed the shares of the corresponding VCS into the covering shares that were generated in step 1; we call the output shares of step 2 the embedded shares. In this way, when we stack a qualified subset of embedded shares the secret image will appear, because the stacking result of covering shares covers all the information of the original share images.

### 4.1.3 Generating the Covering Shares for an Access Structure Using the Dithering Matrices

Suppose the gray-levels of all the pixels in the image $I_0$ are smaller than 4, then the positions corresponding to $D_{00}^0, D_{02}^0, D_{11}^0, D_{12}^0$, and $D_{21}^0$ of all the pixels in the image $I_0'$ are always black after being halftoned by $D_0$, where $D_{ij}^0$ is the entry in the $i$th row and $j$th column of $D_0$. We now give another dithering matrix $D_1$:

$$D_1 = \begin{pmatrix} 1 & 8 & 3 \\ 6 & 4 & 2 \\ 5 & 0 & 7 \end{pmatrix} \tag{4.1}$$

If an image $I_1$ has its pixels with gray-levels smaller than 5, after running Algorithm 4.1, we get that the positions correspond to $D_{01}^1, D_{10}^1, D_{20}^1$, and $D_{22}^1$ of all the pixels in the image $I_1$ are always black. Hence, when we stack the images $I_1'$ and $I_0'$, the resulting image will be an black image, $I_1'$ and $I_0'$ are covering shares. At this point, we embed the share matrices of the (2, 2)-VCS into the images $I_1'$ and $I_0'$.

Generally, in order to construct the covering shares $s_0, s_1, \ldots, s_{n-1}$ for the general access structure $\Gamma_m$ [1], we need to construct $n$ dithering matrices $D_0, D_1, \ldots, D_{n-1}$. By halftoning the input original share images $I_0, I_1, \ldots, I_{n-1}$, we get the covering shares $s_0, s_1, \ldots, s_{n-1}$ satisfying that the stacking results of the qualified covering shares are black images.

Define the positions of the dithering matrix as the elements in the universal set $\xi = \{g_0, g_1, \ldots, g_{n-1}\}$, i.e., the universal set contains the gray-levels in the dithering matrix, where $s$ is the halftone pixel expansion. We denote the sets $A_0, A_1, \ldots, A_{n-1}$ as $n$ subsets of $\xi$, each subset $A_i$ corresponds to a participant $i \in \gamma$ and a covering share $s_i$. For any qualified subset $Q \subset \Gamma_m$, the union of the corresponding subsets of $A_0, A_1, \ldots, A_{n-1}$ covers $\xi$, i.e., $\bigcup_{j \in Q} A_j = \xi$. We call the subsets $A_0, A_1, \ldots, A_{n-1}$ the covering subsets as they correspond to the covering shares, respectively.

Here, we introduce two new concepts: the black ratio for a subset $A_i$ and the average black ratio. Define the black ratio of the covering subset $A_i$ for the universal set $\xi$ to be $\Re(A_i, \Im) = \frac{|A_i|}{|\Im|}$, and define the average black ratio to be $\overline{\Re}(A_i, \Im) = \frac{\sum_{i=1}^{n-1} |A_i|}{|n \cdot \Im|}$. The black ratio of the covering subsets and the average black ratio is expected to be as small as possible.

At this point, it is clear that in order to generate the covering shares, we need three steps: (1) Generate the covering subsets $A_0, A_1, \ldots, A_{n-1}$ given a $\Gamma_m$; (2) Convert the subsets into the dithering matrices $D_0, D_1, \ldots, D_{n-1}$; and (3) Halftone the original share images $I_0, I_1, \ldots, I_{n-1}$ to generate the covering shares $e_0, e_1, \ldots, e_{n-1}$ using $D_0, D_1, \ldots, D_{n-1}$.

Our approach is to construct the covering subsets first for the case of threshold access structure and then extend to the general access structure [1]. In this section, the covering subsets for threshold access structure are called threshold covering subsets and the covering subsets for the general access structure are called general covering subsets.

Recall that $s$ is the halftone pixel expansion, and $n$ is the number of shares. Because $s$ is independent on the value of $n$, we have the following three cases: (1) $s = n$; (2) $s < n$; and (3) $s > n$. First we consider the case $s = n$.

Let $s = n$. Denote the universal set as $\xi = \{g_0, \ldots, g_{n-1}\}$. Define the covering subsets $A_i = \{g_{(0+i) \bmod n}, g_{(1+i) \bmod n}, \ldots, g_{(n-k+i) \bmod n}\}$. We have the following Theorem 4.1.

**Theorem 4.1** *For the universal set $\xi = \{g_0, \ldots, g_{n-1}\}$, we generate $n$ covering subsets $A_0, A_1, \ldots, A_{n-1}$, satisfying that the union of any $k$ out of $n$ subsets is the universal set $\xi$. The black ratio of each covering subset is $\Re(A_i, \xi) = (n-k+1)/n$ for $i = 0, 1, \ldots, n-1$. Furthermore, these covering subsets have the minimum average black ratio $\overline{\Re}(A_i, \xi) = (n-k+1)/n$.*

In the above construction, all the subsets $A_0, A_1, \ldots, A_{n-1}$ have the same cardinality, i.e., have the same black ratio. However, it is not necessary. The following corollary gives a way to change the black ratio of the covering subsets, while the average black ratio remains the same as the original covering subsets. This change will result in that some covering subsets will have their black ratio decreased by sacrificing the black ratio increase of other covering subsets. This does make sense because in practical applications, different covering subsets may have different importance, and hence have different sensitivity on their black ratios.

**Corollary 4.1** *Denote the universal set as* $\xi = \{g_0, \ldots, g_{n-1}\}$, *and* $(k, n)$, *denote the threshold covering subsets generated by Construction 4.1 as* $A_0, A_1, \ldots, A_{n-1}$. *For any two covering subsets* $A_i$ *and* $A_j$, *where* $i \neq j$, *for any element* $x \in A_i$ *and* $x \in A_j$, *we remove* $x$ *from* $A_i$ *and put* $x$ *into* $A_j$, *denote the new constructed subsets as* $A_0, A_1, \ldots, A_{n-1}$, *then the subsets* $A_0, A_1, \ldots, A_{n-1}$ *are still* $(k, n)$ *threshold covering subsets. Furthermore, the average black ratio of* $A_0, A_1, \ldots, A_{n-1}$ *remains the same as that of* $A_0, A_1, \ldots, A_{n-1}$.

We then construct the covering subsets for the cases $s < n$ and $s > n$ for the universal set $\xi = \{g_0, \ldots, g_{n-1}\}$ in Constructions 4.1 and 4.2, respectively.

**Construction 4.1** We take the case $s < n$ into consideration. We make use of the covering subsets $A_0, A_1, \ldots, A_{n-1}$ of Construction 4.1. Let $A'_0, A'_1, \ldots, A'_{n-1}$ be generated by removing the elements $g_0, \ldots, g_{n-1}$ from the covering subsets $A_0, A_1, \ldots, A_{n-1}$, i.e., $A'_i = A_i - \{g_0, \ldots, g_{n-1}\}$, $i = 0, \ldots, n-1$. The subsets $A'_0, A'_1, \ldots, A'_{n-1}$ will satisfy that the union of any $k$ out of $n$ shares will cover the new universal set of $s$ elements, i.e., $\xi = \{g_0, \ldots, g_{s-1}\}$, are the covering subsets $A_0, A_1, \ldots, A_{n-1}$ for the case $s < n$.

**Construction 4.2** We take the case $s > n$ into consideration. We make use of the covering subsets $A_0, A_1, \ldots, A_{n-1}$ of Construction 4.1. First, we add $n - (s \bmod n)$ elements into the universal set $\xi = \{g_0, \ldots, g_{s-1}\}$, denote the $n - (s \bmod n)$ elements as $a_0, a_1, \ldots, a_{n-(s \bmod n)-1}$. Let $s' = s + n - (s \bmod n)$; then we divide the $s'$ elements of the new universal set $\xi' = \{g_0, \ldots, g_{s'-1}\}$ into groups, where each of the $s'/n$ groups has $n$ elements, denote the $s'/n$ groups as $G_0, G_1, \ldots, G_{s'/n}$. For each $G_i$, we treat it as a universal set, and call Construction 4.1 to construct the covering subsets. Then we will have the following subsets: $A_0^1, A_1^1, \ldots, A_{n-1}^1, A_0^2, A_1^2,$ $\ldots, A_{n-1}^2, \ldots, A_0^{s'/n}, A_1^{s'/n}, \ldots, A_{n-1}^{s'/n}$ where we denote $A_i^j$ as the $i$th covering subset belonging to the group $G_j$. Then let the $n$ covering subsets for the universal set $\xi'$, denoted as $A'_0, A'_1, \ldots, A'_{n-1}$, be $A'_0 = A_0^1 \bigcup A_0^2 \bigcup \cdots \bigcup A_0^{s'/n}, A'_1 = A_1^1 \bigcup A_1^2 \bigcup \cdots \bigcup A_1^{s'/n}, \ldots, A'_{n-1} = A_{n-1}^1 \bigcup A_{n-1}^2 \bigcup \cdots \bigcup A_{n-1}^{s'/n}$, and they satisfy that the union of any $k$ out of the $n$ subset will cover the universal set $\xi' = \{g_0, \ldots, g_{s'-1}\}$.

**Corollary 4.2** *For the universal set $\xi = \{g_0, \ldots, g_{s-1}\}$ and the threshold access structure $(k, n)$, the covering subsets constructed by Constructions 4.1 and 4.2 for the cases $s < n$ and $s > n$, respectively, have the minimum average black ratio.*

We now construct the covering subsets for the general access structure $\Gamma_m$ [1]. A simple construction for the general covering subsets is Denote $B \in \Gamma_m$ as a qualified subset and let $min\{|B|, B \in \Gamma_m\}$ be the minimum number of the cardinality of all the qualified subsets $B$ in $\Gamma_m$. Then the construction of the general covering subsets $A_0, A_1, \ldots, A_{n-1}$ is converted into the construction of the $min(\{|B| : B \in \Gamma_m\}, n)$ threshold covering subsets. The constructions of the general covering subsets for the cases $s < n$ and $s > n$ are as same as the construction of the $min(\{|B| : B \in \Gamma_m\}, n)$ threshold covering subsets. This construction is simple; however, the disadvantage of this construction is that it has a high black ratio for each covering subset (i.e., $(n - min\{|B| : B \in \Gamma_m\} + 1)/n$). Take the general access structure $\Gamma_m = \{\{0, 1\}\{1, 2\}\{2, 3\}\}$ as an example, the black ratio for each covering subset will be $(4 - 2 + 1)/4 = 3/4$.

**Construction 4.3** Denote $\Gamma_m$ as the maximal forbidden access structure for the general access structure $(\Gamma_{Qual}, \Gamma_{Forb})$. A cumulative map $(A, \xi)$ for the $\Gamma_{Qual}$ is a finite set $\xi$ along with a mapping $A : \gamma \to 2^\xi$ such that $Q \subseteq \gamma$ for implies that $\bigcup_{\alpha \in Q} A_\alpha = \xi \Leftrightarrow Q \in \Gamma_{Qual}$, where $A_\alpha$ is the subset mapped from $\alpha \in Q$.

We construct a cumulative map $(A, \xi)$ for $\Gamma_{Qual}$ using $\Gamma_M$ as follows: Assume $\Gamma_M = \{F_0, \ldots, F_{t-1}\}$. Let the universal set be $\xi = \{g_0, \ldots, g_{t-1}\}$ and for any $i \in \gamma$, let $A_i = \{g_j | \{i\} \bigcap F_j = \emptyset; 0 \leq j \leq t - 1\}$. For any $X \in Qual$, we have $\bigcup_{i \in X} A_i = \xi$. Note that for any set $X \in \Gamma_{Forb}$, we have $\bigcup_{i \in X} A_i \neq \xi$.

Construction 4.3 produces the general covering subsets with $s = t$ elements. The constructions of the covering subsets of the cases $s < t$ and $s > t$ for general access structure are as same as the threshold ones, i.e., Constructions 4.2 and 4.3. The following example shows how the above constructions work.

According to Construction 4.3, we assume $s = 4$ and since $t = 3$, we add two elements $a_0$ and $a_1$; then we have $s' = 6$, hence the incidence matrix, denoted as $K'$, for the subsets $A'_0, A'_1, A'_2$ and $A'_3$ becomes as follows, where $K'_{ij}$ is the entry of $K'$ at the $i$th row and $j$th column, and is defined as

$$K'_{ij} = \begin{cases} 1 & \text{if } g_i \in A_i \\ 0 & \text{otherwise} \end{cases} \tag{4.2}$$

$$K' = \begin{array}{c} \\ g_0 \\ g_1 \\ g_2 \\ g_3 \\ a_0 \\ a_1 \end{array} \begin{array}{c} A'_0\ A'_1\ A'_2\ A'_3 \\ \left[\begin{array}{cccc} 0 & 1 & 0 & 1 \\ 0 & 1 & 1 & 0 \\ 1 & 0 & 1 & 0 \\ 0 & 1 & 0 & 1 \\ 0 & 1 & 1 & 0 \\ 1 & 0 & 1 & 0 \end{array}\right] \end{array} \tag{4.3}$$

By removing the elements $a_0$ and $a_1$, we get the general covering subsets $A_0'' = \{g_2\}$, $A_1'' = \{g_0, g_1, g_3\}$, $A_2'' = \{g_1, g_2\}$ and $A_3'' = \{g_0, g_3\}$. The black ratios for the four covering subsets are $R(A_0'', \xi) = |A_0''|/|\xi| = 1/4$, $R(A_1'', \xi) = |A_1''|/|\xi| = \frac{3}{4}$, $R(A_2'', \xi) = |A_2''|/|\xi| = \frac{1}{2}$ and $R(A_3'', \xi) = |A_3''|/|\xi| = \frac{1}{2}$, and the average black ratio is $\frac{1}{2}$.

In this part, we will construct the dithering matrices $D_i$ using the covering subsets $A_i$, $i = i_0, i_1, \ldots, n - 1$. The dithering matrix $D_i$ should satisfy that the gray-levels at the positions in $A_i$ of $D_i$ are larger than $s - |A_i|$. As we previously defined, the dithering matrix is a $s(=c \times d)$ integer matrix.

**Construction 4.4**  We define the starting dithering matrix, denoted as $D$. The starting dithering matrix is a random matrix with $s$ entries, where each entry of $D$ contains a gray-level, and each gray-level of $\{0, 1, \ldots, s - 1\}$ appears in $D$ once. Particularly, if $s$ is a square number, we choose a magic square as the starting dithering matrix $D$.

$$
D = \begin{pmatrix}
g_0 & g_1 & \cdots & g_{c-1} \\
g_c & g_{c+1} & \cdots & g_{2c-2} \\
\cdots & \cdots & \cdots & \cdots \\
g_{(d-1)\cdot c} & g_{(d-1)\cdot c+1} & \cdots & g_{s-1}
\end{pmatrix} \tag{4.4}
$$

We construct the dithering matrix $D_i$ using the starting dithering matrix $D$ and the covering subset $A_i$, $i = 0, 1, \ldots, n - 1$. Suppose $A_i = \{g_{i_0}, \ldots, g_{i_{t-1}}\}$. We swap the gray-levels in $A_i$ with the gray-levels $\{s - 1, s - 2, \ldots, s - t\}$. Particularly, one can swap the gray-level $g_{i_j}$ with the gray-level $s - 1 - j$ in $D$ for $A$, where $j = 0, \ldots, t - 1$.

Repeat the above process for all the covering subsets $A_i$, $i = 0, 1, \ldots, n - 1$; we get $n$ dithering matrixes $D_0, D_1, \ldots, D_{n-1}$, respectively. At this point, we halftone the input original share images $I_0, I_1, \ldots, I_{n-1}$, using the dithering matrices $D_0, D_1, \ldots, D_{n-1}$, and hence get the covering shares $s_0, s_1, \ldots, s_{n-1}$. The stacking result of the qualified covering shares will be an black image. However, we have to point out that this construction requires that the gray-levels of all the pixels in each image have to be no larger than $s - |A_i|$, respectively, where $s$ is the halftone pixel expansion, i.e., $s = |\xi|$. This constraint requires the dealer to choose the input images carefully. Images that do not satisfy this requirement need to be darkened before being halftoned. A simple method to darken an image $I_i$ satisfying that the gray-levels of all the pixels in $I_i$ are no larger than $s - |A_i|$ is as follows:

$$
I(x, y) \leftarrow I(x, y) \cdot \frac{a - |A_i|}{max(I_i)} \tag{4.5}
$$

where $I_i(x, y)$ is the gray-level of the pixel at the position $(x, y)$ in $I_i$ and $max(I_i)$ is the largest gray-level of the pixels in $I_i$.

The darkening process will inevitably cause the loss in the visual quality of the shares. So the value of $s - |A_i|$ is expected to be as large as possible, and hence the value of $|A_i|/s$ is expected to be as small as possible, i.e., the black ratio $|A_i|$ is expected to be as small as possible. Hence, the black ratio $R(A_i, \xi) = |A_i|/s$ reflects the requirements on a single input image $I_i$. Furthermore, we introduced the notion average black ratio which reflects the requirements on darkness of all the input images $I_0, I_1, \ldots, I_{n-1}$ from an overall point of view. Another reason we introduce the concept of the average black ratio is one cannot design the threshold covering subsets with all of them having minimum black ratio simultaneously (Corollary 4.1), but one can design the threshold covering subset with minimum average black ratio (Theorem 4.1, Corollaries 4.1 and 4.2), so the average black ratio provides a more appropriate criterion about the effectiveness of the covering subsets.

Note that, after halftoning $I_i$ using $D_i$ of Construction 4.5, the pixels corresponding to the covering subset $A_i$ in dithering matrix $D_i$ will be black pixels. If those pixels are regularly arranged in $D_i$, then some grid patterns are likely to appear in the halftoned shares from an overall point of view [28]. According to our experiments, using random matrix or magic square as the starting dithering matrix $D$ can mitigate this phenomenon. That is the reason for choosing random matrix or magic square as the starting dithering matrix in Construction 4.4.

## 4.1.4 Embedding the Shares of the Corresponding VCS into the Covering Shares

After generating the covering shares, the embedding process is implemented by the following Algorithm 4.1.

Suppose the size of each covering share is $p \times q$. We first divide each covering share into $p \cdot q/t$ blocks with each block containing $t$ subpixels, where $t \geq m$. In case $p \times q$ is not a multiple of $t$, then some simple padding can be applied, for which the detail is skipped here. We choose $m$ positions in each $t$ subpixels to embed the $m$ subpixels of $M$. In this part, we call the chosen $m$ positions that are used to embed

---

**Algorithm 4.1:** The embedding process

**Input** : $n$ covering shares, the corresponding $VCS(C_0, C_1)$ with pixel expansion $m$ and secret image $I$

**Output**: The $n$ embedded shares $e_0, e_1, \ldots, e_{n-1}$

**Step 1**. Dividing the cover sharing into blocks that include $t(\geq m)$ subpixels;
**Step 2**. For all odd $p \in \{0, \ldots, k\}$, call $ADD(p, M^1)$;
**Step 3**. Choose $m$ embedding positions at each block in the $n$ covering shares;
**Step 4**. For each black (resp., white) pixels in $I$, randomly choose a share matrix $M \in C_1 (resp., M \in C_0)$;
**Step 5**. Embed the $m$ subpixels of each row of the share matrix $M$ into the $m$ embedding positions chosen in step 2.

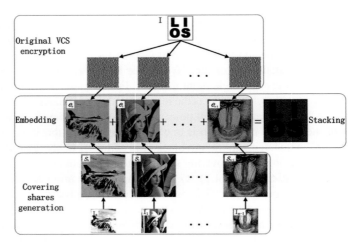

**Fig. 4.1** Diagram of Algorithm 4.1

the secret information as the embedding positions. In order to correctly decode the secret image only by stacking the shares, the embedding positions of all the $n$ covering shares should be the same. At this point, by stacking the embedded shares, the $t - m$ subpixels that have not been embedded by secret subpixels are always black, and the $m$ subpixels that are embedded by the secret subpixels recover the secret image as the corresponding VCS does. Hence, the secret image appears (Fig. 4.1).

Because $t \geq m$, we have the following two cases: When $t = m$, the embedded EVCS degenerates to a VCS, because all the information of the covering shares is covered by the secret subpixels of the share matrices of the corresponding VCS. When $t > m$, we have $\rho = (t - m)/t > 0$, which implies that the scheme is an embedded EVCS. In this embedded EVCS, there are $t - m$ subpixels in the covering shares $s_0, s_1, \ldots, s_{n-1}$ that preserve the information of the original share images $I_0, I_1, \ldots, I_{n-1}$ and the remaining $m$ subpixels carry the secret information of the secret image. Hence, we get to know that the smallest secret image pixel expansion is $m + 1$ when we use the above Algorithm 4.1.

Because the $m$ subpixels in the share matrix correspond to one secret pixel in the secret image, and the $m$ subpixels in the share matrix are embedded into $t$ positions in the $n$ covering shares, we get to know that one pixel in the secret image corresponds to $t$ subpixels of the embedded shares in our construction. Hence, the secret image pixel expansion is $t$ in our construction.

By examining Algorithm 4.1, it is easy to note that the share pixel expansion is different from the secret image pixel expansion. The secret image pixel expansion is independent of the share pixel expansion. Because we choose the block size $t$ to be arbitrarily large (we assume the covering shares can be arbitrarily large), the secret image pixel expansion can be arbitrarily large. In the scheme, because the original share images are only expanded when they are halftoned, the share pixel expansion equals the halftone pixel expansion. We denote as the share pixel expansion or equivalently the halftone pixel expansion. To avoid the image distortion during the halftoning process, we usually let it be a square number.

When the secret image is much smaller than the covering shares, we may have a number of choices of the values of $t$. For a bigger $t$, there are more subpixels (say $t - m$) preserving the information of the covering shares, and hence we have better visual quality for the shares. So there exists a trade-off between the secret image pixel expansion and visual quality of the shares.

Furthermore, for bigger halftone pixel expansion, the dithering matrix can simulate more gray-levels, hence, having better visual quality for the shares. So another trade-off lies between the share pixel expansion and the visual quality of the shares. (Recall that the share pixel expansion is equal to the halftone pixel expansion.)

## 4.1.5 Further Improvements on the Visual Quality of Shares

(1) Reducing the Black Ratio of the Covering Subsets for The Black $s = t$.

The black ratio of $A_i$ requires the gray-levels of all the pixels in the original input images $I_i$ to be no larger than $s - |A_i|$. So, for an input image, the dealer needs first to darken the input image to satisfy the requirement. If the black ratio is high, the darkening process will decrease the visual quality of the covering shares, so the black ratio is expected to be as small as possible. Recall that in the embedding process, $m$ out of every $t$ subpixels in the covering shares are replaced by the subpixels of the basis matrix of the corresponding VCS. Hence, there is no difference whether these $m$ subpixels are black or not in the stacking result of the qualified covering shares. Our method of reducing the black ratio is realized by reducing the number of the elements in the universal set. The universal set is modified as follows: Let the new universal set be $\xi' = \{g_0, \ldots, g_{s-m-1}\}$, which contains $s - m$ elements; recall that the universal set before was $\xi = \{g_0, \ldots, g_{s-1}\}$, which contains $s$ elements; we have $\xi' = \xi$. The stacking result of the qualified covering shares only needs to satisfy that the positions corresponding to the universal set $\xi$ are black.

**Construction 4.5**  The construction of the dithering matrix with reduced black ratio:

**Step 1** Choose the $m(<s)$ embedding positions in the starting dithering matrix, and denote the gray-levels in the embedding positions as $\{g_0, \ldots, g_{m-1}\}$. Remove these positions from the universal set $\xi$, and denote the new universal set as $\xi' = \{g'_0, \ldots, g'_{s-m-1}\}$, i.e., the rest gray-levels other than that in the embedding positions.

**Step 2** Generate the covering subsets $A'_i$, for the universal set $\xi'$, where $i = 0, 1, \ldots, n - 1$.

**Step 3** Convert the covering subsets $A'_i$ into the dithering matrix $D'_i$, where $i = 0, 1, \ldots, n - 1$.

**Step 4** For each dithering matrix $D'_i$, swap the gray-levels $\{g_0, \ldots, g_{m-1}\}$ in the embedding positions with gray-levels $\{s - |A_i| - 1, \ldots, s - |A_i| - m\}$ in a similar way as that of Construction 4.4. Denote the final dithering matrix as $D_i$, where $i = 0, 1, \ldots, n - 1$.

Note that, in Construction 4.5, the reason for Step 4 is as follows: In Step 3, we get the dithering matrix, and after halftoning a share image by $D_i'$, the pixels correspond to gray-levels $\{s - 1, \ldots, s - |A_i|\}$ will be halftoned into black pixels with certainty. Beside these pixels, the pixels correspond to gray-levels $\{s - |A_i| - 1, \ldots, s - |A_i| - m\}$ will be halftoned into black pixels with the largest possibility, compared to that of the rest gray-levels. Hence, if these pixels (correspond to gray-levels $\{s - |A_i| - 1, \ldots, s - |A_i| - m\}$) are replaced by the secret subpixels of the corresponding VCS. The halftoned shares will look brighter than other pixels are replaced.

(2) Reducing the Black Ratio of the Covering Subsets for The Black $s \neq t$.

Denote $lcm(a, b)$ as the least common multiple of the two integers $a$ and $b$. Our method is to construct $(s, t)/s$ dithering matrices for the $i$th input original share image, denoted as $D_{i,0}, D_{i,lcm(s,t)/s-1}$. The $lcm(s, t)/s$ dithering matrices are used to halftone $lcm(s, t)/s$ adjacent pixels of the input original share images at a time. The $lcm(s, t)/s$ dithering matrices are divided into $lcm(s, t)/s$ blocks with $t$ subpixels for each block; we embed $m$ secret subpixels into each block. Hence each dithering matrix has a different universal set. For each universal set, we construct the dithering matrix using the method that is similar to Construction 4.5, respectively. Hence, we get the $lcm(s, t)/s$ dithering matrices for each input original share image. The whole process of generating the dithering matrices is formally described as follows.

**Construction 4.6** The construction of the $lcm(s, t)/s$ dithering matrices for each input original share image for $s \neq t$:

**Step 1**   Concatenate $lcm(s, t)/s$ starting dithering matrices with $s$ entries, and divide these starting dithering matrices into $lcm(s, t)/s$ blocks.

**Step 2**   Choose the $m$ embedding positions in each block.

**Step 3**   Concatenate the $lcm(s, t)/s$ blocks, and divide them into $lcm(s, t)/s$ dithering matrices.

**Step 4**   For each dithering matrix, remove the embedding positions, and the rest of the positions in each dithering matrix constitute the universal set for this dithering matrix.

**Step 5**   Generate the dithering matrixes according to Construction 4.6.

In this section, we give the results for the Algorithm 4.1 and constructions. We also compare the embedded EVCS with many of the well-known EVCSs in the literature.

First, we give the original images that will be used [14]: Lena, Airplane, Baboon, Ruler, Boat, and the secret image. The sizes of these images are $256 \times 256$; they will be scaled to their proper size when necessary. We provide two well-known objective numerical measurements for the visual quality, the peak signal-to-noise ratio (PSNR) and the universal quality index (UQI) [31]. The PSNR is adopted to assess the distortion of each share image with its original halftoned share image (i.e., without the darkening process). In such a way, the PSNR values reflect the effects of a combination of the following possible processes in EVCSs: darkening, embedding, and modification. The PSNR is defined as follows:

$$PSNR = 10 \cdot \log \frac{255^2}{MSE} \qquad (4.6)$$

where *MSE* is the mean squared error. The UQI is adopted to assess the distortion of each share image with its original grayscale share image (after being scaled to the size of shares). Hence, the UQI value reflects the effect of halftoning process besides darkening, embedding, and modification processes in EVCSs.

In this section, we show two methods to generate the covering shares, and proved the optimality on the black ratio of the threshold covering subsets [6–8, 35]. According to comparisons with many of the well known, our construction is flexible in the sense that there exist two tradeoffs between the share pixel expansion and the visual quality of the shares and between the secret image pixel expansion and the visual quality of the shares. Comparisons on the experimental results show that the visual quality of the share of the proposed embedded EVCS is competitive with that of many of the well-known EVCSs in the literature.

## 4.2 Probabilistic Visual Cryptography Scheme (PVCS)

**Definition 4.2** Let $k$ and $n$ be positive integers satisfying $2 \leq k \leq n$. The two collections of $n \times 1$ binary matrices $(C_0, C_1)$ constitute a probabilistic threshold visual cryptography scheme $(k, n)$-PVCS [19, 24, 25, 29, 31–33, 35–37], if the following properties are satisfied:

**Contrast.** For any $s \in C_0$, denote $p(w, k)$ as the probability that the dot operation $(\cdot)$ of any $k$ out of the $n$ rows of $s$ is 1, and for any $s \in C_1$, denote $p(b, k)$ as the probability that the dot operation $(\cdot)$ of any $k$ out of the $n$ rows of $s$ is 1, then $p(w, k) < p(b, k)$.

**Security.** For any $i_1 < i_2 < \cdots < i_t$ in $\{1, 2, \ldots, n\}$ with $t < k$, the values of the two probabilities $p(w, t)$ and $p(b, t)$ for the collections $C_0$ and $C_1$ are the same.

**Definition 4.3** Average Contrast of the $(k, n)$-PVCS is defined as

$$\alpha_{(p(b,k),\, p(w,k))} = \frac{p(b, k) - p(w, k)}{p(b, k) \cdot (1 - p(b, k)) + p(w, k) \cdot (1 - p(w, k))} \qquad (4.7)$$

where the parameters $p(b, k)$ and $p(w, k)$ are the probabilities that the dot operation $(\cdot)$ of any $k$ out of the $n$ rows of the matrices in the collections $C_1$ and $C_0$ is 1, respectively.

Hence overall, the clearness of the recovered secret image of the PVCS is the same as the clearness of the recovered secret image of the DVCS. However, because of the probabilistic nature of PVCS, it has a thin line problem, i.e., a thin solid line in the secret image is usually recovered as a dotted line in the recovered secret image. The reason is that part of the black pixels in the thin solid line are falsely represented by the white pixels in the recovered secret image. Hence, the PVCS has the disadvantage in displaying the details of the secret image, such as the thin lines and scattered pixels.

## 4.3  Size-Invariant VCS (SIVCS)

In this section, by examining the known SIVCS', we observe that visual quality of the recovered secret image is reflected by both the average contrast and the variance of the darkness levels [4, 5]. Given a fixed average contrast, the recovered secret image with a smaller variance has better visual quality, especially the evenness of the recovered secret image. In this section, we thoroughly verify, analytically and experimentally, the effectiveness of the variance to be a criterion for evaluating the visual quality of the recovered secret image. And based on the observation, we present two ME-SIVCSs (Constructions 4.3 and 4.4) under different security levels (ME-SIVCS-1 and ME-SIVCS-2) [9], where the proposed schemes satisfy the following properties.

- For both constructions, the share images and the recovered secret images are size invariant.
- For both constructions, the visual quality of the recovered secret images is improved compared with that of the P-SIVCS, which is realized by reducing the variance of the darkness levels of each block in the recovered secret image.
- Construction 4.3 avoids the thin line problems TLP-1 and TLP-2. Construction 4.4 avoids all the thin line problems TLP-1, TLP-2, and TLP-3.
- Both constructions are for general $(k, n)$ access structure.

**Definition 4.4**  $(k, n, t)$-ME-SIVCS-1. A $(k, n, t)$-multipixel encryption size-invariant visual cryptography scheme [21] encrypts a block of $t$ adjacent pixels at a time, where $t$ should not be too large and the chosen of the $t$ pixels does not relate to the content of the secret image. For the encryption of any two blocks $B$ and $B'$ in the secret image, a $(k, n, t)$-ME-SIVCS-1 generates $n$ shares $s_1, \ldots, s_n$ satisfying:

**Contrast**. Denote $v$ and $v'$ as the vectors that consist of the secret pixels at $B$ and $B'$, respectively, and denote $v_p$ and $v'_p$ as their corresponding vectors that are on the shares $s_p$ for $p = 1, \ldots, n$. Without loss of generality, suppose $w(v) > w(v')$, then for any $k$ out of $n$ shares $Q = \{s_{q_1}, \ldots, s_{q_k}\}(\subseteq \{s_1, \ldots, s_n\})$, let $v_Q = v_{q_1} OR, \ldots, OR v_{q_k}$ and $v'_Q = v'_{q_1} OR, \ldots, OR v'_{q_k}$, then stacking result satisfies $w(v_Q) > w(v'_Q)$, where $w(v_Q)$, for example, is the average value of $w(v_Q)$ for all the possible values of $v_Q$.

**Security**. For any less than $k$ shares $F = \{s_{f_1}, \ldots, s_{f_d}\}(\subset \{S_1, \ldots, S_n\})$ where $d < k$, let $v_F = v_{f_1} OR, \ldots, OR v_{f_d}$, and $v'_F = v'_{f_1} OR, \ldots, OR v'_{f_d}$, then the darkness levels of $v_F$ and $v'_F$ have the same statistical characteristics regardless whatever the secrets are. Particularly, it satisfies $\mu(w(v_F)) = \mu(w(v'_F))$ and $\sigma(w(v_F)) = \sigma(w(v'_F))$, where $\mu(\cdot)$ denotes the mathematical expectation and $\sigma(\cdot)$ denotes the variance.

Note that we require each block of ME-SIVCS consists of adjacent pixels. The reason is that our human visual system (HVS) only average adjacent pixels to a gray-level area. And in Definition 4.4, the reason for $t$ should not be too large that the security condition guarantees the stacking results of less than $k$ shares will be a noise like image on the condition that there are a large number of blocks in the stacked result image.

In Definition 4.4, the contrast condition ensures that the secret image can be recovered by stacking any $k$ out of $n$ shares from an overall view point. And the security condition ensures the stacking result of less than $k$ shares is a noise image. Note that the security condition of the definition does not guarantee the unconditional security as the traditional VCS does (except when $t = 1$). However, consider that VCSs are usually useful in such scenarios that are lack of computers. It is very hard for human to get useful information about the secret only by observing a noise image especially when computers are not accessible. In such cases, the security condition is enough to secure the secrets. From other side, the weakened security condition provided possibilities to improve the visual quality of the recovered image, which may be more important for such scenarios that are lack of computers.

However, we still give the formal definition of ME-SIVCS with unconditional security condition as follows.

**Definition 4.5** $(k, n, t)$-ME-SIVCS-2. A $(k, n, t)$-multipixel encryption size-invariant visual cryptography scheme [21] encrypts a block of $t$ adjacent pixels at a time, where the chosen of the $t$ pixels does not relate to the content of the secret image. For the encryption of any two blocks $B$ and $B'$ in the secret image, a $(k, n, t)$-ME-SIVCS-2 generates $n$ shares $s_1, \ldots, s_n$ satisfying:

**Contrast.** Denote $v$ and $v'$ as the vectors that consist of the secret pixels at $B$ and $B'$, respectively, and denote $v_p$ and $v'_p$ as their corresponding vectors that are on the shares $s_p$ for $p = 1, \ldots, n$. Without loss of generality, suppose $w(v) > w(v')$, then for any $k$ out of $n$ shares $\{s_{q_1}, \ldots, s_{q_k}\}(\subseteq \{s_1, \ldots, s_n\})$, let $v_Q = v_{q_1}OR, \ldots, ORv_{q_k}$ and $v'_Q = v'_{q_1}OR, \ldots, ORv'_{q_k}$, then stacking result satisfies $avg(w(v_Q)) > avg(w(v'_Q))$, where $avg(w(v_Q))$ is the average value of $w(v_Q)$ for all the possible values of $v_Q$.

**Security.** Denote $CF$ and $CF'$ as the collections of all the possible submatrices of any less than $k$ shares for blocks $B$ and $B'$, respectively, then $CF$ and $CF'$ are indistinguishable since they contain the same submatrices with the same frequencies.

The construction of $(k, n)$-P-SIVCS is described as follows.

**Construction 4.7** $((k, n)$-P-SIVCS) Let the $n \times m$ matrices $M_0$ and $M_1$ be the basis matrices of a $(k, n)$-D-SEVCS. The collections $C_0$ and $C_1$ of the $(k, n)$-P-SIVCS consist of all the $m$ columns in $M_0$ and $M_1$, respectively.

According to Construction 4.7, when the dealer encrypts a black (resp. white) pixel, he just needs to choose a column in $M_1$ (resp. $M_0$) randomly, and distributes its rows to the $n$ participants. And it is easy to verify that Construction 4.7 satisfies the Definition 4.5, where we have $p(1, k) = h/m$ and $p(0, k) = l/m$. ($h$ and $l$ are the darkness level thresholds of the corresponding $(k, n)$-D-SEVCS) [35].

The $(k, n, m)$-ME-SIVCS takes a secret image as input, and outputs $n$ share images. Suppose the secret image is divided into $q$ blocks of $m$ pixels. The $(k, n, m)$-ME-SIVCS is described as follows.

**Construction 4.8** $((k, n, m)$-ME-SIVCS). Let the $n \times m$ matrices $M_0$ and $M_1$ be the basis matrices for a $(k, n)$-D-SEVCS. The following steps encrypt a block of $m$ secret pixels at a time. Denote $b$ as the number of the black pixels in the block, and $m$ as the pixel expansion of the corresponding D-SEVCS and also is the block size. Denote $E[b]$ as the number of blocks that have $b$ black pixels and have already been encrypted.

1. $E[b] \leftarrow 0$ for $b = 1, 2, \ldots, m$
2. For $i = 0$ $to$ $q - 1$ do the following
3. /*Suppose the $i$th block in the secret image is Bb*/
4. If $E[b] \bmod m < b$ then encrypt $B_b$ by $M_1$ after permuting its columns randomly
5. Else encrypt $B_b$ by $M_0$ after permuting its columns randomly
6. $E[b] \leftarrow E[b] + 1$

For a block of $m$ pixels which has $b$ black pixels, Construction 4.2 shows a method to encrypt these $m$ pixels with the basis matrices $M_0$ and $M_1$, where the use of basis matrix $M_1$ takes a proportion of $b/m$ and that of $M_0$ is $(m - b)/m$.

## 4.4 A ME-SIVCS that Satisfies ME-SIVCS-2 Security

A $(k, n, m)$-ME-SIVCS takes a secret image as input, and outputs $n$ share images. Suppose the secret image is divided into $q$ blocks of $m$ pixels. The $(k, n, m)$-ME-SIVCS under ME-SIVCS-2 security is described as follows.

**Definition 4.6** $((k, n, m)$-ME-SIVCS under ME-SIVCS-2 security) Denote $M_0$ and $M_1$ as the basis matrices of the corresponding D-SEVCS under the definition of VCS, the following steps encrypt a $B_{m,b}$ block at a time, where $b$ is the number of the black pixels, $m$ is the pixel expansion of the corresponding D-SEVCS and also is the block size.

1. $E[b] \leftarrow b$ for $b = 1, 2, \ldots, m$
2. $N[b] \leftarrow m$ for $b = 1, 2, \ldots, m$
3. For $i = 0$ to $q - 1$ do the following
4. /* Suppose the $i$th block in the secret image is $B_{m,b}$ */
5. If Random($N[b]$) $< E[b]$ then
6. Encrypt $B_{m,b}$ by $M_1$ after permuting its columns randomly
7. $N[b] \leftarrow N[b] - 1$
8. $E[b] \leftarrow E[b] - 1$
9. Else
10. Encrypt $B_{m,b}$ by $M_0$ after permuting its columns randomly
11. $N[b] \leftarrow N[b] - 1$
12. If $N[b] = 0$ then $E[b] \leftarrow b, N[b] \leftarrow m$

**Remark.** In Construction 4.3, the function Random($N[b]$) generates a random number between 0 and $N[b] - 1$. $N[b]$ and $E[b]$ together guarantee that for every $m$ of $B_{m,b}$ blocks, there are exactly $b$ of them are encrypted by $M_1$. And for each block, both $M_0$ and $M_1$ have chances to be chosen for encryption.

We compare the values of the variances of the above Constructions 4.1 and 4.3. According to Construction 4.3, we have every $m$ of $B_{m,b}$ blocks are encrypted by $M_1$ for $b$ times and by $M_0$ for $(m - b)$ times, which means that a $B_{m,b}$ block is encrypted by $M_1$ with a probability of $b/m$ and by $M_0$ with a probability of $(m - b)/m$ and that is the same as that of Construction 4.2. We hence have the variance of a $B_{m,b}$ block is $\delta_{m,b}^3 = \frac{b(m-b)(h-l)^2}{m^2}$, which implies that for most reasonable values of $m$, $h$, and $l$, we have $\delta_{m,b}^3 \leq \delta_{m,b}^1$ i.e., the visual quality of the recovered secret image of Construction 4.3 is better than that of Construction 4.1 on block size $m$ for most reasonable values of $m$, $h$, and $l$.

**Theorem 4.2** *The Construction 4.3 generates a $(k, n, m)$-ME-SIVCS under ME-SIVCS-2 security.*


## 4.5 A ME-SIVCS that Satisfies ME-SIVCS-1 Security

Denote $M[i]$, $i = 0, \ldots, m - 1$, as the $i$th column of M. Suppose the secret image is divided into $p \times q$ blocks of $r \times s$ pixels. The $(k, n, r \times s)$-ME-SIVCS under ME-SIVCS-1 security is constructed as follows:

**Construction 4.9** (($k, n, rs$)-ME-SIVCS under ME-SIVCS-1 security).

Denote $M_0$ and $M_1$ as the basis matrices of the corresponding $D$-SEVCS under Definition of VCS. The following steps encrypt a $B_{r \times s, b}$ block of $r \times s$ pixels at a time, where $b$ is the number of black pixels among them and $r \times s$ is the block size satisfying $m|rs$ and $m|b$, i.e., $m$ is a divisor of both $rs$ and $b$.

1. For $p = 0$ to $I_{Height}/s - 1$;  /*$I_{Height}$ is the height of the secret image */
2. For $q = 0$ to $I_{Width}/r - 1$;  /*where $I_{Width}$ is the width of the secret image*/
3. /*Suppose the block at the position $(q, p)$ in the secret image is $B_{r \times s,b}$*/
4. For $i = 0$ to $b - 1$
5. Choose a black pixel $p_i$ that has not been encrypted in $B_{r \times s,b}$ randomly
6. Encrypt $p_i$ using $M_1[i \bmod m]$
7. For $j = 0$ to $rs - b - 1$
8. Choose a white pixel $p_j$ that has not been encrypted in $B_{r \times s,b}$ randomly
9. Encrypt $p_j$ using $M_0[j \bmod m]$

**Remark.** First, we compare the values of the variance of Constructions 4.1 and 4.4. According to Construction 4.4, the dealer encrypts the black and white pixels separately. Take the encryption of black pixels as example, the dealer randomly choose a black pixel, and encrypts this pixel by a column of $M_1$. For the $b$ black pixels, each column of $M_1$ is used by $b/m$ times, the process is equivalent to that the $b$ black pixels are encrypted by $b/m$ random permutations of $M_1$. Similarly, $rs - b$ white pixels are encrypted by $(rs - b)/m$ random permutations of $M_0$. We have that the darkness level of a $B_{r \times s,b}$ block, denoted by $d$, is always a fixed value, i.e., $d = b/m \cdot h + (rs - b)/m \cdot l$. We then get that the mathematical expectation of the darkness level of $B_{r \times s,b}$, denoted by $d'$, is $d' = b/m \cdot h + (rs - b)/m \cdot l$. Hence, the variance of the darkness levels of $B_{r \times s,b}$ in the recovered secret image is $\delta^4_{rs,b} = 1 \cdot (d - d')^2 = 0$. Recall the variance of the darkness levels of $B_{r \times s,b}$ for Construction 4.1 is $\delta^1_{rs,b} = [b \cdot h \cdot (m-h) + (r \times s - b) \cdot l \cdot (m-l)]/m^2$, i.e., $\delta^4_{rs,b} \leq \delta^1_{rs,b}$. Hence, the visual quality of the recovered secret image of Construction 4.4 is better than that of Construction 4.1 on the block size $rs$.

At last, we give the following theorem for Construction 4.4.

**Theorem 4.3** *The Construction 4.4 generates a $(k, n, rs)$-ME-SIVCS under ME-SIVCS-1 security.*

We have to point out that, Construction 4.4 gets fine visual quality at the cost of security. However, we claim that its security is enough for the common application scenarios of VCS. It is very difficult for human eyes to extract useful information of the fine secret image even with computers.

Generally, the condition of Construction 4.4 that $m|rs$ is easy to fulfill, for example, we choose $r \times s = 2 \times m$. However, for the condition $m|b$, some blocks in the secret image may not satisfy the condition. Hence, we need to modify the secret image to satisfy the condition. The error diffusion algorithm is a kind of halftone technique that the output image has nice visual quality.

The following algorithm generates an image that each block of the image satisfies that the number of black pixels in the block is a multiple of $m$.

---

**Algorithm 4.2:** The image processing algorithm

---

**Input** : The secret image and the basis matrices for a black and white $(k, n)$-VCS, $M_0$ and
$M_1$, which have pixel expansion $m$.
**Output**: The shares $S_i$ for $i = 1, \ldots, n$.

**Step 1**. Initialize the $\frac{I_{Height}}{s} \times \frac{I_{Width}}{r}$ error matrix $E$, such that all its entities equal 0;
**Step 2**. For $p = 0$ to $I_{Height}/s - 1$; /*where $I_{Height}$ is the height of the secret image; */
**Step 3**. For $q = 0$ to $I_{Width}/r - 1$; /*where $I_{Width}$ is the width of the secret image; */
**Step 4**. /*Suppose the block at the position $(q, p)$ in the secret image is $B_{r \times s, b}$ */
**Step 5**. $b \leftarrow b \bmod m$;
**Step 6**. $b - E[q][p] < m - b$;
**Step 7**. Choose $b$ black pixels in $B_{r \times s, b}$ randomly and convert them into white pixels;
**Step 8**. $E[q + 1][p] \leftarrow E[q + 1][p] + \frac{3}{8}(E[q][p] - b)$
**Step 9**. $E[q + 1][p + 1] \leftarrow E[q + 1][p + 1] + \frac{1}{4}(E[q][p] - b)$
**Step 10**. $E[q][p + 1] \leftarrow E[q][p + 1] + \frac{3}{8}(E[q][p] - b)$
**Step 11**. Else
**Step 12**. Choose $m - b$ white pixels in $B_{r \times s, b}$ randomly and convert them into black pixels;
**Step 13**. $E[q + 1][p] \leftarrow E[q + 1][p] + \frac{3}{8}(E[q][p] + m - b)$
**Step 14**. $E[q + 1][p + 1] \leftarrow E[q + 1][p + 1] + \frac{1}{4}(E[q][p] + m - b)$
**Step 15**. $E[q][p + 1] \leftarrow E[q][p + 1] + \frac{3}{8}(E[q][p] + m - b)$

---

According to the above algorithm, for the $B_{r \times s, b}$ block, either $b \bmod m$ black pixels
are converted into white pixels, or $m - (b \bmod m)$ white pixels are converted into
black pixels, i.e., the number of black pixels in $B_{r \times s, b}$ is either turned to $b - (b \bmod m)$
or turned to $b + m - (b \bmod m)$, and for both cases, the number of black pixels is a
multiple of $m$. Hence, the condition of Construction 4.4 is satisfied.

The two proposed ME-SIVCSs are easily extended to the general access structure
size-invariant visual cryptography scheme [21], or the size-invariant visual cryptography scheme with meaningful shares, or color size-invariant visual cryptography
scheme [8], given that the corresponding D-SEVCS is the general access structure
D-SEVCS, and the meaningful share D-SEVCS, and the color D-SEVCS.

## 4.6 Threshold VCS (TVCS)

Traditionally, VCS was based on the OR operation, where the shares are printed on
transparencies. The physical meaning of the OR operation is that when the shares
(printed on the transparencies) are stacked together [1, 3, 7, 13–18, 22, 30], their
pixels perform the OR operation, i.e., the stacking of two white pixels (with values
0) will result in a white pixel, and the stacking of two black pixels (with values 1)
will result in a black pixel, and the stacking of one white pixel and one black pixel
will result in a black pixel (0 OR 1 = 1).

Tuyls et al. presented a new physical model for VCS, which corresponds to a complicated underlying operation. One special case of the operation is the XOR operation. The main idea is to insert a new liquid crystal (LC) layer into a liquid crystal display (LCD) which already have an LC layer. So, such a model contains five layers, they are the backlight, first polarizer [3], first LC layer, second LC layer, and second polarizer. Depending on the voltage applied on an LC cell, this LC cell will rotate the polarization of the light that enters it over a certain angle [3]. Denote the angle rotated by the cell of the first LC layer as $\alpha_1 \in [0, \pi]$ and $\alpha_2 \in [0, \pi]$ for that of the cell of the second LC layer. Then the total angle rotated by the two LC layers is $\alpha = \alpha_1 + \alpha_2$. The second polarizer only emits the light coming from the first polarizer. Let $I_r$ denote the normalized intensity of the recovered pixel, we have

$$I_r(\alpha) = \cos^2(\alpha) = \cos^2(\alpha_1 + \alpha_2) \tag{4.8}$$

When $\alpha_1, \alpha_2 \in [0, \pi/2]$, since $\cos^2(\pi) = \cos^2(0) = 1$, and $\cos^2(\pi/2) = 0$, the model forms a visual cryptography model with the underlying operation XOR.

Since LC layers are driven electronically (as in LCDs), when an LC layer is used as a share of a VCS, it is easily updated, which leads to a practical updating mechanism. When the shares of the VCS (actually the LC layers) are used to recover the original secret image, the process will be rather simple, it only needs to stack the LC layers together. It is noted that the interaction with the LC layers is purely optical, which avoids digital data exchange. These traits make this model practical.

### 4.6.1 Definitions of TVCS

In this section, we will give some definitions about visual cryptography under the operation '·', which may be the OR operation, or the XOR operation, or the mod 3 addition operation of this article. We will restrict ourselves to images only consisting of black and white pixels and encode pixels one at a time. In order to share a complete image, the scheme has to be applied on all the pixels in the image.

By a $(k, n)$-TVCS, we mean a scheme in which a secret image (black and white) is divided into $n$ shares which are distributed to $n$ participants. Any subgroup of $k$ out of $n$ participants can recover the secret image, but any subgroup consisting of less than $k$ participants cannot get any information about the secret image other than the size of the secret image.

For a vector $v \in GF^m(2)$, we denote by $w(v)$ the number of 1s in the vector $v$ (i.e., $w(v)$ is the Hamming weight of $v$). A $(k, n)$-TVCS consists of two collections of $n \times m$ binary share matrices $C_0$ and $C_1$. Since the two collections of share matrices $C_0$ and $C_1$ uniquely determine the $(k, n)$-TVCS; hence for the simplicity of description, we denote a $(k, n)$-TVCS by its specific $(C_0, C_1)$. To share a white (resp. black) pixel, the dealer (the one who sets up the system) randomly chooses one of the matrices in $C_0$ (resp. $C_1$) and distributes its rows (shares) to the $n$ participants of the scheme. Formally, we give the definition of the $(k, n)$-TVCS as follows.

**Definition 4.7** Let $k, n, m$, and $h$ be nonnegative integers satisfying $2 \leq k \leq n$ and $1 \leq h \leq m$. The two collections of $n \times m$ binary matrices $(C_0, C_1)$ constitute a $(k, n)$-TVCS if there exists a value $\alpha(>0)$ satisfying:

**Contrast**. For any $s \in C_0$, the '$\cdot$' operation of any $k$ out of the $n$ rows of $s$ is a vector $v$ that satisfies $w(v) \leq (h - \alpha \cdot m)$.

**Contrast**. For any $s \in C_1$, the '$\cdot$' operation of any $k$ out of the $n$ rows of $s$ is a vector $v$ that satisfies $w(v) \leq h$.

**Security**. For any $i_1 < i_2 < \cdots < i_t$ in $\{1, 2, \ldots, n\}$ with $t < k$, the two collections of $t \times m$ matrices $D_j, j = 0, 1$, obtained by restricting each $n \times m$ matrix in $C_j$ to rows $i_1, i_2, \ldots, i_t$, are indistinguishable in the sense that they contain the same matrices with the same frequencies.

In the above Definition 4.7,

1. The '$\cdot$' operation is the underlying operation, which can be the OR operation, or the XOR operation or the mod 3 addition operation.
2. $h$ and $\alpha \cdot m$, $(h \leq \alpha \cdot m)$ are the thresholds of the scheme, $h$ is called whiteness level and $\alpha \cdot m$ $(h \leq \alpha \cdot m)$ is called the darkness level under the '$\cdot$' operation.
3. $m$ is called the pixel expansion of the scheme.
4. $\alpha$ is called the contrast, the value of $\alpha$ should be larger than 0. Since the contrast may differ with different underlying operations, in order to differentiate the contrast under different underlying operations, we will use the notations $\alpha_{OR}$, $\alpha_{XOR}$ and $\alpha_{\text{mod } 3}$, respectively.

Note that $0 < \alpha \leq 1$. Generally, the pixel expansion $m$ is expected to be as small as possible and the contrast $\alpha$ is expected to be as large as possible.

As in Definition 4.7, the first two contrast conditions ensure that the participants will be able to distinguish the black and white pixels, and the third condition ensures the security of the scheme.

### 4.6.2  Basis Matrix

**Definition 4.8** (*Basis matrix of TVCS*) Let $k, n, m$, and $h$ be nonnegative integers satisfying $2 \leq k \leq n$ and $1 \leq h \leq m$. Two $n \times m$ binary matrices $M_0$ and $M_1$ are called basis matrices of a $(k, n)$-TVCS, if there exists a value $\alpha(>0)$ satisfying:

**Contrast**. The '·' operation of any $k$ out of the $n$ rows of $M^0$ is a vector $v$ that satisfies $w(v) \leq (h - \alpha \cdot m)$.

**Contrast**. The '·' operation of any $k$ out of the $n$ rows of $M^1$ is a vector $v$ that satisfies $w(v) \geq h$.

**Security**. For any $i_1 < i_2 < \cdots < i_t$ in $\{1, 2, \ldots, n\}$ with $t < k$, the two collections of $t \times m$ matrices $D_j, j = 0, 1$, obtained by restricting $M^j$ to rows $i_1, i_2, \ldots, i_t$ are equal up to a column permutation.

Note that we obtain the collections $C_0$ and $C_1$ by permuting the columns of $M^0$ and $M^1$ in all possible ways, respectively. Denote $P(M)$ as the collection of all the column permutations of a matrix $M$, then we have $C_0 = P(M^0)$ and $C_1 = P(M^1)$. This approach of the construction of TVCS will have small memory requirements (it keeps only the basis matrices) and is efficient (to choose a matrix in $C_0$ (resp. $C_1$), it only needs to generate a column permutation of the basis matrix). In this section, if each of the collections $C_i$, for $i = 0, 1$, of a $(k, n)$-TVCS is generated by only one basis matrix, we call such a $(k, n)$-TVCS as the basis matrix $(k, n)$-TVCS.

## 4.7 Construction of $(k, n)$-TVCS

In this section, we will prove that the basis matrices constructed by that algorithm constitute a $(k, n)$-TVCS for both OR and XOR operations. Droste's algorithm is as follows: First, we give a subroutine $ADD(p, M)$ which is used to add each restriction of $k$ rows of a matrix $M$ every column with $p$ 1s by adding columns to the entire matrix $M$, where a matrix is considered as a collection of columns.

**Definition 4.9** $(ADD(p, M))$ (1) If $p \leq k - p$, add all the columns with $q = p$ 1s to $M$, i.e., the number of columns in $M$ is increased by $C_n^q$.
(2) If $p > k - p$, add all the columns with $q = p + n - k$ 1s to $M$, i.e., the number of columns in $M$ is increased by $C_n^q$.

The subroutine $ADD(p, M)$ makes it easy to construct basis matrices $M^0$ (resp. $M^1$) whose restrictions to $k$ rows always contain every even (resp. odd) column (an even (resp. odd) column is a column that contains even (resp. odd) number of 1s). When every even (resp. odd) column is removed once from every restriction of $M^0$ (resp. $M^1$), the remaining columns maintain the same, i.e., those remaining columns are unchanged regardless which $k$ rows are restricted, and whether they are from $M^0$ or $M^1$. Hence the remaining columns of every restriction of $M^0$ which are not remaining columns of every restriction of $M^1$, called the rest of $M^0$ have to be added to every restriction of $M^1$ and vice versa. In most cases, these added columns will create new rests which cause new columns to be added. The algorithm has the following form.

---

**Algorithm 4.3:**

---

**Input**  : The parameters $k$ and $n$, and two empty basis matrices $M^0$ and $M^1$, where the basis
matrices $M^0$ and $M^1$ are considered as collections of columns;
**Output**: The basis matrices $M^0$ and $M^1$ for a $(k, n)$-TVCS;

**Step 1.** For all even $p \in \{0, \ldots, k\}$, call $ADD(p, M^0)$;
**Step 2.** For all odd $p \in \{0, \ldots, k\}$, call $ADD(p, M^1)$;
**Step 3.** While the rests of $M^0$ and $M^1$ are not empty, denote the Hamming weight of the
columns (restricted to $k$ rows) in the rest of $M^0$ (resp. $M^1$) as $p_1, \ldots, p_s$ (resp., $p_1, \ldots, p_s$)
(a) Add to $M^0$ all columns adjusting the rest of $M^1$ by calling $ADD(p_i, M^0)$, for all
$i \in \{1, \ldots, s\}$
(b) Add to $M^1$ all columns adjusting the rest of $M^0$ by calling $ADD(p_i, M^1)$, for all
$i \in \{1, \ldots, s\}$

---

Execute Step 3 until the rests of $M^0$ and $M^1$ are empty. We then show that Algorithm 4.3 also generates a $(k, n)$-TVCS under the XOR operation, i.e., under the visual cryptography model of Tuyls.

**Theorem 4.4** *Algorithm 4.3 generates the basis matrices of a $(k, n)$-TVCS $M^0$ and $M^1$ which works both under the OR and XOR operations.*

The next theorem shows a structural property of the scheme constructed by Algorithm 4.3.

**Theorem 4.5** *The basis matrices $M^0$ and $M^1$ constructed by Algorithm 4.3 have the same number of 1s (Hamming weight) in each row. The contrast $\alpha_{OR}$, $\alpha_{XOR}$ and the pixel expansion $m$ satisfy: $\alpha_{OR} \cdot m = 1$ and $\alpha_{XOR} \cdot m = 2k - 1$.*

Theorem 4.5 shows that there exists a $(k, n)$-TVCS with each row having the same number of 1s. It will be seen that such a scheme is useful in the construction of TEVCS.

In fact, there are many techniques in the literature to reduce the pixel expansion of the VCS. First, Blundo et al., Hofmeister et al. and Verheul et al. analyzed the structure of the TVCS and tried to get the bounds of the contrast and the pixel expansion. However, because of the complexity of the structure of TVCS, they only got the smallest pixel expansion given the largest contrast for the $(2, n)$ access structure. Second, Koga et al. found a new way to represent the basis matrices of TVCS using polynomials. They found some TVCS with good contrast and pixel expansion properties by exhaustive search [27]. Third, Ito et al., Yang et al. and Cimato et al. show a technique to reduce the pixel expansion of TVCS to 1 [11, 12].

Their method is realized by randomly choosing one column of the basis matrices to encode a secret pixel in the secret image. However, the disadvantage of this method is that a secret pixel is only correctly recovered with probability $p$, i.e., the reduced scheme does not satisfy the contrast conditions of Definitions 4.8 and 4.9, and hence is not a TVCS in the traditional sense any more. In such a case, the human eyes

cannot recover the secret image precisely, and many details of the secret image are
lost. We call this pixel expansion reducing method the probabilistic method [19].

In this section, we present a method to further reduce the pixel expansion of the
$(k, n)$-TVCS constructed by Algorithm 4.3. Our pixel expansion reducing method is
similar to the probabilistic method in the sense that we also restrict the share matrices
of an original TVCS to a number of rows, however, the characteristic of our method
is that we find a proper value of pixel expansion which is smaller than the original
pixel expansion of the TVCS while the scheme with the smaller pixel expansion still
satisfies the contrast conditions of Definitions 4.8 and 4.9, i.e., the human eyes still
recover the secret image precisely. The experimental results show that our method
significantly reduces the pixel expansion of the TVCS generated in Sect. 3.1 under
the XOR operation.

First, we give the following Lemma 4.1.

**Lemma 4.1** *Let $M^0$ and $M^1$ be the basis matrices of a $(k, n)$-TVCS. Let $s(\leq m)$ be a
positive integer. By restricting to s out of m columns of the basis matrices (there are $C_m^s$
combinations), and permuting the submatrices' columns, we get two sets of matrices
$P(M_1^0), P(M_2^0), \ldots, P(M_{C(m,s)}^0)$ and $P(M_1^1), P(M_2^1), \ldots, P(M_{C(m,s)}^1)$, which satisfy
the security condition of Definition 4.9.*

Now we give the theorem to reduce the pixel expansion of the $(k, n)$-TVCS:

**Theorem 4.6** *Let $M^0$ and $M^1$ be the basis matrices of a $(k, n)$-TVCS. For the
submatrix generated by restricting to any k rows in $M^0$, denote a as the maximum number of columns, where the stacking result of the entries of these columns
are 1s, and for the submatrix generated by restricting to any k rows in $M^1$,
denote b as the maximum number of columns, where the stacking result of the
entries of these columns are 0s. Let $t(\leq m - a - b)$ be a positive integer. By
restricting to $a + b + t$ columns of $M^0$ and $M^1$, and permuting the submatrices'
columns, the collections of share matrices $\{P(M_1^0), P(M_2^0), \ldots, P(M_{C(m,a+b+t)}^0)\}$
and $\{P(M_1^1), P(M_2^1), \ldots, P(M_{C(m,a+b+t)}^1)\}$ form a $(k, n)$-TVCS with pixel expansion
$a + b + t$ and contrast $\alpha = t/(a + b + t)$.*

According to Theorem 4.6, we now give the experimental results for the $(k, n)$-
TVCS generated by Algorithm 4.3 with the underlying operation XOR. Table 4.1
shows the reduced pixel expansion using Theorem 4.6 when $t = 1$ [29]. These
experimental results show that the construction of Theorem 4.6 is more efficient,
with respect to the pixel expansion, than the known results under the XOR operation.
For example, the pixel expansion of the schemes is: for the case $(3, n)$-TVCS, the
pixel expansion is $m = 2 \cdot n - 2$, and for the case $(4, n)$-TVCS the pixel expansion
is $m = n^2 - 2 \cdot n$. Furthermore, the reduced pixel expansion of the $(k, n)$-TVCS is
expressed as $m - 2^{k-1} + 1$, where $m$ is the pixel expansion.

**Table 4.1** The reduced pixel expansion for the $(k, n)$-TVCS generated by Algorithm 4.3 with the underline operation XOR

| k/n | 2 | 3 | 4 | 5 | 6 | 7 | 8 | 9 | 10 |
|---|---|---|---|---|---|---|---|---|---|
| 2 | 1 | 2 | 3 | 4 | 5 | 6 | 7 | 8 | 9 |
| 3 | | 1 | 3 | 5 | 7 | 9 | 11 | 13 | 15 |
| 4 | | | 1 | 8 | 17 | 28 | 41 | 56 | 73 |
| 5 | | | | 1 | 15 | 33 | 55 | 81 | 111 |
| 6 | | | | | 1 | 39 | 97 | 189 | 289 |
| 7 | | | | | | 1 | 77 | 193 | 357 |
| 8 | | | | | | | 1 | 188 | 513 |
| 9 | | | | | | | | 1 | 374 |
| 10 | | | | | | | | | 1 |

## 4.8 Concolorous TVCS

In this section, we propose a concolorous TVCS under the visual cryptography model of Tuyls, where the shares are concolorous and the secret image is recovered by stacking the qualified shares as well as the TVCS does.

### 4.8.1 The Model of Concolorous TVCS

As described before, the angles of rotating the corresponding cells in $LC_1$ and $LC_2$ are denoted by $\alpha_1$ and $\alpha_2$ (the first and the second LC layer), respectively [10, 20]. If we restrict $\alpha_1$ and $\alpha_2$ be chosen from the set $\{\pi/3, 2\pi/3\}$, value of the angle of the total polarization rotation will be from $\{2\pi/3, \pi, 4\pi/3, \ldots\}$ [3]. Because the period of the function $f = \cos^2(x)$ is $\pi$, so the value of the angle of the total polarization rotation will actually be from $\{\pi/3, 2\pi/3, \pi\}$. Because of $\cos^2(\alpha_1) = \cos^2(\pi/3) = \frac{1}{4} = \cos^2(2\pi/3) = \cos^2(\alpha_2)$, i.e., the intensity of the recovered pixel of $\alpha_1$ and $\alpha_2$ is equal, so the shares are concolorous. In such a way, the intensity of the recovered pixel of $\alpha$ will only have two values $\cos^2(\pi/3) = \cos^2(2\pi/3) = 1/4$ and $\cos^2(\alpha) = 1$. We define the recovered pixel by the angle of rotation $\alpha$ as a white pixel and the pixel by the angle $\pi/3$ or $2\pi/3$ as a black pixel. Using such construction of TVCS, one will get concolorous shares while the stacking results will be black and white images. Map $\pi/3$ to 1, $2\pi/3$ to 2 and $\alpha$ to 0. Then the underlying operation of such schemes will be equivalent to the mod 3 addition operation. Because the entries of the share matrix only have two possible values (1 and 2), so we make use of the binary matrix to study the concolorous TVCS.

## 4.8.2 The Existence and Construction of Concolorous TVCS

In this part we will show that the concolorous $(k, n)$-TVCS with an odd $k$ does not exist, and the construction of $(k, n)$-TVCS with an even $k$ is generated from the traditional construction of black and white $(k, n)$-TVCS.

Denote a black and white $(k, n)$-TVCS as $(C_0, C_1)$. Substitute all the 0s of all the share matrices in $C_0'$ and $C_1'$ by 2s, we get $C_0$ and $C_1$, respectively.

The length of the columns of a concolorous $(k, n)$-TVCS is $n$, we sort these columns by the number of 2s and denote the number of the columns in $C_0'$ which have $i$ number of 2s as $x_i$ and that in $C_1$ as $y_i$. Denote $M(\subset \{0, \ldots, n\})$ as the set of the subscripts of the columns $x_i$ and $y_i$, where the stacking of all the entries equals 0 mod 3.

We now discuss the existence of the concolorous $(k, n)$-TVCS with $k$ odd. Without loss of generality, let $(C_0, C_1)$ be a concolorous $(n, n)$-TVCS. First we give the following lemma.

**Lemma 4.2** *The following equations must have solutions if there exists a concolorous $(n, n)$-TVCS $(C_0', C_1')$:*

$$n \cdot x_0 + x_1 = n \cdot y_0 + y_1$$
$$(n - 1) \cdot x_1 + 2 \cdot x_2 = (n - 1) \cdot y_1 + 2 \cdot y_2$$
$$\ldots \ldots$$
$$x_{n-1} + n \cdot x_n = y_{n-1} + n \cdot y_n$$
$$\sum_{j \in M} x_j < \sum_{j \in M} y_j$$
*where $x_i \geq 0$, $y_i \geq 0$, $i \in \{0, \ldots, n\}$.*

Note it is clear that less than $(n \geq 1)$ shares contain no more information than that of $(n \geq 1)$ shares. Hence, we only need to consider the case of $(n \geq 1)$ shares, which is enough for the proof of Theorem 4.7. Next, we show the existence of concolorous $(k, n)$-TVCS with $k$ odd.

**Theorem 4.7** *The concolorous $(k, n)$-TVCS with $k$ odd does not exist.*

Denote $M[X]$ as the $|X| \times m$ submatrix obtained from $M$ by restricting to the rows in $X$. The following Theorem 4.8 holds.

**Theorem 4.8** *Let $M^0$ and $M^1$ be two $n \times m$ binary matrices. The matrices $M^0$ and $M^1$ are basis matrices of a weak $(k, n)$-TVCS with pixel expansion $m$ if and only if for all subsets $X$ consisting of $k$ rows, there exists a binary matrix $D_X$ and an integer $h_X$ such that $D_X$ is a submatrix of both $M^0[X]$ and $M^1[X]$, all the even columns appear in $\frac{M^0[X]}{D_X}$ with multiplicity $h_X$, and all the odd columns appear in $\frac{M^1[X]}{D_X}$ with multiplicity $h_X$, where multiplicity of a column means the number of the columns.*

The above theorem involves a concept of 'weak TVCS' which is coincidence with our definition of TVCS in Definitions 4.8 and 4.9. So the above theorem holds for the $(k, n)$-TVCS under Definitions 4.8 and 4.9 as well.

The following theorem proves the existence of the concolorous $(k, n)$-TVCS with even $k$. It actually gives a concrete construction of a concolorous $(k, n)$-TVCS with even $k$ based on the known black and white basis matrix $(k, n)$-TVCS (recall that the basis matrix TVCS means that the collection $C_0$ (resp. $C_1$) is generated by only one basis matrix).

**Theorem 4.9** *The concolorous $(k, n)$-TVCS with even $k$ is constructed by substituting the 0s of the share matrices of a black and white basis matrix $(k, n)$-TVCS by 2s, which implies that its pixel expansion remains the same with the black and white basis matrix $(k, n)$-TVCS. More precisely, denote a black and white basis matrix $(k, n)$-TVCS as $(C_0, C_1)$, substitute all the 0s of all the matrices in $C_0$ and $C_1$ by 2s, we get $C_0'$ and $C_1'$, respectively. For the case $k \bmod 4 = 0$, the newly constructed concolorous $(k, n)$-TVCS is $(C_0', C_1')$. For the case $k \bmod 4 = 2$, the newly constructed concolorous $(k, n)$-TVCS is $(C_1', C_0')$.*

It is easy to verify that the basis matrices $M_k^0$ and $M_k^1$ satisfy the security condition of Definition 4.9. So we only need to prove the contrast condition.

In this section, we will show how to construct concolorous $(k, n)$-TVCS with smaller pixel expansion from an existing concolorous $(k, n)$-TVCS. Because the concolorous $(k, n)$-TVCS are under the mod 3 addition operation, from Theorem 4.9, we have the following corollary.

**Corollary 4.3** *Let $M^0$ and $M^1$ be the basis matrices of a concolorous $(k, n)$-TVCS. For the submatrix generated by restricting to any $k$ rows in $M^0$, denote $a$ as the maximum number of columns, where the stacking result of the entries of these columns are 1 or 2, and for the submatrix generated by restricting to any $k$ rows in $M^1$, denote $b$ as the maximum number of columns, where the stacking result of the entries of these columns are 0. Let $t(\leq m - a - b)$ be a positive integer. By restricting to $a + b + t$ columns of $M^0$ and $M^1$, the collections of share matrices $\{P(M_1^0), P(M_2^0), \ldots, P(M_{C(m,a+b+t)}^0)\}$ and $\{P(M_1^1), P(M_2^1), \ldots, P(M_{C(m,a+b+t)}^1)\}$ form a concolorous $(k, n)$-TVCS with pixel expansion $a + b + t$ and contrast $t/(a + b + t)$.*

Corollary 4.3 shows a construction of concolorous $(k, n)$-TVCS with smaller pixel expansion.

# 4.9  Construction of $(k, n)$-TEVCS

## 4.9.1  The Model

In this section, we introduce a method to construct threshold-extended visual cryptography based on a known construction of TVCS where the underlying operation is XOR or OR [35]. We denote '*' as the OR or XOR operation. Note that, the proposed

TEVCS may result in different collections of share matrices depending on whether the underlying operation is OR or XOR.

For the TEVCS, we start with $n + 1$ images (the first $n$ are associated with the $n$ participants, whereas the last one is the secret image) to obtain $n$ shares that they are meaningful, i.e., participants are able to see the image on their share. In general, we denote by $C_c^{c_1...c_n}$, the collection of matrices from which the dealer chooses a matrix to encode, where $c, c_1, \ldots, c_n \in \{1, 0\}$. For $i = 1, \ldots, n$, $c_i$ is the color of the pixel on the $i$th original share image, and $c$ is the color of the secret image. Hence, to realize a TEVCS we need to construct $2^n$ pairs of such collections $(C_0^{c_1...c_n}, C_1^{c_1...c_n})$, each pair is for each possible combination of white and black pixels in the $n$ original share images. Formally, a $(k, n)$-TEVCS is defined as follows.

**Definition 4.10**  Let $k, n, m,$ and $h$ be nonnegative integers satisfying $2 \leq k \leq n$ and $1 \leq h \leq m$. A family of $2^n$ pairs of collections of $n \times m'$ binary matrices $\{(C_0^{c_1...c_n}, C_1^{c_1...c_n})\}_{c_1,...,c_n \in \{1,0\}}$ constitute a $(k, n)$-TEVCS if there exist values $\alpha_F(>0)$, $\alpha_S(>0)$ and $h$ satisfying:

**Contrast**.  For any $M \in C_0^{c_1...c_n}$ the '∗' of any $k$ out of $n$ rows of $M$ is a vector $v$ that satisfies $w(v) \leq (h - \alpha_F \cdot m)$, and for any $M \in C_1^{c_1...c_n}$, we have $w(v) \geq h$.

**Security**.  For any $i_1 < i_2 < \cdots < i_t$ in $\{1, 2, \ldots, n\}$ with $t < k$, the two collections of $t \times m$ matrices $D_j^{c_1,...,c_n}$ with $j \in \{0, 1\}$, obtained by restricting each $n \times m$ matrix in $C_j^{c_1...c_n}$ to rows $i_1, i_2, \ldots, i_t$ are indistinguishable in the sense that they contain the same matrices with the same frequencies.

**Contrast**.  After the original images are encoded, they are still meaningful. More precisely, for any $i \in \{1, 2, \ldots, n\}$ and any $c, c_1, \ldots, c_{i-1}, c_{i+1}, \ldots, c_n \in \{0, 1\}$, denote $M[i]$ as the $i$th row of $M$, we have.

$$\min_{M \in M_0} \omega(M[i]) - \max_{M \in M_0} \omega(M[i]) \geq \alpha_s \cdot m' \qquad (4.9)$$

where

$$M_0 = \bigcup_{c,c_1,...,c_n \in [0,1]} C_c^{c_1...c_{i-1}1c_{i+1}c_n} \qquad (4.10)$$

$$M_1 = \bigcup_{c,c_1,...,c_n \in [0,1]} C_c^{c_1...c_{i-1}0c_{i+1}c_n} \qquad (4.11)$$

In the above Definition 4.10, $\alpha_F$ and $\alpha_S$ are the contrast of $m$ the recovered secret image and the contrast of the shares, respectively, and $m'$ is the pixel expansion. Note that we use $m'$ to differentiate the notation $m$ which is the pixel expansion of the $(k, n)$-TVCS with random shares.

In Definition 4.10, the first and second conditions correspond to the contrast and security conditions of Definition 4.10. The third condition implies that the original images are not 'modified', i.e., after we encode the $n$ original images using the $2^n$ pairs of collections $\{(C_0^{c_1 \cdots c_n}, C_1^{c_1 \cdots c_n})\}$, where $c_1, \ldots, c_n \in \{0, 1\}$, participants will recognize their own image.

Note that for the $(k, k)$-TEVCS with underlying operation OR, the values of $\alpha_F$, $\alpha_S$, and $m'$ satisfy the following conditions $2^{k-1}\alpha_F + k/(k-1) \cdot \alpha_S \leq 1$ and $m' \geq 2^{k-1} + 2$. However, for the $(k, k)$-TEVCS with underlying operation XOR, the values of $\alpha_F$, $\alpha_S$ and $m'$ may not satisfy the conditions.

## 4.9.2 Constructions of $(k, n)$-TEVCS

In this section, we give the following theorem to construct the $(k, n)$-TEVCS based on a known $(k, n)$-TVCS (also called the corresponding $(k, n)$-TVCS) satisfying that all the rows of the share matrices have the same Hamming weight, and the underlying operation of the proposed TEVCS is '$*$', which is OR or XOR operation.

**Theorem 4.10** *The scheme $(C_0^{c_1 \cdots c_n}, C_1^{c_1 \cdots c_n})c_1, \ldots, c_n \in \{0, 1\}$ constructed by the following steps is a $(k, n)$-TEVCS with underlying operation '$*$'.*

**Step 1** *Let $C_0$ and $C_1$ be the collections of the $(k, n)$-TVCS with underlying operation '$*$', which satisfy that all the rows of the share matrices have the same Hamming weight. Denote $\alpha_*$ as its contrast which can be $\alpha_{OR}$ or $\alpha_{XOR}$, and denote $m$ as its pixel expansion.*

**Step 2** *Construct an $n \times l$ matrix $D^{c_1 \cdots c_n}$ as follows ($l$ is an integer satisfying $1 \leq l < \alpha_* \cdot m$): For $i = 1$ to $n$ do*
*If $c_i = 1$ then set all the entries of row $i$ of $D^{c_1 \cdot c_n}$ to 1.*
*Else set the entry of row $i$ of $D^{c_1 \cdots c_n}$ to 0.*

**Step 3** *The collections $C_0^{c_1 \cdots c_n}$ and $C_1^{c_1 \cdots c_n}$ are obtained as follows:*
*$C_0^{c_1 \cdots c_n} = \{M | D^{c_1 \cdots c_n}\}$ for all $M \in C_0$,*
*$C_1^{c_1 \cdots c_n} = \{M | D^{c_1 \cdots c_n}\}$ for all $M \in C_1$.*

Furthermore, in Theorem 4.10, if the corresponding $(k, n)$-TVCS is a $(k, n)$-TVCS both under the OR and XOR operations, and satisfies $1 \leq l < \alpha_{OR} \cdot m$ and $1 \leq l < \alpha_{XOR} \cdot m$, then the newly constructed $(k, n)$-TEVCS is a $(k, n)$-TEVCS both under the OR and XOR operations. If only one of the inequalities $1 \leq l < \alpha_{OR} \cdot m$ and $1 \leq l < \alpha_{XOR} \cdot m$ holds, then the newly constructed $(k, n)$-TEVCS works only under either the OR or the XOR operation.

## 4.10 A Security-Enriched VCS

In this section, we present a general method to let the VC shares carry more secrets, the technique is to use cipher output of private-key systems as the input random numbers of VC scheme; meanwhile, the encryption key could be shared, the shared keys could be associated with the VC shares. After this operation, VC scheme and secret sharing scheme [30] are merged with the private-key system.

The main contribution of this section is the random inputs of VC scheme could be applied to carry covert data, the ciphertext of those private-key system-based encryption algorithms could be considered as random inputs of a VC scheme, hence it increases the amount of secret shared by VCS. Using Shamir's secret sharing scheme [26], the encryption key is able to be shared into $n$ subkeys that could be associated with the corresponding shares. We call this scheme as the enriched secret sharing VC scheme (ESSVCS), or three-in-one VCS. The scheme articulately combined the two secret sharing schemes and private-key encryption scheme together. The secret shared by the ESSVCS includes two parts: secret and covert data. Figures 4.2 and 4.3 illustrate the encryption and decryption procedures. The reasonabilities, possiblities, and potential problems will be discussed.

In Fig. 4.2, we encrypt a plaintext $S_{plaintext}$ using the key $S_{Key}$ so as to generate the ciphertext $S_{ciphertext}$ via the function $En(S_{Key}, S_{plaintext})$, the ciphertext $S_{ciphertext}$ could be used as a VCS share to split a visual secret $S_1$ using $(k, n)$-VCS scheme, so as to get

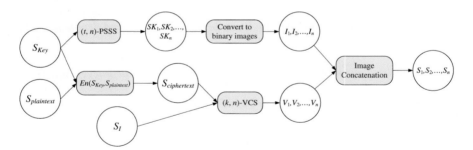

**Fig. 4.2** The encryption process of the $(k, t, n)$-ESSVCS

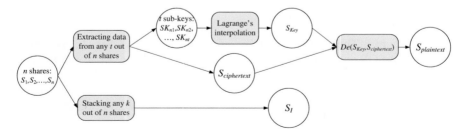

**Fig. 4.3** The decryption process of the $(k, t, n)$-ESSVCS

the visual shares $V_1, V_2, \ldots, V_n$; on the other hand, the key $S_{Key}$ could be shared using the polynomia-based secret sharing scheme (PSSS) namely $(t, n)$-PSSS to get the subkeys $SK_1, SK_2, \ldots, SK_n$; we could convert the subkeys to binary images, so we could get the imagelets $I_1, I_2, \ldots, I_n$; we now concatenate the imagelets $I_1, I_2, \ldots, I_n$ and the visual shares $V_1, V_2, \ldots, V_n$ together to get the visual shares $S_1, S_2, \ldots, S_n$.

In Fig. 4.3, we decrypt the corresponding secrets in Fig. 4.2 using the $n$ shares $S_1, S_2, \ldots, S_n$, we superimpose the $n$ shares and get the secret $S_1$, we extract data from any $t$ out of $n$ shares so as to get the secret $S_{cipertext}$ and $t$ subkeys $SK_1, SK_2, \ldots, SK_n$, we use the Lagrange's algorithm to interpolate the key $S_{Key}$, the key $S_{Key}$ and the cipertext $S_{cipertext}$ work together to decrypt the plaintext $S_{plaintext}$ using the function $De(S_{Key}, S_{cipertext})$. The reasons to guarantee this step will be explained in the following sections.

In order to share the covert data, we need to employ computational devices. By utilizing a $(k, t, n)$-ESSVCS $(k \leq t)$, the VC scheme that carries additional covert data where any $k$ out of $n$ participants visually recovers the secret by stacking the shares, any $t$ out of $n$ participants restore the additional covert data by computation. There are two computer-aided VCSs schemes, one is called two-in-one image secret sharing scheme (TiOISSS), which is able to reveal a secret image by stacking the shares and restore a much finer gray image by computation. Li et al. improved Yang et al.'s TiOISSS by gray mixing model. Fang et al. also tried to make use of the pseudorandom inputs to carry confidential data. Unfortunately, the scheme is only for $(2, 2)$ access structure.

The presented $(k, t, n)$-ESSVCS is a multi-threshold secret sharing scheme [35]. $k$ out of $n$ members share one secret, whereas a majority of participants $t \leq n$ access the additional secret. By comparing our ESSVCS and any 2D encoding methods, we find that decoding a secret totally relies on a computing device using any 2D encoding methods. If participants are in the scenario where there is no such computing devices, they cannot extract any information. But with our ESSVCS scheme, the participants could stack the shares and get part of the secret. Hence, our proposed ESSVCS scheme will have much wider application.

## 4.10.1 PSSS

Shamir introduced the $(t, n)$-PSSS $(t \leq n)$ to share the secret data into $n$ shares [15]. Any $t$ shares are used to reconstruct the secret, but any $t - 1$ or less shares get no information about the secret. To share the secret, it randomly generates a $(t - 1)$-degree polynomial using modular arithmetic

$$f(x) = (a_0 + a_1 x + \cdots + a_{t-1} x^{t-1}) \bmod p \qquad (4.12)$$

where $a_0$ is replaced by the secret data, $p$ is a prime number greater than $a_0$ and $n$. The coefficients $a_1, a_2, \ldots, a_{t-1}$ are randomly chosen from a uniform distribution over the integers in $[1, p)$. Then we could generate $n$ shares $(x_i, f(x_i)), i = 1, 2, \ldots, n$.

Later, with any $t$ out of the $n$ shares, we uniquely determine a $(t-1)$-degree polynomial as follows,

$$f(x) = \sum_{j=1}^{t} f(j) \prod_{i=1, i\neq j}^{t} \frac{x-j}{j-i} \qquad (4.13)$$

Particularly, the coefficient $a_0$ of the polynomial $f(x)$ is decrypted (Lagrange's interpolation). However, any $t-1$ or fewer shares cannot uniquely determine a $(t-1)$-degree polynomial. Hence no information about the secret is revealed.

*Example 4.1 (The Shamir's (2, 3)-PSSS)* In a $(2, 3)$-PSSS [26], the prime number $p$ is chosen as 251. Let the secret number be 45, which is in the range of $(0, p-1)$. In the sharing process, the secret number 45 replaces the constant coefficient of a 1-degree polynomial, and another coefficient, for example 145, is randomly chosen in $(1, p-1)$. Therefore, we generate a 1-degree polynomial as follows:

$$f(x) = (45 + 145x) \bmod 251$$

Then we generate three shares $(x_i, f(x_i))$, where $x_i$ is the ID of the $i$th participant. Without loss of generality, let $i$ be the ID of the $i$th participant, we have three shares $(1, 190)$, $(2, 84)$, and $(3, 229)$.

In the revealing process, any two out of three shares uniquely determine a 1-degree polynomial by Eq. (4.13). Finally, the secret number 45 is decrypted.

### 4.10.2 ESSVCS

In this section, we first propose a construction of the ESSVCS scheme by taking the pseudorandom inputs as a subchannel, and then study some relevant issues of the ESSVCS: (1) The pseudorandomness that the input of VCS requires; (2) The sufficient conditions to uniquely determine a share matrix in the set $C_i$ for $i = 0, 1$; (3) The bandwidth of the subchannel; and (4) The method to decode the ciphertext of ESSVCS scheme.

#### 4.10.2.1 Construction of General $(k, t, n)$-ESSVCS

The main idea of this proposed scheme is to treat the private-key encryption algorithm as the pseudorandom generator of VCS. Thus the VCS naturally carries the additional covert data encrypted by the private-key algorithm. In this section, we take the VCS proposed as the building block. In practical, the encryption algorithm is the AES or Twofish, etc. The cipher block chaining (CBC) encryption mode is employed. The encryption key $S_{Key}$ in ESSVCS is shared by $(t, n)$-PSSS into $n$

subkeys $SK_1, SK_2, \ldots, SK_n$. Therefore, any $t$ or more subkeys could be used to reveal the secret key, while any $t - 1$ or less subkeys together could restore the secret key.

Before showing the construction, we need to present the assumption that participants know the access structure they belong to, i.e., the $i$th participant knows by himself/herself that (s)he is the $i$th participant. Usually, the access structure of a VCS is not one part of secret, therefore this assumption is reasonable.

**Construction**

Encryption Process of $(k, t, n)$-ESSVCS;

**Input**   The secret image $S_I$, covert data $S_{Plaintext}$ and the secret key $S_{Key}$.
**Output**  $n$ shares.
**Step 1**  Encrypt the covert data $S_{plaintext}$ using the key $S_{Key}$, $S_{ciphertext} = En(S_{Key}, S_{plaintext})$;
**Step 2**  Share the secret image $S_I$ into $n$ shares $V_1, V_2, \ldots, V_n$ using the $(k, n)$-VCS, where the encrypted data from the Step 1 is employed as the pseudo-random input of the $(k, n)$-VCS;
**Step 3**  Share $S_{Key}$ into $n$ subkeys $SK_1, SK_2, \ldots, SK_n$ using $(t, n)$-PSSS, then convert these subkeys into binary images $I_1, I_2, \ldots, I_n$, and concatenate $I_i$, $(i = 1, 2, \ldots, n)$ with share $V_i$ to get the final share $S_i$.

Decryption process of $(k, t, n)$-ESSVCS:

**Input**   Any $t$ shares where $k \leq t$.
**Output**  The secret image $S_I$ and the covert data $S_{plaintext}$.
**Step 1**  Stack any $k$ shares to get the recovered secret image $S_I$;
**Step 2**  Determine the share matrices which are used to encrypt the secret image for each pixel by $t$ shares, and hence get the ciphertext $S_{ciphertext}$;
**Step 3**  Extract $t$ subkeys from $t$ shares, then reconstruct the secret key $S_{Key}$ by Lagrange's interpolation.
**Step 4**  Decrypt the ciphertext. $S_{ciphertext}$ using the $S_{Key}$, $S_{plaintext} = De(S_{Key}, S_{ciphertext})$.

**Remarks** In practical, key length of the AES or Twofish scheme, usually, is 128 bits. Therefore, each subkey is generated and converted into a 128 bits binary image which only takes a small area in the share.

For the $(k, t, n)$-ESSVCS, by stacking $k$ shares, we reconstruct the secret image $S_I$. If one obtains $t$ rows, (s)he can uniquely determine a share matrix and hence obtain the ciphertext, where 'can uniquely determine a share matrix' means that there only exists one share matrix in $C_i$ ($i = 0, 1$) that contains these $t$ rows (and 'cannot uniquely determine' means there exist more than one share matrices that contain these $t$ rows, hence we cannot determine which one is chosen by the dealer when encrypting the secret pixel). In another word, in order to get the ciphertext one needs $t$ shares.

Security of the $(k, t, n)$-ESSVCS is based on the security of the encryption algorithm and that of VCS and PSSS scheme. Particularly, if an hacker wants to know the secret image, (s)he needs at least $k$ shares; if (s)he wants to know the covert data encrypted by the encryption algorithm, (s)he needs at least $t$ shares to extract the ciphertext and the secret key.

The VCS requires pseudorandom number inputs to guide the choice of VC share matrices. Denote the share matrices in $C_i$ as $S_0^i, \ldots, S_{|C_i|-1}^i$, and $P(S_j^i)$ for $i = 0, 1$ and $j = 0, 1, \ldots, |C_i| - 1$ as the probability choosing the share matrix $S_j^i$. Hence inputs of the pseudorandom numbers should guarantee that

$$P(S_0^i) = P(S_1^i) = \cdots = P(S_{|C_i|-1}^i) \tag{4.14}$$

In order to choose a share matrix pseudorandomly in $C_i$, the dealer needs at least $\log_2 |C_i|$ bits pseudorandom numbers (we will take the case that $\log_2 |C_i|$ is not an integer into consideration). Denote $B(j)$ as the binary representation of integer $j$ with length $\log_2 |C_i|$, i.e., $B(j)$ is the binary string that represents $j$. Without loss of generality, we assume that when the pseudorandom number input is $B(j)$, the dealer chooses the share matrix $S_j^i$ to encrypt the secret pixel $i$. Denote $P(B(j))$ as the probability of generating the binary string $B(j)$. According to the Eq. (4.14), we have

$$P(B(0)) = P(B(1)) = \cdots = P(B(|C_i| - 1)) \tag{4.15}$$

In fact, ciphertext of AES or Twofish satisfies the Eq. (4.15), because they have passed the serial test. Therefore, we take AES or Twofish as the pseudorandom generator. This is also the ground truth that why we do not use the covert data directly to guide the generation of shares.

To make things simple and clear, we give the following example for $(2, 2, 2)$-ESSVCS:

*Example 4.2* The sets of share matrices of $(2, 2, 2)$-ESSVCS are as follows:

$$C_0 = \left\{ \begin{bmatrix} 10 \\ 10 \end{bmatrix}, \begin{bmatrix} 01 \\ 01 \end{bmatrix} \right\} and C_1 = \left\{ \begin{bmatrix} 10 \\ 01 \end{bmatrix}, \begin{bmatrix} 01 \\ 10 \end{bmatrix} \right\}$$

The principle of choosing share matrix is if the pseudorandom input is 0, we choose the first share matrix in $C_0$ or $C_1$; if the pseudorandom input is 1, we choose the second option. Figure 4.4 presents an illustration for the procedure of the $(2, 2, 2)$-ESSVCS.

In Fig. 4.4, a secret image having $64 \times 128$ pixels is split into Share 1 and Share 2. Size of the shares and the recovered secret image is $129 \times 128$. Since the length of each subkey is 128 bits, it only takes one line at the bottom of each share to attach the subkeys. Length of the ciphertext $S_{ciphertext}$ encrypted in the shares is $2^{13}$ bits, i.e., the subchannel is used to carry extra $2^{13}$ bits of covert data. In the first step of the reconstruction, the secret image is visually revealed by stacking two shares. In the second step, two subkeys $SK_1$ and $SK_2$ are extracted from the last row of two shares, and then we restore the secret key $S_{Key}$ by Lagrange's interpolation. With further observation, the ciphertext is obtained by the uniquely determined share matric by

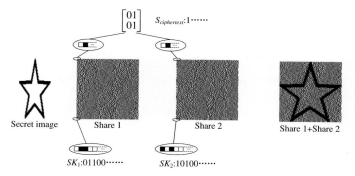

**Fig. 4.4**   The procedure of the (2, 2, 2)-ESSVCS

share blocks. For example, the first block of share 1 is constituted by two subpixels '0' and '1', and the first block of share 2 is also constituted by two subpixels '0' and '1'. Therefore, we determine the share matrix, which is the second share matrix $C_0$ and the recovered ciphertext is '1'. Finally, we get the covert data $S_{plaintext}$ by decrypting the ciphertext $S_{ciphertext}$.

### 4.10.2.2   Uniquely Determine a Share Matrix

For the $(n, n)$-VCS, if one has all the $n$ shares, (s)he uniquely determines the share matrices used when sharing the secret image $S_I$ and hence to know the ciphertext.

We then focus our discussion on the $(k, n)$-VCS with $k < n$; we find that, for the VCS, $n - 1$ rows uniquely determine a share matrix in the set $C_0$ (resp. $C_1$). The following theorem shows this result.

**Theorem 4.11**   *Denote $M_0$ and $M_1$ be the basis matrices constructed by $(k, n)$-VCS, and denote $C_0$ and $C_1$ be the sets of share matrices generated from $M_0$ and $M_1$, respectively. If every $t$ rows of a share matrix in $C_i$ $(i = 0, 1)$ uniquely determines a share matrix in $C_i$, then $t \geq n - 1$.*

*Proof First*, for the case of $t = n$, it obviously uniquely determines an $n$-row matrix from its $n$ rows.

*Second*, we show any $n - 1$ rows uniquely determine a share matrix. According to the construction, number of the 1's of each column in the basis matrix $M_0$ is from the set $T_0 = \{a | 0 \leq a \leq \lfloor \frac{k}{2} \rfloor, a \bmod 2 = 0\} \bigcup \{a + n - k | \lfloor \frac{k}{2} \rfloor < a \leq k, a \bmod 2 = 0\}$, and number of 1's of each column in the basis matrix $M_1$ is from the set $T_1 = \{a | 0 \leq a \leq \lfloor \frac{k}{2} \rfloor, a \bmod 2 = 1\} \bigcup \{a + n - k | \lfloor \frac{k}{2} \rfloor < a \leq k, a \bmod 2 = 1\}$. Hereafter, $\lfloor x \rfloor$ is the largest integer that is no greater than $x$ and $\lceil x \rceil$ is the smallest integer no less than $x$.

Because $k < n$, when one has $n - 1$ rows of a share matrix $M$, he stacks $k$ shares and hence knows the secret pixel. Without loss of generality, suppose the secret pixel is black. We determine last row of the share matrix $M$ as follows: for the column $p_i$ of $M$, where $i \in \{1, \ldots m\}$, denote number of 1's of the $n - 1$ rows in column $p_i$ as $h$, then we have the entry of the last rows of column $p_i$ be 0 if $h \in T_1$ and be 1 if $h + 1 \in T_1$. Hence, the last row is uniquely determined by the $n - 1$ rows, because the participants know the access structure they belong to, the share matrix will be uniquely determined.

*Third*, we prove any $n - 2$ rows cannot uniquely determine a share matrix. Consider the construction, we have that the basis matrix $M_1$ contains all the columns with Hamming weight are equal to 1. Let $A$ be a share matrix in $C_1$. Without loss of generality, there exist two different columns $c_1$ and $c_2$ in $A$, whose Hamming weights are equaled to 1. Denote the position of 1 in column $c_1$ (resp. $c_2$) be $p_1$ (resp. $p_2$), we have $p_1 \neq p_2$. Let $X = \{1, 2, \ldots, n\} \backslash \{p_1, p_2\}$, then, by restricting all the rows of columns $c_1$ and $c_2$ in $X$, we get two same subcolumns. Suppose $B$ is a matrix generated by exchanging positions of columns $c_1$ and $c_2$ in $A$, then $B$ is also a share matrix in $C_1$. Therefore, by restricting all the rows of $A$ and $B$ in $X$, we are able to get two same submatrices. Namely, the $n - 2$ rows of share matrix $A$ (the rows restricted in $X$) cannot uniquely determine a share matrix. Obviously, it also cannot uniquely determine a share matrix from less than $n - 2$ rows.

*Example 4.3* In a $(2, 3)$-VCS constructed by Droste's method, we have two basis matrices as follows:

$$M_0 = \begin{bmatrix} 010 \\ 010 \\ 010 \end{bmatrix}, M_1 = \begin{bmatrix} 100 \\ 010 \\ 001 \end{bmatrix}$$

Obviously, we generate three (resp. six) share matrices from basis matrix $M_0$ (resp. $M_1$). When we have two rows of a share matrix, we need to uniquely determine the share matrix. By the definition of VCS, any two rows of a share matrix reveal the secret pixel. From Theorem 4.11, we have the number of 1's of each column in basis matrix $M_0$ (resp. $M_1$) constructs the set $T_0 = 0, 3$ (resp. $T_1 = 1$). If the secret pixel is white (resp. black), the share matrix is constructed by permuting basis matrix $M_0$ (resp. $M_1$). Since all rows of $M_0$ are the same, we uniquely determine the share matrix from its two rows if it is constructed by $M_0$. If the share matrix is constructed by $M_1$, we also uniquely determine the share matrix from its two rows by counting the number of 1's of each column. For example, if we have two rows of a share matrix like

$$B = \begin{bmatrix} 010 \\ 100 \end{bmatrix}$$

Because the number of 1's in each column is in the set $T_1 = 1$, we determine the third row of the share matrix as [001]. However, if we have only one row of a share matrix, we cannot determine the secret pixel, and also cannot uniquely determine the share matrix. For example, if we have one row of a share matrix, like [010]. There are three share matrices, which may share the same row. These three share matrices are shown as follows:

$$B^1 = \begin{bmatrix} 010 \\ 010 \\ 010 \end{bmatrix}, B^2 = \begin{bmatrix} 010 \\ 100 \\ 001 \end{bmatrix}, B^3 = \begin{bmatrix} 010 \\ 001 \\ 100 \end{bmatrix}$$

Therefore, in a $(2, 3)$-VCS, a share matrix is determined by any 2 rows.

Theorem 4.11 presents an explicit method to uniquely determine a share matrix in $C_i$ ($i = 0, 1$), and in light of the above discussion, we have the following theorem:

**Theorem 4.12** *Let* $t = n - 1$, *then Construction 4.9 generates a* $(k, n - 1, n)$-*ESSVCS.*

For general basis matrix visual cryptography $(C_0, C_1)$, denote $C_i^{All}$ as a set of all the possible columns that appear in the share matrices of $C_i$ ($i = 0, 1$). For any set of participants $X \subseteq P$, denote $M'$ as a submatrix which is generated by restricting to the rows in $X$ of a share matrix in $C_i$. *First*, we have the following lemma

**Lemma 4.3** *For every column* $c'$ *of* $M'$, *if there exists only one column* $c \in C_i^{All}$ *such that* $c[X] = c'$, *then the submatrix* $M'$ *uniquely determines a share matrix in* $C_i$, *where* $c[X]$ *is the subcolumn generated by restricting to the rows in* $X$ *of* $c$.

*Proof* (Reduction to absurdity) Suppose $M'$ cannot uniquely determine a share matrix in $C_i$, i.e., there exist two different share matrices, denoted by $M_a$ and $M_b$, such that $M_a[X] = M_b[X] = M'$, where $M_a[X]$ is the submatrix generated by restricting to the rows in $X$ of $M_a$. Since $M_a$ and $M_b$ are different share matrices, there exists at least one column that is different for $M_a$ and $M_b$. Denote this column in $M_a$ is $c_a$ and that in $M_b$ is $c_b$, i.e., $c_a \neq c_b$. Because of $M_a[X] = M_b[X]$, we have $c_a[X] = c_b[X]$, which is contradict to the assumption that there exists only one column $c \in C_i^{All}$ such that $c[X] = c'$. Hence, $M'$ uniquely determines a share matrix in $C_i$.

According to Lemma 4.3, we present a general discussion for basis matrix $(k, n)$-VCS, denote $c_p, c_q \in C_i^{All}$ as two different columns, and denote $X_{pq}^i (\subset P)$ as the set of the participants such that for each $x \in X_{pq}^i$ satisfying $c_p[x] = c_q[x]$, where $c_p[x]$ is the $x$th entry of $c_p$. Then we have the following theorem:

**Lemma 4.4** *Let* $t = max\{|X_{pq}^i| + 1\}$ *for* $p \neq q$, $1 \leq p, q \leq m$ *and* $i = 0, 1$, *then a submatrix of* $t$ *rows of a share matrix in* $C_i$ *uniquely determines a share matrix in* $C_i$.

*Proof* Let $c'$ be a column of the submatrix $M'$ which is generated by restricting $t$ rows of a share matrix in $C_i$ ($i = 0, 1$). Denote a set of the participants of these $t$ rows as $X$, i.e., $|X| = t$, where $t = max\{|X_{pq}| + 1\}$. We prove that there only exists one column $c$ of $M$ such that $c[X] = c'$.

**Reduction to absurdity.** Suppose there exist two columns $c_a$ and $c_b$ such that $c_a[X] = c_b[X] = c'$, we see that $c_a$ and $c_b$ have $t$ entries with the same values, i.e., $t = |X_{ab}|$, which is impossible because $t = max\{|X_{pq}| + 1\}$ which implies $t > |X_{ab}|$.

According to Lemma 4.3, we have that a submatrix $M'$ with $t$ rows uniquely determine a share matrix in $C_i$.

According to Lemma 4.4, and let us recall that we have assumed $t \geq k$. (another reason that we assume $t \geq k$ that, if $t < k$, then $t$ participants cannot decide the submatrix of their $t$ shares is from $C_0$ or $C_1$, and hence it may not get the ciphertext either); we hence get the following theorem immediately.

For a $(k, n)$-VCS, any $k - 1$ or less shares cannot get any information of the secret image. In another word, any $t(t < k)$ shares cannot decide the $t$-row submatrix is from $C_0$ or $C_1$, and hence we cannot uniquely determine the share matrix. Therefore, it is reasonable to assume $t \geq k$. Further with Lemma 4.4, we get the following theorem.

**Theorem 4.13** *For a basis matrix $(k, n)$-VCS, there exists a $(k, t, n)$-ESSVCS where $t = max\{k, |X_{pq}^i| + 1\}$, $p \neq q$, $1 \leq p, q \leq m$ and $i = 0, 1$.*

According to Theorem 4.13, we also examined other two known constructions of $(k, n)$-VCS, and found that the two constructions have $t = n - 1$ (the same as the results in Theorem 4.11). Because they both take the canonical matrices as building block, where the canonical matrices mean the matrices that all the columns of a given weight occur with the same frequency. And for the canonical matrices that have a column $c_i$ with $x$ 1's and $n - x$ 0's where $0 < x < n$, there exists a column $c_j$ such that only two entries are different from $c_i$, which implies $|X_{ij}| = n - 2$, and hence $t = n - 1$.

#### 4.10.2.3  Bandwidth of ESSVCS Scheme

We define bandwidth of the ESSVCS as the maximum amount of covert data it carries through its subchannel. Denote columns in the basis matrix $M_i$ as $c_1, \ldots, c_e$ and multiplicities of these columns are $a_1, \ldots, a_e$, let us recall that we have the number of share matrix in $C_i$ being $|C_i| = \frac{(\sum_{i=1}^{e} a_i)!}{\prod_{i=1}^{e} a_i!}$ for $i \in \{0, 1\}$. To choose a share matrix in $C_i$, one needs at least $\log_2 |C_i|$ pseudorandom bits theoretically. By determining the share matrix which is chosen when encrypting the secret image in $C_i$, one can determine at most $\log_2 |C_i|$ bits information theoretically. Hence, the amount of the additional covert data that are carried by the secret pixel $i$ is at most $\log_2 |C_i|$ bits theoretically. We list the number of the share matrices $|C_i|$ of the VCS constructed in the Tables 4.2 and 4.3 as follows.

Actually, in practical, a pseudorandom number generator only generates integer number of pseudorandom bits, and ciphertexts are also represented by integer number of bits. However, the values of $\log_2 |C_i|$ are rarely integers, which means that some share matrices cannot be chosen by integer number of the pseudorandom bits, and it is hard to determine all the $\log_2 |C_i|$ ciphertext bits, hence results in wasting of the pseudorandom resources. So from the practical viewpoint, the amount of the covert data carried by the ESSVCS is impossible to reach the theoretical value.

**Table 4.2**  The number of share matrices in $C_0$

| $kn$ | 2 | 3 | 4 | 5 | 6 | 7 | 8 | 9 | 10 |
|---|---|---|---|---|---|---|---|---|---|
| 2 | 2 | 3 | 4 | 5 | 6 | 7 | 8 | 9 | 10 |
| 3 | | $4!$ | $\frac{6!}{2!}$ | $\frac{8!}{3!}$ | $\frac{10!}{4!}$ | $\frac{12!}{5!}$ | $\frac{14!}{6!}$ | $\frac{16!}{7!}$ | $\frac{18!}{8!}$ |
| 4 | | | $8!$ | $\frac{15!}{3!2!}$ | $\frac{24!}{6!3!}$ | $\frac{35!}{10!4!}$ | $\frac{48!}{15!5!}$ | $\frac{63!}{21!6!}$ | $\frac{80!}{28!7!}$ |
| 5 | | | | $16!$ | $\frac{30!}{3!(2!)^6}$ | $\frac{48!}{6!(3!)^7}$ | $\frac{70!}{10!(4!)^8}$ | $\frac{96!}{15!(5!)^9}$ | $\frac{126!}{21!(6!)^{10}}$ |
| 6 | | | | | $32!$ | $\frac{70!}{4!(2!)^{21}3!}$ | $\frac{128!}{10!(3!)^{28}6!}$ | $\frac{210!}{20!(4!)^{36}10!}$ | $\frac{320!}{35!(5!)^{45}15!}$ |
| 7 | | | | | | $64!$ | $\frac{140!}{4!(2!)^{28}(3!)^8}$ | $\frac{256!}{10!(3!)^{36}(6!)^9}$ | $\frac{420!}{20!(4!)^{45}(10!)^{10}}$ |
| 8 | | | | | | | $128!$ | $\frac{315!}{5!(3!)^{36}(2!)^{36}4!}$ | $\frac{640!}{15!(6!)^{45}(3!)^{45}10!}$ |
| 9 | | | | | | | | $256!$ | $\frac{630!}{5!(3!)^{45}(2!)^{120}(4!)^{10}}$ |
| 10 | | | | | | | | | $512!$ |

**Table 4.3**  The number of share matrices in $C_1$

| $kn$ | 2 | 3 | 4 | 5 | 6 | 7 | 8 | 9 | 10 |
|---|---|---|---|---|---|---|---|---|---|
| 2 | $2!$ | $3!$ | $4!$ | $5!$ | $6!$ | $7!$ | $8!$ | $9!$ | $10!$ |
| 3 | | $4!$ | $\frac{6!}{2!}$ | $\frac{8!}{3!}$ | $\frac{10!}{5!}$ | $\frac{12!}{5!}$ | $\frac{14!}{6!}$ | $\frac{16!}{7!}$ | $\frac{18!}{8!}$ |
| 4 | | | $8!$ | $\frac{15!}{(2!)^5}$ | $\frac{24!}{(3!)^6}$ | $\frac{35!}{(4!)^7}$ | $\frac{48!}{(5!)^8}$ | $\frac{63!}{(6!)^9}$ | $\frac{80!}{(7!)^{10}}$ |
| 5 | | | | $16!$ | $\frac{30!}{3!(2!)^6}$ | $\frac{48!}{6!(3!)^7}$ | $\frac{70!}{10!(4!)^8}$ | $\frac{96!}{15!(5!)^9}$ | $\frac{126!}{21!(6!)^{10}}$ |
| 6 | | | | | $32!$ | $\frac{70!}{(3!)^7(2!)^7}$ | $\frac{128!}{(6!)^8(3!)^8}$ | $\frac{210!}{(10!)^9(4!)^9}$ | $\frac{320!}{(15!)^{10}(5!)^{10}}$ |
| 7 | | | | | | $64!$ | $\frac{140!}{4!(2!)^{28}(3!)^8}$ | $\frac{256!}{10!(3!)^{36}(6!)^9}$ | $\frac{420!}{20!(4!)^{45}(10!)^{10}}$ |
| 8 | | | | | | | $128!$ | $\frac{315!}{(4!)^9(2!)^{84}(3!)^9}$ | $\frac{640!}{(10!)^{10}(3!)^{120}(6!)^{10}}$ |
| 9 | | | | | | | | $256!$ | $\frac{630!}{5!(3!)^{45}(2!)^{120}(4!)^{10}}$ |
| 10 | | | | | | | | | $512!$ |

In fact, if the secret pixels are encrypted only one at each time, in order to choose a share matrix pseudorandomly in $C_i$, one needs at least $\lceil \log_2 |C_i| \rceil$ pseudorandom bits, and its length of the ciphertext is at most $\lfloor \log_2 |C_i| \rfloor$ bits. To fully make use of the pseudorandom resources, we propose to encrypt $q$ secret pixels at a time, i.e., the *q-pixel encryption model*. Let $q = a_0 + a_1$, where $a_0$ is denoted as the number of white pixels and $a_1$ as the number of black pixels, the effectiveness of using *q-pixel encryption model* rather than *1-pixel encryption model* is as follows.

*First*: the number of pseudorandom bits required to choose the share matrices when the *q-pixel encryption model* is $\lceil a_0 \log_2 |C_0| + a_1 \log_2 |C_1| \rceil$, and it satisfies

$$\lceil a_0 \log_2 |C_0| + a_1 \log_2 |C_1| \rceil \leq a_0 \lceil \log_2 |C_0| \rceil + a_1 \lceil \log_2 |C_1| \rceil \qquad (4.16)$$

which implies less pseudorandom bits are required using the *q-pixel encryption model* than the 1-*pixel encryption model*.

*Second*: the number of pseudorandom bits determined by the share matrices when encrypting $q$ secret pixels at each time is $\lfloor a_0 \log_2 |C_0| + a_1 \log_2 |C_1| \rfloor$, and it satisfies

$$\lfloor a_0 \log_2 |C_0| + a_1 \log_2 |C_1| \rfloor \geq a_0 \lfloor \log_2 |C_0| \rfloor + a_1 \lfloor \log_2 |C_1| \rfloor \qquad (4.17)$$

which implies more pseudorandom bits are determined using the *q-pixel encryption model* than the 1-*pixel encryption model*.

A problem for the *q-pixel encryption model* is when encrypting more secret pixels at a time, the encryption scheme becomes more complex. So there exists a trade-off for the value of $q$.

To make things clear, we present the following example for a $(2, 2, 3)$-ESSVCS:

*Example 4.4*  For the sets

$$C_0 = \left\{ \begin{bmatrix} 100 \\ 100 \\ 100 \end{bmatrix}, \begin{bmatrix} 010 \\ 010 \\ 010 \end{bmatrix}, \begin{bmatrix} 001 \\ 001 \\ 001 \end{bmatrix} \right\} \qquad (4.18)$$

$$C_1 = \left\{ \begin{bmatrix} 100 \\ 010 \\ 001 \end{bmatrix}, \begin{bmatrix} 100 \\ 001 \\ 010 \end{bmatrix}, \begin{bmatrix} 010 \\ 100 \\ 001 \end{bmatrix}, \begin{bmatrix} 010 \\ 001 \\ 100 \end{bmatrix}, \begin{bmatrix} 001 \\ 100 \\ 010 \end{bmatrix}, \begin{bmatrix} 001 \\ 010 \\ 100 \end{bmatrix} \right\} \qquad (4.19)$$

We have, from theoretic point of view, the amount of information bits that are carried by a white secret pixel is $\log_2 |C_0| = \log_2 3$ and by a black secret pixel is $\log_2 |C_1| = \log_2 6$. And for 10 secret pixels with 5 white secret pixels and 5 black secret pixels the value will be $5 \log_2 3 + 5 \log_2 6 \approx 20.85$.

However, in practical, for the 10-*pixel encryption model*, where $a_0 = 5$ and $a_1 = 5$ as example, we have the amount of information that is carried is $\lfloor \log_2 3^5 + \log_2 6^5 \rfloor = 20$, which is more than 1-*pixel encryption model*, where the corresponding value is $5\lfloor \log_2 3 \rfloor + 5\lfloor \log_2 6 \rfloor = 15$.

At this point, we calculate the bandwidth of the ESSVCS as follows:

**Theorem 4.14**  *For a secret image $S_I$ which consists of $n_w$ white pixels and $n_b$ black pixels, the bandwidth $W$ of the ESSVCS is $W = \lfloor n_w \log_2 |C_0| + n_b \log_2 |C_1| \rfloor$, and it is achieved when using the $q_a$-pixel encryption model where $q_a = n_w + n_b$.*

*Proof*  For the $q_a$-*pixel encryption model* where $q_a = n_w + n_b$, which implies encrypt all the secret pixels in the secret image at each time. And it is clear that the amount of covert data carried by such ESSVCS is $W = \lfloor n_w \log_2 |C_0| + n_b \log_2 |C_1| \rfloor$. We only need to prove that $W$ reaches its maximum when using the $q_a$-*pixel encryption model*, i.e., if one divides all the pixels in the secret image into several parts, and encrypts these parts, respectively, the amount of covert data carried is less than the $q_a$-*pixel encryption model*.

Without loss of generality, let $q_a = q_1 + q_2$ (i.e., divide into two parts) and suppose encryption of the secret image $S_I$ is realized using $q_1$-*pixel encryption model* and $q_2$-*pixel encryption model*, and let $q_1 = a_0 + a_1$, $q_2 = b_0 + b_1$, where $a_0$, $b_0$ are the number of white pixels and $a_1$, $b_1$ are the number of black pixels. We have that the total number of pseudorandom bits is $\lfloor a_0 \log_2 |C_0| + a_1 \log_2 |C_1| \rfloor + \lfloor b_0 \log_2 |C_0| + b_1 \log_2 |C_1| \rfloor$, which is not greater than $\lfloor (a_0 + b_0) \log_2 |C_0| + (a_1 + b_1) \log_2 |C_1| \rfloor = \lfloor n_w \log_2 |C_0| + n_b \log_2 |C_1| \rfloor$. Hence, the theorem is true.

### 4.10.2.4 On Decoding the Ciphertext

For ESSVCS, in order to encrypt the secret pixels and decode the ciphertext, one needs to set a bijection between the set of pseudorandom numbers (ciphertext) and the set of share matrices. A simple way to realize that is to generate a table which contains all the share matrices and their corresponding random numbers. When the dealer generates the shares, (s)he needs to generate a pseudorandom number and find the corresponding share matrix by table-lookup, then (s)he can encrypt the shares using the share matrix. When decoding the ciphertext, the participants get the share matrices according to the Theorem 4.11, and find the corresponding numbers by table-lookup, hence, they get the ciphertext. Disadvantage of this decoding method is the table requires us to store all the share matrices in sets $C_0$ and $C_1$, and hence it has large memory requirements. In this subsection, we propose a decoding method which is more efficient than the above-mentioned method.

The proposed decoding method contains two subroutines: the first is $MTN(S)$, which takes a share matrix in $C_i$ ($i = 0, 1$) as its input and generates a number between 1 and $m!$, the second is $NTM(N)$, which takes a number between 1 and $m!$ as its input and generates a share matrix $S$. The subroutines $MTN(S)$ and $NTM(N)$ form a bijection between the set of the share matrices and the set of numbers between 1 and $m!$.

Using $MTN(S)$ and $NTM(N)$, when the dealer encrypts a secret pixel $p$, (s)he first generates a pseudorandom number between 1 and $m!$, and then consults the subroutine $NTM(N)$ to generate a share matrix in $C_i$ ($i = 0, 1$), and encrypts the secret pixel $p$ using the share matrix. When the participants decode the ciphertext, they first generate the share matrix according to Theorem 4.11, and consult the subroutine $MTN(S)$ to get the ciphertext.

Denote the columns of the basis matrix as $c_1, \ldots, c_m$, first we take the case that $c_1, \ldots, c_m$ are pairwise into consideration. In this part, we treat a matrix as a set of columns. The subroutine $MTN(S)$ which outputs a number between 1 and $m!$ given a share matrix $S$ as its input is

**Subroutine: MTN(S)**

> For $i = 1$ to $m - 1$
> Find $c_i$ in $S$, assume that $c_i$ is the $J_i$th column of $S$
> Delete $c_i$ from $S$
> Output $N = 1 + \sum_{i=1}^{m-1} ((m - i)!)(J_i - 1)$

The subroutine $NTM(N)$ which outputs a share matrix $S$ given a number between 1 and $m!$ as its input is

**Subroutine: NTM(N)**

> Initial $S$ as an empty matrix
> $N_0 \leftarrow N - 1$
> For $i = 1$ to $m - 1$
> $\quad J_i \leftarrow \lfloor \frac{N_{i-1}}{(m-i)!} \rfloor + 1$
> $\quad N_i \leftarrow N_{i-1} - (J_i - 1)((m - i)!)$
> Insert $c_m$ to $S$ as its 1st column
> For $i = m - 1$ to $1$
> $\quad$ Insert column $c_i$ into $S$ as its $J_i$th column
> Output $S$

According to the subroutines $MTN(S)$ and $NTM(N)$ above, we have the following theorem:

**Theorem 4.15** *The subroutines $MTN(S)$ and $NTM(N)$ form a bijection between the set of share matrices in $C_i$ ($i = 0, 1$) and the set of numbers between 1 and $m!$.*

*Proof* Because in subroutines $MTN(S)$ and $NTM(N)$, we represent the share matrices by the positions of its columns $(J_1, J_2, \ldots, J_{m-1})$ where $1 \le J_i \le m + 1 - i$ for $i = 1, 2, \ldots, m - 1$, we only need to prove that $MTN(S)$ and $NTM(N)$ form a bijection between the sets $X = \{(J_1, J_2, \ldots, J_{m-1}) | 1 \le J_i \le m + 1 - i \text{ for } i = 1, 2, \ldots, m - 1\}$ and $Y = \{1, 2, \ldots, m!\}$. Denote $f : X \to Y$ as a map from $X$ to $Y$, we prove that $f$ is a bijection.

*First*, given a number in $Y$, according to $NTM(N)$, there exists a $(J_1, J_2 \ldots, J_{m-1})$, hence $f$ is a surjection.

*Second*, for any two different elements in $X$, $J = (J_1, J_2, \ldots, J_{m-1})$ and $J' = (J'_1, J'_2, \ldots, J'_{m-1})$ such that $J \ne J'$, we prove that their corresponding numbers $f(J)$ and $f(J')$ are different.

According to $MTN(S)$, we have $f(J) = 1 + \sum_{i=1}^{m-1} ((m - i)!)(J_i - 1)$ and $f(J') = 1 + \sum_{i=1}^{m-1} ((m - i)!)(J'_i - 1)$. Denote $i^*$ as the smallest number that $J_{i^*} \ne J'_{i^*}$, without loss of generality, we suppose $J_{i^*} > J'_{i^*}$, i.e., $J_{i^*} - J'_{i^*} \ge 1$. Thus, we have

$$f(J) - f(J') = \sum_{i=1}^{m-1} ((m - i)!)(J_i - J'_i)$$

$$= (m - i^*)!(J_{i^*} - J'_{i^*}) + \sum_{i=i^*+1}^{m-1} ((m - i)!)(J_i - J'_i)$$

$$\ge (m - i^*)! + \sum_{i=i^*+1}^{m-1} ((m - i)!)(J_i - J'_i)$$

Because $1 \leq J_i, J_i' \leq m + 1 - i$, we have $-(m - i) \leq J_i - J_i' \leq m - i$, hence

$$f(J) - f(J') \geq (m - i^*)! - \sum_{i=i^*+1}^{m-1} ((m - i)!)(m - i)$$
$$= (m - i^*)! - ((m - i^*)! - 1)$$
$$= 1$$

Therefore, $f(J) - f(J') \neq 0$, we have $f$ is an injection. Hence, $f$ is a bijection and the theorem follows.

*Example 4.5* For a $(2, 3)$-VCS, the basis matrix $M_1$ has three different columns. $M_1$ and its three columns $c_1, c_2, c_3$ are shown as follows:

$$M_1 = \begin{bmatrix} 100 \\ 010 \\ 001 \end{bmatrix}, c_1 = \begin{bmatrix} 1 \\ 0 \\ 0 \end{bmatrix}, c_2 = \begin{bmatrix} 0 \\ 1 \\ 0 \end{bmatrix}, c_3 = \begin{bmatrix} 0 \\ 0 \\ 1 \end{bmatrix}$$

From subroutines $MTN(S)$ and $NTM(N)$, we construct a bijection between the set of share matrices generated by $M_1$ and the set of numbers between 1 and 3!. The detailed bijection is shown as follows:

$$No.1: \begin{bmatrix} 100 \\ 010 \\ 001 \end{bmatrix}, No.2: \begin{bmatrix} 100 \\ 001 \\ 010 \end{bmatrix}, No.3: \begin{bmatrix} 010 \\ 100 \\ 001 \end{bmatrix}$$

$$No.4: \begin{bmatrix} 001 \\ 100 \\ 010 \end{bmatrix}, No.5: \begin{bmatrix} 010 \\ 001 \\ 100 \end{bmatrix}, No.6: \begin{bmatrix} 001 \\ 010 \\ 100 \end{bmatrix}$$

For the case that there are identical columns in the basis matrix, which means that there are identical share matrices in the $m!$ permutations of the basis matrix. Suppose there are $e$ different columns in the basis matrix, and the multiplicities of these columns are $a_1, a_2, \ldots, a_e$. Denote $N_d$ as the number of the different share matrices in $C_i$, then we have $N_d = \frac{(\sum_{i=1}^{e} a_i)!}{\prod_{i=1}^{e} a_i!}$, for $i \in \{0, 1\}$. Each share matrix appears $\frac{m!}{N_d}$ times in the $m!$ permutations.

Furthermore, according to the subroutine $MTN(S)$, each permutation corresponds to a number between 1 and $m!$, we divide these $m!$ numbers into $N_d$ groups, where each group contains $\frac{m!}{N_d}$ numbers, and the numbers in one group correspond to an identical share matrix. We hence form an array of length $N_d$ by choosing the smallest number of each group. Denote this array as $A$, and denote $S_1^i, S_2^i, \ldots, S_{N_d}^i$ as the different share matrices in the set $C_i$, the following subroutine generates $A$:

**Subroutine: MC**

    Initial an empty array $A$
    For $j = 1$ to $N_d$

For $q = 1$ to $m$

 Find the first $c_q$ in $S_j^i$ from left to right, assume that $c_q$ is the $J_q$th column of $S_j^i$

 Delete $c_q$ from $S_j^i$

$$A[j] \leftarrow 1 + \sum_{q=1}^{m-1} ((m-q)!)(J_q - 1)$$

To differentiate the two cases, whether there exist and do not exist identical columns, we denote $MTN$-d$(S)$ and $NTM$-d$(N)$ as the corresponding subroutines for the case that there exist identical columns:

## Subroutine: MTN-d(S)

$A \leftarrow MC$

For $q = 1$ to $m$

 Find the first $c_q$ in $S_j^i$ from left to the right, assume that $c_q$ is the $J_q$th column

of $S_j^i$

 Delete $c_q$ from $S_j^i$

$$N' \leftarrow 1 + \sum_{q=1}^{m-1} ((m-q)!)(J_q - 1)$$

For $r = 1$ to $N_d$

 if $A[r] = N'$

  Output $r$

## Subroutine: NTM-d(N)

$A \leftarrow MC$

$N' \leftarrow A[N]$

$S \leftarrow NTM(N')$

Output $S$

According to the Theorem 4.15, we have, each group only has one smallest number. Hence the array $A$ is a bijection from the set $\{1, 2, \dots, N_d\}$ and the set of the smallest numbers in each group. Furthermore, because each group corresponds to a different share matrix, we have, the $MTN$-d$(S)$ and $NTM$-d$(N)$ form a bijection between the set $\{1, 2, \dots, N_d\}$ and the set of share matrices $\{S_1^i, S_2^i \dots, S_{N_d}^i\}$. We summarize this result as the following theorem:

**Theorem 4.16** *The subroutines MTN-d$(S)$ and NTM-d$(N)$ form a bijection between the set of share matrices in $C_i$ ($i = 0, 1$) and the set of numbers between 1 and $N_d$.*

*Example 4.6* For a $(2, 3)$-VCS, there are identical columns in basis matrix $M_0$. $M_0$ and its two different columns $c_1$ and $c_2$ with multiplicities 1 and 2 are shown as follows:

$$M_1 = \begin{bmatrix} 100 \\ 100 \\ 100 \end{bmatrix}, c_1 = \begin{bmatrix} 1 \\ 0 \\ 0 \end{bmatrix}, c_2 = \begin{bmatrix} 0 \\ 0 \\ 0 \end{bmatrix}$$

From subroutines $MTN - d(S)$ and $NTM - d(N)$, we construct a bijection between the set of share matrices generated by $M_0$ and the set of numbers between 1 and 3. The detailed bijection is shown as follows:

$$No.1: \begin{bmatrix} 100 \\ 100 \\ 100 \end{bmatrix}, No.2: \begin{bmatrix} 100 \\ 010 \\ 001 \end{bmatrix}$$

The above subroutines are more efficient than the simple table-lookup method. Particularly, for the case that the columns $c_1, c_2, \ldots, c_m$ are pairwise different, the subroutines $MTN(S)$ and $NTM(N)$ are efficient, because they only need fixed memory requirements. For the case that there are identical columns in $c_1, c_2, \ldots, c_m$, the memory requirement of the subroutines $MTN - d(S)$ and $NTM - d(N)$ relates to the value of $m$. Because they only need to store the indexes of the share matrices $A[1], A[2], \ldots, A[N_d]$ [31], they are more efficient than the simple table-lookup method. Furthermore, the table (the array $A$ in Subroutine $MC$) is previously generated and reusable.

## 4.11 Exercises

(1) Embedded EVCS in this chapter is based on traditional VCS. Give a new embedded EVCS based on probabilistic VCS.
(2) Explain the differences between $(k, n)$-P-SIVCS and $(k, n, m)$-ME-SIVCS.
(3) Please compare the definition of $(k, n, t)$-ME-SIVCS-1 with the definition of $(k, n, t)$-ME-SIVCS-2 and explain their differences.
(4) Please generate the basis matrices of $(3, 4)$-VCS using Algorithm 4.3.
(5) How are the polynomial-based secret sharing scheme and the encryption algorithm added into the security-enriched VCS?

## References

1. Ateniese G, Blundo C, Santis AD, Stinson DR (1996) Visual cryptography for general access structures. Inf Comput 129:86–106
2. Ateniese G, Blundo C, Santis AD, Stinson DR (2001) Extended capabilities for visual cryptography. ACM Theory Comput Sci 250(1–2):143–161
3. Biham E, Itzkovitz A (1997) Visual cryptography with polarization. In: Proceedings of CRYPTO'98
4. Blundo C, Santis A, Stinson DR (1999) On the contrast in visual cryptography schemes. J Cryptol 12(4):261–289

5. Blundo C, Bonis A, Santis A (2001) Improved schemes for visual cryptography. Des Codes Cryptogr 24:255–278
6. Blundo C, D'Arco P, Santis A, Stinson DR (2003) Contrast optimal threshold visual cryptography schemes. SIAM J Discret Math 16(2):224–261
7. Bose M, Mukerjee R (2010) Optimal $(k, n)$ visual cryptographic schemes for general $k$. Des Codes Cryptogr 55:19–35
8. Chang CY (2000) Visual cryptography for color images. Masters thesis. National Central University, Taiwan
9. Chen YF, Chan YK, Huang CC, Tsai MH, Chu YP (2007) A multiple-level visual secret-sharing scheme without image size expansion. Inf Sci 177:4696–4710
10. Chen TH, Tsao KH, Wei KC (2008) Multiple-image encryption by rotating random grids. In: Proceedings of international conference on intelligent systems design and applications, vol 3, pp 252–256
11. Cimato S, Prisco R, Santis A (2005) Optimal colored threshold visual cryptography schemes. Des Codes Cryptogr 35:311–335
12. Cimato S, Prisco RD, Santis AD (2006) Probabilistic visual cryptography schemes. Comput J 49(1):97–107
13. Degara-Quintela N, Perez-Gonzalez F (2003) Visible encryption: using paper as a secure channel, security and watermarking of multimedia contents. In: Proceedings of SPIE'03, vol 5020
14. Droste S (1996) New results on visual cryptography. In: Proceedings of CRYPTO'96, vol 1109. Springer, New York, pp 401–415
15. Eisen PA, Stinson DR (2002) Threshold visual cryptography schemes with specified whiteness levels of reconstructed pixels. Des Codes Cryptogr 25:15–61
16. Ehrsam WF, Meyer CHW, Smith JL, Tuchman WL (1976) Message verification and transmission error detection by block chaining
17. Fang P, Lin JC (2006) Visual cryptography with extra ability of hiding confidential data. J Electron Imaging 15(2):023020
18. Floyd RW, Steinberg L (2006) Visual cryptography with extra ability of hiding confidential data. J Electron Imaging 15(2):023020
19. Hsu HC, Chen TS, Lin YH (2004) The ringed shadow image technology of visual cryptography by applying diverse rotating angles to hide the secret sharing. Netw Sens Control 2:996–1001
20. Krause M, Simon Hu (2003) Determining the optimal contrast for secret sharing schemes in visual cryptography. Comb Probab Comput 12(3):285–299
21. Kuwakado H, Tanaka H (2004) Size-reduced visual secret sharing scheme. IEICE Trans Fundam E87-A(5):1193–1197
22. Lin SJ, Chen SK, Lin JC (2010) Flip visual cryptography (FVC) with perfect security, conditionally-optimal contrast, and no expansion. J Vis Commun Image Represent 21(8): 900–916
23. Liu F, Wu CK (2011) Embedded meaningful share visual cryptography schemes. IEEE Trans Inf Forensics Secur 6(2):307–322
24. Liu F, Wu CK, Lin XJ (2010) A new definition of the contrast of visual cryptography scheme. Inf Process Lett 110:241–246
25. Naor M, Shamir A (1995) Visual cryptography. In: Proceedings of EUROCRYPT'94. LNCS, vol 950. Springer, New York, pp 1–12
26. Shamir A (1979) How to share a secret. Commun ACM 22(11):612–613
27. Shyu SJ (2006) Efficient visual secret sharing scheme for color images. Pattern Recognit 39(5):866–880
28. Shyu SJ (2007) Image encryption by random grids. Pattern Recognit 40:1014–1031
29. Shyu SJ, Huang SY, Lee YK, Wang RZ, Chen K (2007) Sharing multiple secrets in visual cryptography. Pattern Recognit 40(12):3633–3651
30. Wu HC, Chang CC (2005) Sharing visual multi-secrets using circle shares. Comput Stand Interfaces 28:123–135
31. Xhou W, Bovik AC (2002) A universal image quality index. IEEE Signal Process Lett 9(3): 81–84

32. Yang CN (2004) New visual secret sharing schemes using probabilistic method. Pattern Recognit Lett 25:481–494
33. Yang CN, Chen TS (2005) Aspect ratio invariant visual secret sharing schemes with minimum pixel expansion. Pattern Recognit Lett 26:193–206
34. Yang CN, Chen TS (2005) Size-adjustable visual secret sharing schemes. IEICE Trans Fundam E88-A(9):2471–2474
35. Yang CN, Chen TS (2006) New size-reduced visual secret sharing schemes with half reduction of shadow size. IEICE Trans Fundam E89-A(2):620–625
36. Yang CN, Chen TS (2007) Visual secret sharing scheme: prioritizing the secret pixels with different pixel expansions to enhance the image contrast. Opt Eng 46(9):097005
37. Yang CN, Ciou CB (2010) Image secret sharing method with two-decoding-options: lossless recovery and previewing capability. Image Vis Comput 28:1600–1610
38. Zhou Z, Arce GR, Crescenzo GD (2003) Halftone visual cryptography. IEEE ICIP 521–524

# Chapter 5
# Various Color Schemes of Visual Cryptography

## 5.1 Introduction

Visual cryptography scheme (VCS) is a kind of secret-sharing scheme that allows the encryption of a secret image into $n$ shares that are distributed to $n$ participants [9, 24, 25]. The beauty of such a scheme is that the decryption of the secret image requires neither the knowledge of cryptography nor complex computation. Color visual cryptography has become an interesting research topic after the formal introduction of visual cryptography by Naor and Shamir in 1995 [6]. The authors propose a color $(k, n)$-VCS using the visual cryptography model of Naor and Shamir with no pixel expansion [8, 10, 14, 30], and a color $(k, n)$-extended visual cryptography scheme $((k, n)$-EVCS) using the visual cryptography model of Naor and Shamir with pixel expansion the same as that of its corresponding black-and-white $(k, n)$-EVCS [2]. Furthermore, this chapter presents a black-and-white $(k, n)$-VCS and a black-and-white $(k, n)$-EVCS based on the visual cryptography model of Tuyls. Based on the black-and-white schemes, the authors propose a color $(k, n)$-VCS and a color $(k, n)$-EVCS based on the same visual cryptography model, whose pixel expansions are the same as that of their corresponding black-and-white $(k, n)$-VCS and $(k, n)$-EVCS, respectively. The authors also give the experimental results of the proposed schemes, and compare the proposed scheme with known schemes in the literature.

The color visual cryptography (VCS) based on the visual cryptography model of Naor and Shamir has been studied by many researchers [28, 29]. The first approach to implement color VCS is to print the colors in the secret image on the transparencies directly. The expected color appears by hiding the colors using a special black color, or by showing the mixed color according to the subtractive and additive color models [32]. Unfortunately, this approach has the following disadvantages. First, it often generates color VCS with large pixel expansion. Second, the approach can only represent a small number of colors, the reason being that the pixel expansion of the color VCS generated by this approach is related to the number of colors in the recovered secret image, and the pixel expansion grows rapidly when the number of colors in the recovered secret image increases. Hence, given a reasonable pixel expansion

© Springer International Publishing Switzerland 2015
F. Liu and W.Q. Yan, *Visual Cryptography for Image
Processing and Security*, DOI 10.1007/978-3-319-23473-1_5

in the practical sense (which cannot be too large), the recovered secret image can only represent a small number of colors. Third, the color model of this approach assumes that the stacking of pixels with the same color will result in a pixel that has the same color (such an assumption is used to simplify the constructions). However, this is not true. The stacking of some lighter pixels will result in a darker pixel. For example, the stacking of two red pixels will result in a wine pixel different from the original red pixel. This is the color darkening phenomenon because of stacking the pixels with the same color [9].

The second approach to implement color visual cryptography is to convert a color image into black-and-white images on the three color channels (red, green, blue or equivalently cyan, magenta, yellow), respectively, and then apply the black-and-white VCS to each of the color channels. This method can obtain smaller pixel expansion but requires the halftone process [33], which decreases the quality of the secret image and often results in the expansion of the input images [12, 30, 33].

The third approach to implement color visual cryptography and recover the secret image perfectly requires very little computation. Their method utilizes the binary representation of the color of a pixel and encrypts the secret image at the bit level. However, the method has pixel expansion $m$ and needs the assistance of computing devices for decrypting, and can only be applied in the visual cryptography model of Naor and Shamir.

The color VCS using the visual cryptography model of Tuyls is attractive as it has good color, resolution, and contrast properties [3, 21]. For example, the $(n, n)$-VCS in the visual cryptography model can recover the secret image perfectly. However, the color VCS for general $(k, n)$ access structure has not been studied [1], not to mention the color EVCS.

In general, a $(k, n)$-EVCS takes a secret image and $n$ original share images as input and output $n$ shares that satisfy the following three conditions: first, any $k$ out of $n$ shares can recover the secret image; second, any less than $k$ shares cannot obtain any information about the secret image other than the size of the secret image; and third, all the shares are meaningful images. Besides, a color $(k, n)$-EVCS should fulfill the condition that the secret image, the original share images, the shares, and the recovered secret image are all colorful. Because all the constructions of color EVCS of this study take their corresponding black-and-white EVCS as building blocks [18, 19], in this section, we give some definitions about the black-and-white EVCS. Note that, for the black-and-white EVCS, the color of a pixel has only two possible values, black and white.

We denote $C_c^{c_1,\ldots,c_n}$ as the collection of matrices from which the dealer chooses a matrix to encrypt, where $c, c_1, \ldots, c_n \in \{1, 0\}$. For $i = 1, \ldots, n$, $c_i$ is the color of the pixel on the $i$th original share image, and $c$ is the color of the secret image. Hence, to implement a black-and-white $(k, n)$-EVCS, we have to construct $2^n$ pairs of such collections $(C_0^{c_1,\ldots,c_n}, C_1^{c_1,\ldots,c_n})$, one for each possible combination of white-and-black pixels in the $n$ original share images. A black-and-white $(k, n)$-EVCS is defined as follows.

**Definition 5.1** A family of $2^n$ pairs of collections of $n \times m'$ binary matrices $\{(C_0^{c_1,\ldots,c_n}, C_1^{c_1,\ldots,c_n})\}_{c_1,\ldots,c_n \in \{1,0\}}$, constitute a black-and-white $(k, n)$-EVCS if there exist values $\alpha_F (> 0)$, $\alpha_S (> 0)$ and $h$ satisfying:

**Contrast** for any $M \in C_0^{c_1,\ldots,c_n}$, the '$\cdot$' operation of any $k$ out of $n$ rows of $M$ is a vector $v$ that satisfies $w(v) \leq (h - \alpha_F \cdot m')$, and for any $M \in C_1^{c_1,\ldots,c_n}$, we have $w(v) \geq h$.

**Security** for any $i_1, i_2, \ldots, i_t \in \{1, 2, \ldots, n\}$ with $t < k$, the two collections of $t \times m'$ matrices $D_j^{c_1,\ldots,c_n}$, $j = 0, 1$, obtained by restricting each $t \times m'$ matrix in $C_j^{c_1,\ldots,c_n}$ to rows $i_1, i_2, \ldots, i_t$, are indistinguishable in the sense that they contain the same matrices with the same frequencies.

**Contrast** after the original share images are encrypted, the shares are still meaningful. Formally, for any $i \in \{1, 2, \ldots, n\}$ and any $c, c_1, \ldots, c_{i-1}, c_{i+1}, \ldots, c_n \in \{0, 1\}$, with the $i$th row of $M$ denoted as $M[i]$, we have

$$\min_{M \in M_1} \omega(M[i]) - \max_{M \in M_0} \omega(M[i]) \geq \alpha_S \cdot m', \tag{5.1}$$

where

$$M_1 = \bigcup_{c, c_1, \ldots, c_n \in \{0,1\}} C_c^{c_1 \cdots c_{i-1}^1 c_{i+1} \cdots c_n} \tag{5.2}$$

$$M_0 = \bigcup_{c, c_1, \ldots, c_n \in \{0,1\}} C_c^{c_1 \cdots c_{i-1}^0 c_{i+1} \cdots c_n} \tag{5.3}$$

In the above Definition 5.1, $m'$ is the pixel expansion of the black-and-white $(k, n)$-EVCS. $\alpha_F$ and $\alpha_S$ are the contrast of the recovered secret image and that of the shares, respectively [21].

We take EVCS into consideration, where $C_c^{c_1,\ldots,c_n}$ ($c, c_1, \ldots, c_n \in \{0, 1\}$) are constructed from the $n \times m'$ basis matrices $S_c^{c_1,\ldots,c_n}$. The set $C_c^{c_1,\ldots,c_n}$ consists of the $m!$ matrices obtained by applying all permutations to the columns of $S_c^{c_1,\ldots,c_n}$. Denote $p(S_c^{c_1,\ldots,c_n})$ as a random column permutation of $S_c^{c_1,\ldots,c_n}$.

In Definition 5.1, the first and second conditions correspond to the contrast and security conditions of Definition 5.1, and the third condition implies that the original share images are not 'modified', that is, after we encrypt the $n$ original images by using the $2^n$ pairs of collections $\{(C_0^{c_1,\ldots,c_n}, C_1^{c_1,\ldots,c_n})\}$, where $c_1, \ldots, c_n \in \{0, 1\}$, the encrypted shares are still meaningful.

## 5.2  Basic Principles of Color Models

The additive and subtractive color models are widely used to describe the constitutions of colors. In the additive color model, the three primary colors are red, green, and blue (RGB), with the desired colors obtained by mixing different RGB channels [17]. By controlling the intensity of red (resp, green, or blue) channel, we can modulate the amount of red (resp, green, or blue) in compound light. The more the mixed-colored light, the more the brightness of the light. Mixing the red, green, and blue channels of equal intensities results in white color light. The computer screen is a good example of the additive color model [17]. In the subtractive color model, the color is represented by applying the combinations of colored light reflected from the surface of an object (because most objects do not radiate by themselves) [31]. For example, taken an apple under natural light, the surface of the apple absorbs the green and blue parts of the natural light and reflects the red light to human eyes and, thus, it becomes a red apple. By mixing cyan (C) with magenta (M) and yellow (Y) pigments, we can produce a wide range of colors. The more the pigment added, the lower the intensity of the light, and thus the darker the light [17]. This is why it is called the subtractive model. $C$, $M$, and $Y$ are the three primitive colors of pigment that cannot be composed from other colors.

In the computer, a natural color image can be divided into three color channels: red, green, and blue (or equivalently cyan, magenta, and yellow) [26], and each channel will constitute a gray-level image, where each pixel can be represented by a binary value of 8 bits [11]. Denote $x(p, q) = [x_{(p,q)_1}, x_{(p,q)_2}, x_{(p,q)_3}]$ as the color of a pixel located at the position $(p, q)$ of a color image of size $K_1 \times K_2$ for $p = 1, 2, \ldots, K_1$ and $q = 1, 2, \ldots, K_2$. Let $t$ describe the color channel (e.g., $t = 1$ for red, $t = 2$ for green, and $t = 3$ for blue) and the color component $x_{(p,q)_t}$ is coded with a binary value of 8 bits allowing $x_{(p,q)_t}$ to be an integer between 0 and $2^8 - 1 = 255$ and, hence, the color of the pixel $x_{(p,q)}$ can be expressed in a binary form as follows:

$$x_{(p,q)} = \sum x^i_{(p,q)} \cdot 2^{8-i} \tag{5.4}$$

where $x^i_{(p,q)} = [x^i_{(p,q)_1}, x^i_{(p,q)_2}, x^i_{(p,q)_3}] \in \{0, 1\}^3$ denote the binary vector at the $i$th bit level, with $i = 1$ denoting the most significant bit and $i = 2$ denoting the second most significant bit. In this way, a natural color image [26] is divided into 24 binary images.

By the gray level of a pixel [11] we mean that the darkness of the pixel appears for each color channel. In this study, we divide the distance between a black and a white pixel, for each color channel, into 256 gray levels. Define the gray level 0 for a complete white pixel, and the gray level 255 for a complete black pixel. Note that this definition of black-and-white pixels is just the opposite to their traditional definitions on the computer. Based on this definition, the 1's and 0's in the binary representation of the gray level correspond to black-and-white bits, respectively, which is consistent with their traditional definitions in visual cryptography.

Because we divide 256 gray levels for each color channel, each color channel can be expressed by a binary vector of 8 bits. To construct such a color VCS, different bit levels should be assigned with different gray levels in order to represent the target color (gray level) [11]. For example, we can print a pixel with a gray level $\alpha_1$ for the most significant bit, and $\alpha_2$ for the second most significant bit in the visual cryptography model of Naor and Shamir. For VCS in the visual cryptography model of Tuyls, we rotate through an angle $(\alpha_1/256 \cdot \pi/2)$ for the most significant bit, and through $(\alpha_2/256 \cdot \pi/2)$ for the second most significant bit, and so on, where $\alpha_i \in [0, 255]$, for $i \in \{1, \ldots, 8\}$ [7, 16].

Then, we show the principles of the color superimposition for the visual cryptography model of Naor and Shamir and those of Tuyls, respectively. To simplify the discussion, we take one color channel as an example.

First, for the visual cryptography model of Naor and Shamir, the basic principle of the color by superimposing two pixels is defined as follows: for a pixel with a gray level $\alpha_i$ and a pixel with a gray level $\alpha_j$, the gray level of the resulting pixel by stacking the two pixels will be $(255 - (255 - \alpha_i)(255 - \alpha_j)/255)$. This definition of color superimposition is widely accepted.

Second, for the visual cryptography model of Tuyls, the basic principle of the color by superimposing the shares is defined as follows: for a pixel with a gray level $\alpha_i$ and a pixel with a gray level $\alpha_j$, which are implemented by rotating the angles $(\alpha_i/256 \cdot \pi/2)$ and $(\alpha_j/256 \cdot \pi/2)$ for the first and the second LC layers, respectively, the gray level of the superimposition of the two pixels will be $\alpha_i + \alpha_j$, which is implemented by rotating through an angle $(\alpha_i + \alpha_j)/256 \cdot \pi/2$ [7, 16].

Denote $M_0$ and $M_1$ as the $n \times m$ basis matrices for a black-and-white $(k, n)$-VCS which satisfy Definition 5.1. Denote $b$ as the number of the black pixels in a block of $m$ pixels. Denote $e_b$ as the number of blocks, with $b$ black pixels that have already been encrypted. The multi-pixel encryption method encrypts a block of $m$ pixels at a time and can be described as follows:

---

**Algorithm 5.1**: The multi-pixel encryption method

---

**Input**  : The secret image and the basis matrices for a black-and-white $(k, n)$-VCS, $M_0$ and $M_1$, which have pixel expansion $m$.
**Output**: The shares $S_i$ for $i = 1, \ldots, n$.

**Step 1**. Set $e_b \neq 0$ for $b = 1, 2, \ldots, m$;
**Step 2**. Pick up a block of $m$ pixels, $p_1, p_2, \ldots, p_m$, in the secret image, and denote $b$ as the number of black pixels among them;
**Step 3**. Put the $m$ subpixels in the $i$th row of $P(M)$ to the corresponding positions of $p_1, p_2, \ldots, p_m$ in the $i$th share for $i = 1, \ldots, n$, where $P(M)$ is a random column permutation of $M$ and the basis matrix $M$ is decided as follows:
if $e_b \bmod m < b$ then $M \leftarrow M_1$
else $M \leftarrow M_0$
**Step 4**. Set $e_b \leftarrow e_b + 1$;
**Step 5**. Repeat Steps 2, 3, and 4 until all the pixels of the secret image are encrypted and output the $n$ shares $S_i$ for $i = 1, \ldots, n$.

---

For a block of $m$ pixels that have $b$ black pixels, Algorithm 5.1 shows a method to encrypt these $m$ pixels with the basis matrices $M_0$ and $M_1$, where $M_0$ contributes with a probability of $b/m$ and $M_1$ contributes with a probability of $(m-b)/m$ exactly. By such a method, the recovered secret image has a better visual effect than the scheme.

The security of the multi-pixel encryption method has been proved by Hou and Tu [15]; we refer to their result by the following Theorem 5.1.

**Theorem 5.1** *Algorithm 5.1 generates $n$ shares $S_i$ for $i = 1, \ldots, n$, where less than $k$ out of these $n$ shares cannot obtain any information about the secret image other than the size of the secret image.*

Note that the multi-pixel encryption is a method to reduce the pixel expansion while maintaining better visual effect [15, 22, 30]. However, for the encryption of a single pixel, the generated shares do not satisfy the contrast conditions of Definition 5.1 since a white pixel may occasionally be wrongly represented by a black pixel and vice versa.

## 5.3  Color VCS and Color EVCS in the Traditional Visual Cryptography Model

Usually, a color visual cryptography model has large pixel expansion. In this section we provide a construction of color $(k, n)$-VCS and a construction of color $(k, n)$-EVCS in the visual cryptography model of Naor and Shamir [18]. For the proposed color $(k, n)$-VCS, the advantages of the scheme are as follows: it takes a natural image as input [26], which does not need the halftone process [13] and has no pixel expansion [8, 10, 14, 30]. For the proposed color $(k, n)$-EVCS, the advantages of this scheme are as follows: it implements the color $(k, n)$-EVCS with pixel expansion $m$ for general access structures and does not require the halftone process (recall that $m$ is the pixel expansion of the corresponding black-and-white $(k, n)$-EVCS) [1, 12].

Construction 5.1 below constructs the color $(k, n)$-VCS by Steps 1, 2, 3, and 4 and constructs the color $(k, n)$-EVCS by Steps 1′, 2′, 3, and 4:

**Construction 5.1**  Constructions of the color $(k, n)$-VCS and the color $(k, n)$-EVCS in the visual cryptography model of Naor and Shamir:

**Setup**  Denote the $n \times m$ matrices $M_0$ and $M_1$ as the basis matrices of a corresponding black-and-white $(k, n)$-VCS in the visual cryptography model of Naor and Shamir. Denote the $n \times m'$ matrices $M_c^{c_1, \ldots, c_n}$ as the basis matrices of a corresponding black-and-white $(k, n)$-EVCS in the visual cryptography model of Naor and Shamir, where $c, c_1, \ldots, c_n \in \{0, 1\}$. Denote $a_j$ as the gray level of 1's at bit-level $j$, $j \in \{1, 2, \ldots, 8\}$.

**Output** The shares $S_i$ for $i = 1, \ldots, n$.

**Step 1** Represent the gray levels of each color channel ($C$, $M$ and $Y$, respectively) of all the pixels in the secret image by vectors of 8 bits, that is, the secret image is divided into 8 bit levels and each bit level forms a binary image.

**Step 1′** Represent the gray levels of each color channel ($C$, $M$ and $Y$, respectively) of all the pixels in the secret image (resp. the $n$ original share images) by vectors of 8 bits, that is, the secret image (resp. the $n$ original share images) is divided into 8 bit levels and each bit level forms a binary image.

**Step 2** For each bit-level $j$ and each color channel, choose a block of $m$ pixels in the binary secret image, and encrypt the $m$ bits by applying Algorithm 5.1 for the color channels $C$, $M$, and $Y$ and bit-levels $j \in \{1, 2, \ldots, 8\}$, respectively, in which the 1's in $M_0$ or $M_1$ is replaced by the gray level $a_j$ leaving the 0's intact.

**Step 2′** For each bit-level $j$ and each color channel, encrypt a bit by $P(M_c^{c_1, \ldots, c_n})$ for the color channels $C$, $M$, and $Y$ and bit levels $j \in \{1, 2, \ldots, 8\}$, respectively, in which $P(M_c^{c_1, \ldots, c_n})$ is a random column permutation of $M_c^{c_1, \ldots, c_n}$ and replace the 1's in $P(M_c^{c_1, \ldots, c_n})$ by the gray level $a_j$ and leave the 0's intact.

**Step 3** Repeat Steps 1 and 2 (resp. 1′ and 2′) until all the pixels in the secret image have been encrypted. Then we obtain the shares $s_{i,t}^1, s_{i,t}^2, \ldots, s_{i,t}^8$ where $i \in \{1, 2, \ldots, n\}$, $t \in \{C, M, Y\}$ and the share $s_{i,t}^j$ is denoted as the share for the participant $i$ at the bit-level $j$ for the color channel $t$.

**Step 4** Each participant $i$ is distributed with a share $S_i$, where $S_i$ is generated by stacking the shares at the different bit levels and of the different color channels $s_{i,C}^1$, $s_{i,C}^2, \ldots, s_{i,C}^8, s_{i,M}^1, s_{i,M}^2, \ldots, s_{i,M}^8, s_{i,Y}^1, s_{i,Y}^2, \ldots, s_{i,Y}^8$ for $i \in \{1, 2, \ldots, n\}$.

In Construction 5.1, Steps 1 and 1′ divide the secret image (resp. the $n$ original shares images) into 8 bit levels and three color channels. In fact, the color images stored in the computer, such as the bitmap image file, are of this format. Then, in Steps 2, 2′ and 3, we encrypt each bit level and color channel, respectively. More specifically, when we encrypt the binary secret image at bit-level $j$ by applying the corresponding black-and-white $(k, n)$-VCS, for the bit-level $j$, we print pixels with gray level $a_j$ for the 1's of $M_0$, $M_1$ and $M_c^{c_1, \ldots, c_n}$, and leave the pixel intact for the 0's of $M_0$, $M_1$ and $M_c^{c_1, \ldots, c_n}$. Then we construct 24 shares in total for each participant, that is, the shares $s_{i,C}^1, s_{i,C}^2, \ldots, s_{i,C}^8, s_{i,M}^1, s_{i,M}^2, \ldots, s_{i,M}^8, s_{i,Y}^1, s_{i,Y}^2, \ldots, s_{i,Y}^8$. The final shares for the participants are constructed by superimposing the 24 shares in Step 4. One can easily observe that shares at bit-level $j$ can recover the $j$th binary image (bit level) of the secret image visually. Thus, by superimposing the shares of all the bit levels, the original secret image appears visually with all the bit levels.

We need to point out that, taking the characteristic of our human visual system into consideration, the dealer does not need to generate all the shares for all the bit levels, since the information about a higher bit level is not as important as that of a lower bit level for our human visual system, that is, the dealer only generates the shares for several lower bit levels in the practical sense.

In Step 2, Algorithm 5.1 encrypts a block of $m$ pixels at a time by using the $m$ columns of the basis matrices, which results in no pixel expansion [8, 10, 14, 30]. For general color $(k, n)$-VCS, one can make use of the basis matrices of the corresponding black-and-white $(k, n)$-VCS and so on.

In Step 2, because the encryption uses the $n \times m$ basis matrix $M_c^{c_1,\ldots,c_n}$, this later scheme results in the pixel expansion $m$, that is, the same as that of the corresponding black-and-white EVCS. For general color $(k, n)$-EVCS, one can make use of the basis matrices of the corresponding black-and-white $(k, n)$-EVCS.

As for the security of Construction 5.1, according to Definition 5.1, and Theorem 5.1, we have the following theorem.

**Theorem 5.2** *Construction 5.1 generates n shares $S_i$ for $i = 1, \ldots, n$, where less than k out of n shares cannot get any information about the secret image other than the size of the secret image.*

For the color VCS in the visual cryptography model of Naor and Shamir, the 0's in the transparencies for all bit levels are intact (i.e., with gray level 0), and the 1's for the bit-level $j$ is assigned with gray level $a_j$. Hence, the distance between the 0's and 1's for bit-level $j$ is $a_j$. The larger the value of $a_j$, the more apparent is the difference between black-and-white pixels at bit-level $j$. For two bit-levels $i$ and $j$, where $i$ and $j$ should satisfy $a_i > a_j$. For example, the gray levels of the most and the second most significant bits $a_1$ and $a_2$ should satisfy $a_1 > a_2$, and the larger the value of $(a_1 - a_2)$, the more apparent the most significant bits appear in the recovered secret image, and vice versa. Hence, for different types of secret images, the dealer should choose the gray levels carefully for different applications.

In the ideal subtractive color model, the stacking of the qualified color shares can recover the secret image visually [27]. However, such an ideal subtractive color mixture is impractical because of the properties of the ink. To alleviate this phenomenon, we propose to divide the color into three channels $C$, $M$, and $Y$, and print each channel of the color on adjacent pixels, respectively. Superimposition of the same color channel results in better visual effect. However, this method will expand the output images three times (Fig. 5.1).

In this section, we will prove that the basis matrices constructed by the algorithm is also a $(k, n)$-VCS in the XOR operation, which is under the visual cryptography model of Tuyls. Droste's algorithm can be described as follows.

First, we give a subroutine $ADD(p, M)$ that is used to add each restriction of $k$ rows of a matrix $M$ to every column with $p$ 1's by adding columns to the entire matrix $M$, where a matrix is considered as a collection of columns.

**Definition 5.2** $(ADD(p, M))$ (1) If $p \leq k - p$, add all the columns with q = p 1's to $M$, that is, the number of columns of $M$ is increased by $\binom{n}{q}$.

**(a)**                    **(b)**

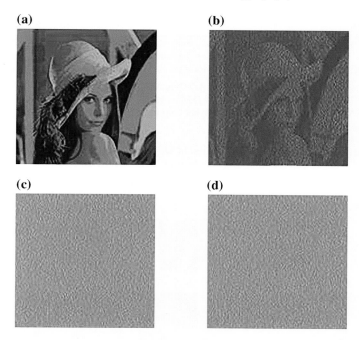

**(c)**                    **(d)**

**Fig. 5.1** Experimental results of the color (2, 2)-VCS with no pixel expansion in the visual cryptography model of Naor and Shamir (size of the secret image is $256 \times 256$). **a** Original secret image; **b** Resulting image by superimposing (**c**) and (**d**); **c** Encrypted shares; **d** Encrypted shares

(2) If $p > k - p$, add all the columns with $q = p + n - k$ 1's to $M$, that is, the number of columns of $M$ is increased by $\binom{n}{q}$.

The subroutine $ADD(p, M)$ makes it easy to construct basis matrices $M_0$ (resp. $M_1$) whose restrictions to $k$ rows always contain every even (resp. odd) column (an even column is one that contains even number of 1's; an odd column is one that contains odd number of 1's). When every even (resp. odd) column is removed once from every restriction of $M_0$ (resp. $M_1$), the remaining columns maintain the same, i.e., the remaining columns are unchanged regardless of which $k$ rows are restricted, and whether they are from $M_0$ or $M_1$. Hence, the remaining columns of every restriction of $M_0$, which are not remaining columns of every restriction of $M_1$, called the rest of $M_0$, have to be added to every restriction of $M_1$ and vice versa. In most cases, these added columns will create new rests which cause new columns to be added. The algorithm has the following form:

---

**Algorithm 5.2**:

---

**Input** : The parameters $k$ and $n$, and two empty basis matrices $M_0$ and $M_1$, where the basis matrices $M_0$ and $M_1$ are considered as collections of columns;
**Output**: The basis matrices $M_0$ and $M_1$ for a $(k, n)$-VCS;

**Step 1.** For all even $p \in \{0, \ldots, k\}$, call $ADD(p, M_0)$;
**Step 2.** For all odd $p \in \{0, \ldots, k\}$, call $ADD(p, M_1)$;
**Step 3.** While the rests of $M_0$ and $M_1$ are not empty:
if $e_b \bmod m < b$, then $M \leftarrow M_1$
else $M \leftarrow M_0$
(a) Add to $M_0$ all columns adjusting the rest of $M_1$ by calling ADD.
(b) Add to $M_1$ all columns adjusting the rest of $M_0$ by calling ADD.
Execute Step 3 until the rests of $M_0$ and $M_1$ are empty.

---

**Fig. 5.2** Experimental results of the color (2, 2)-EVCS with pixel expansion of 4 in the visual cryptography model of Naor and Shamir (Size of the secret image is $200 \times 200$) **a** Original two share image; **b** Original two share image; **c** Original secret image; **d** Encrypted shares; **e** Encrypted shares; **f** Resulting image by superimposing the shares (**d**) and (**e**)

Then we show that Algorithm 5.2 also generates a $(k, n)$-VCS under the XOR operation, that is, in the visual cryptography model of Tuyls (Fig. 5.2).

**Theorem 5.3** *Algorithm 4.2 generates the basis matrices of a $(k, n)$-VCS, $M_0$ and $M_1$, in XOR operation.*

*In this section, we propose a black-and-white $(k, n)$-EVCS in the visual cryptography model of Tuyls, that is, using XOR operation, as follows:*

Denote $S_c^{c_1, \ldots, c_n}$ as the basis matrix for the $n$ original share images that have color $c_1, \ldots, c_n$ and the secret image that has color $c$ for $c_1, \ldots, c_n, c \in \{0, 1\}$. Denote the binary matrices $M_0$ and $M_1$ as the basis matrices of a black-and-white $(k, n)$-VCS in operation XOR, where all the rows of $M_0(resp.M_1)$ have the same Hamming weight. Denote $a$ as its contrast and $m$ as its pixel expansion.

---

**Algorithm 5.3**:

**Input**   : The parameters $k$ and $n$, and two empty basis matrices $M_0$ and $M_1$, where the basis
matrices $M_0$ and $M_1$ are considered as collections of columns;
**Output**: The basis matrices $M_0$ and $M_1$ for a $(k, n)$-VCS;

**Step 1**. Construct an $n \times l$ matrix $D$ as follows ($l$ is an integer satisfying $1 \leq l < a \cdot m$):
For $i = 1$ to $n$ do
{If $c_i = 1$, then set all the entries of row $i$ in $D$ to 1:
   else set all the entries of row $i$ in $D$ to 0:
}
**Step 2**. The basis matrices $S_c^{c_1,\ldots,c_n}$ are obtained by concatenating the matrix $D$ with $M_0$ and
$M_1$ that is:
IF $c = 0$, THEN $S_c^{c_1,\ldots,c_n} = [M_0, D]$;
IF $c = 1$, THEN $S_c^{c_1,\ldots,c_n} = [M_1, D]$;
where the notation $[M, D]$ means the concatenation of the two matrices $M$ and $D$.

---

It is easy to verify that the above construction generates a general black-and-white
$(k, n)$-EVCS under operation XOR, and the basis matrices $M_0$ and $M_1$ can be the
basis matrices. If $a \cdot m = 1$ holds, then we can replace $M_0$ and $M_1$ with the matrices
$[M_0, M_0]$ and $[M_1, M_1]$, respectively. Note that the basis matrices always satisfy
$a \cdot m = 1$; hence, we can let $l = 1$ for any access structure [1]. In fact, Algorithm 4.3
is not restricted to threshold EVCS only; it can be applied to the general access
structure EVCS given that $M_0$ and $M_1$ are the basis matrices of the general access
structure VCS. Because of the lack of VCS in the general access structure, the work
only takes the threshold access structure for the case of EVCS into consideration.
However, if such a VCS of the general access structure exists, then our approach can
be applied to generate the corresponding EVCS under operation XOR directly.

Formally, we have the following theorem:

**Theorem 5.4**  *Algorithm 4.3 generates the basis matrices $S_c^{c_1,\ldots,c_n}$ for a black-and-
white $(k, n)$-EVCS under operation XOR, where $c, c_1, \ldots, c_n \in \{0, 1\}$.*

The visual cryptography model of Tuyls is interesting for reasons of good resolution, contrast, and color properties [3, 4, 21]. The color $(n, n)$-VCS on this visual
cryptography model can recover the secret image perfectly. However, there is no
known color VCS for general $(k, n)$-VCS, not to mention the color EVCS in this
visual cryptography model. In this section, we provide the constructions of color
VCS and color EVCS in the visual cryptography model of Tuyls.

The following construction constructs the color $(k, n)$-VCS by Steps 1, 2, 3 and
4 and constructs the color $(k, n)$-EVCS by Steps 1, 2, 3, and 4:

**Construction 5.2**  Constructions of the color $(k, n)$-VCS and the color $(k, n)$-EVCS
using the visual cryptography model of Tuyls:

**Setup** Denote the $n \times m$ matrices $M_0$ and $M_1$ as the basis matrices of a corresponding black-and-white $(k, n)$-VCS using the visual cryptography model of Tuyls,
and denote the $n \times m_0$ matrices $M_c^{c_1,\ldots,c_n}$ as the basis matrices of a corresponding

black-and-white $(k, n)$-EVCS using the visual cryptography model of Tuyls, where $c, c_1, \ldots, c_n \in \{0, 1\}$. Denote $a_j$ as the gray level of 1's and $b_j$ as the gray level of 0's at bit-level $j$.

**Output** The shares $S_i$ for $i = 1, \ldots, n$.

**Step 1** Represent the gray levels of each color channel (R, G, and B, respectively) of all the pixels in the secret image by vectors of 8 bits, that is, the secret image is divided into 8 bit levels, and each bit level forms a binary image.

**Step 1'** Represent the gray levels of each color channel (R, G, and B, respectively) of all the pixels in the secret image (resp, the $n$ original share images) by vectors of 8 bits, that is, the secret image (resp, the $n$ original share images) is divided into 8 bit levels, and each bit level forms a binary image.

**Step 2** For each bit-level $j$ and each color channel, encrypt a bit by $P(M_0)$ and $P(M_1)$ for the color channels R, G, and B and bit-levels $j \in \{1, 2, \ldots, 8\}$, respectively, where $P(M_0)$, $P(M_1)$ are the random column permutations of $M_0$, $M_1$, and replace the 1's in $P(M_0)$, $P(M_1)$ by the gray level $a_j$ and the 0's by the gray level $b_j$.

**Step 2'** For each bit-level $j$ and each color channel, encrypt a bit by $P(M_c^{c_1, \ldots, c_n})$ for the color channels R, G, and B and bit levels $j \in \{1, 2, \ldots, 8\}$, respectively, where $P(M_c^{c_1, \ldots, c_n})$ is a random column permutation of $M_c^{c_1, \ldots, c_n}$, and replace the 1's in $P(M_c^{c_1, \ldots, c_n})$ by the gray level $a_j$ and the 0's by the gray level $b_j$.

**Step 3** Repeat Steps 1 and 2 (resp. 1 and 2) until all the pixels in the secret image have been encrypted. Then we obtain the shares $s_{i,t}^1, s_{i,t}^2, \ldots, s_{i,t}^8$, where $i \in \{1, 2, \ldots, n\}$, $t \in \{R, G, B\}$, and the share $s_{i,t}^j$ is denoted as the share for the participant $i$ at the bit-level $j$ for the color channel $t$.

**Step 4** Each participant $i$ is distributed with a share $S_i$, where $S_i$ is generated by stacking the shares at the different bit levels and of the different color channels $s_{i,R}^1$, $s_{i,R}^2, \ldots, s_{i,R}^8, s_{i,G}^1, s_{i,G}^2, \ldots, s_{i,G}^8, s_{i,B}^1, s_{i,B}^2, \ldots, s_{i,B}^8$ for $i \in \{1, 2, \ldots, n\}$.

Construction 5.2 looks similar to Construction 5.1, except the differences in the color channels and the basis matrices $M_0$, $M_1$ and $M_c^{c_1, \ldots, c_n}$. However, Construction 5.1 cannot be applied properly using the visual cryptography model of Tuyls, because of the differences in choosing the values of the gray levels, which is caused by the different color model. For the case of the construction of the color VCS using the visual cryptography model of Naor and Shamir, we only need to choose the gray levels for the 1's of each bit level, and leave the pixels of the 0's intact. However, for the case of using the visual cryptography model of Tuyls, we have to choose the gray levels for both the 1's and 0's of each bit-level $j$, that is, the values of $a_j$ and $b_j$. We notice that, by choosing different gray levels for the bit levels, we will obtain quite different visual effects. However, finding a formula to determine the proper values for $a_j$ and $b_j$ is rather complicated for the general $(k, n)$-VCS [5, 20], which heavily depends on the contents of the secret image, the observer's experiences, the access structure, and the intensity function of the visual cryptography model of Tuyls (i.e., the function $I_r(a) = \cos^2(a_1 + a_2)$) [1] and so on.

However, some basic rules should be satisfied, for example as follows. First, the distance between $a_j$ and $b_j$ should be larger than the distance between $a_{j+1}$ and $b_{j+1}$, that is $|a_j - b_j| > |a_{j+1} - b_{j+1}|$, which means that the information about bit-level $j$ should be more apparent than that of bit-level $j + 1$. Second, the average intensity of a white pixel, which contains $m(m_0)$ subpixels, should be larger than that of a black pixel, that is, a white pixel should be lighter than a black pixel.

In Step 2, because the encryption uses the $n \times m$ basis matrices $M_0$ and $M_1$, this scheme results in the pixel expansion of $m$, that is, the same as that of its corresponding black-and-white VCS. For general color $(k, n)$-VCS, one can make use of the basis matrices of the corresponding black-and-white VCS and so on [5].

In Step $2'$, because the encryption uses the $n \times m'$ basis matrix $M_c^{c_1, \ldots, c_n}$, this later scheme results in a pixel expansion of $m'$, that is, the same as that of its corresponding black-and-white EVCS. For general color $(k, n)$-EVCS, one can make use of the corresponding basis matrices [5].

With regard to the security of Construction 5.2, we give the following theorem on the security of the proposed color VCS and color EVCS (Fig. 5.3).

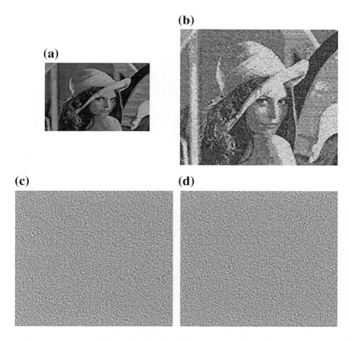

**Fig. 5.3** Experimental results of the color $(2, 3)$-VCS using the visual cryptography model of Tuyls. **a** Original secret image; **b** Resulting image by superimposing the shares (**c**) and (**d**); **c** Encrypted shares; **d** Encrypted shares; Other shares and recovered secret image are omitted; size of the secret image is $256 \times 170$

**Table 5.1** Comparisons with known results in the literature

| Constructions | $C_1$ | $C_2$ | $C_3$ | $C_4$ | $C_5$ | $C_6$ | $C_7$ | $C_8$ |
|---|---|---|---|---|---|---|---|---|
| Cimato 1 | N/A | – | – | – | No | Yes | No | No |
| Cimato 2 | $C_k^n 2^{k-2}$ | – | – | – | No | Yes | Yes | No |
| Hou&Tu 2 | 1 | – | – | – | Yes | No | Yes | No |
| Lukac&Plataniotis | m | – | – | – | No | No | Yes | Yes |
| Shyu | $\lceil \log c \rceil \cdot m$ | – | – | – | No | Yes | No | No |
| Verhoul&Tilborg | $q^{k-1}(q \geq c)$ | – | – | – | No | Yes | No | No |
| Yang&Laih | $c \cdot m$ | – | – | – | No | Yes | No | No |
| Koga&Yamamoto | N/A | – | – | – | No | Yes | No | No |
| Koga | N/A | – | – | – | No | Yes | No | No |
| Ishihala&Koga | N/A | – | – | – | No | Yes | No | No |
| Yang&Chen | 1 | – | – | – | No | No | No | No |

**Theorem 5.5** *Construction 5.2 generates n shares $S_i$ for $i = 1, 2, \ldots, n$, where less than k out of these n shares cannot get any information about the secret image other than the size of the secret image.*

In this section, we compare our constructions of color $(k, n)$-VCS and color $(k, n)$-EVCS with known results in the literature. In Table 5.1, the comparisons are based on the following criteria:

$C_1$: the pixel expansion of color $(k, n)$-VCS using the visual cryptography model of Naor and Shamir;

$C_2$: the pixel expansion of color $(k, n)$-EVCS using the visual cryptography model of Naor and Shamir;

$C_3$: the pixel expansion of color $(k, n)$-VCS using the visual cryptography model of Tuyls;

$C_4$: the pixel expansion of color $(k, n)$-EVCS using the visual cryptography model of Tuyls;

$C_5$: whether or not the construction is based on the halftone technique;

$C_6$: whether or not the increase in the number of colors of the recovered secret image will increase the pixel expansion;

$C_7$: whether or not the color model of the construction considers the color darkening phenomenon during stacking of pixels with the same color;

$C_8$: whether or not the recovery of the secret image requires the assistance of computing devices (Fig. 5.4).

For criteria $C_1$, $C_2$, $C_3$, and $C_4$, it is clear that a smaller share is easier to carry and preserve, or requires less memory. Hence, the pixel expansion is expected to be as small as possible.

For criterion $C_5$, we need to point out that the halftone technique usually expands the size of the secret image and degrades the quality of the secret image [16, 23]. In fact, the halftone technique without image expansion does exist, however, in such a

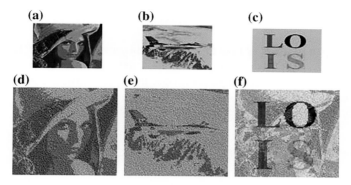

**Fig. 5.4** Experimental results of the color (2, 2)-EVCS under the visual cryptography model of Tuyls. **a** Original image; **b** Original image; **c** Original image and secret image; **d** Encrypted shares; **e** Encrypted shares; **f** Resulting image by superimposing the share (**d**) and (**e**)

case, it is equivalent to pick out the most significant bits of each pixel in the secret image, and abandon all the other information about the secret image, which results in a serious degeneration in the visual effect of the secret image.

For criterion $C_6$, it is worthy to point out that, if the increase in the number of colors increases the pixel expansion, then the recovered secret image can only have a small number of colors in the practical sense.

For criterion $C_7$, it is more practical if a color model considers the phenomenon of color darkening when stacking the pixels with the same color. For criterion $C_8$, the beauty of the VCS is its simplicity; hence, it is better not to rely on the assistance of computing devices when recovering the secret image.

In Table 5.1, $c$ is the number of colors and $m$ and $m'$ are the pixel expansions of the corresponding black-and-white $(k, n)$-VCS and $(k, n)$-EVCS that are used as building blocks. The N/A in the $C_1$ column indicates that the corresponding constructions do not provide an explicit expression to calculate the pixel expansion for their color $(k, n)$-VCS. The '–' in the $C_2$, $C_3$, and $C_4$ columns indicates that the corresponding criteria do not apply.

According to the above comparisons, the advantages of our constructions can be seen as follows. First, the pixel expansion of our constructions is small, our constructions have the ability to represent all colors, and our color model considers the phenomenon of color darkening when stacking the pixels with the same color, which makes our constructions more practical [9]. Second, our constructions do not need the halftone process while maintaining a small pixel expansion [12, 14, 30]. Third, our constructions do not need the assistance of computing devices. Furthermore, our constructions can generate VCS and EVCS for general $(k, n)$ threshold access structure [1].

Unfortunately, the color EVCS proposed above all have the disturbing phenomenon, that is, part of the information about the original share images may appear in the recovered secret image. It is hard to eradicate such a phenomenon, but it is possible to find a method to weaken it. This challenging problem is left as an open problem.

Another open problem is how to determine the gray levels of the bit-levels $a_i$ and $b_i$ ($i \in \{1, \ldots, 8\}$), which is quite complicated and depends on the different color model, the content of the secret image, the access structure, the observers' experiences, and so on [1, 11].

## 5.4 Exercises

(1) There are three construction approaches for color visual cryptography. Give some examples to show their advantages and disadvantages.
(2) Explain the differences between the subtractive and additive color models.
(3) Analyze the definition of contrast in the proposed color VCS.

## References

1. Ateniese G, Blundo C, Santis AD, Stinson DR (1996) Visual cryptography for general access structures. Inf Comput 129:86–106
2. Ateniese G, Blundo C, Santis AD, Stinson DR (2001) Extended capabilities for visual cryptography. ACM Theory Comput Sci 250(1–2):143–161
3. Blundo C, Santis A, Stinson DR (1999) On the contrast in visual cryptography schemes. J Cryptol 12(4):261–289
4. Blundo C, D'Arco P, Santis A, Stinson DR (2003) Contrast optimal threshold visual cryptography schemes. SIAM J Discret Math 16(2):224–261
5. Bose M, Mukerjee R (2010) Optimal $(k, n)$ visual cryptographic schemes for general $k$. Des Codes Cryptogr 55:19–35
6. Chang CY (2000) Visual cryptography for color images. Masters thesis. National Central University (Taiwan)
7. Chen TH, Tsao KH, Wei KC (2008) Multiple-image encryption by rotating random grids. In: International conference on intelligent systems design and applications, vol 3, pp 252–256
8. Chen YF, Chan YK, Huang CC, Tsai MH, Chu YP (2007) A multiple-level visual secret-sharing scheme without image size expansion. Inf Sci 177:4696–4710
9. Cimato S, Prisco RD, Santis AD (2007) Colored visual cryptography without color darkening. Theory Comput Sci 374:261–276
10. Droste S (1996) New results on visual cryptography. In: Proceedings of CRYPTO'96, vol 1109, Springer, New York, pp 401–415
11. Fang WP (2009) Non-expansion visual secret sharing in reversible style. Int J Comput Sci Netw Secur 9(2):204–208
12. Hou YC, Chang CY, Lin F (1999) Visual cryptography for colour images based on colour decomposition. In: Proceedings of 5th conference on information management, pp 584–591
13. Hou YC, Chang CY, Tu SF (2001) Visual cryptography for color images based on halftone technology. In: Proceedings of international conference on information systems, analysis and synthesis (World Multiconference on Systemics, Cybernetics and Informatics)
14. Hou YC (2003) Visual cryptography for color images. Pattern Recognit 36:1619–1629
15. Hou YC, Tu CF (2004) Visual cryptography techniques for colour images without pixel expansion. J Inf Technol Soc 1:95–110

16. Hsu HC, Chen TS, Lin YH (2004) The ringed shadow image technology of visual cryptography by applying diverse rotating angles to hide the secret sharing. Netw Sens Control 2:996–1001
17. Ishihara T, Koga HA (2003) visual secret sharing scheme for color images based on mean value-color mixing. IEICE Trans Fundam E86-A:194–197
18. Ito R, Kuwakado H, Tanaka H (1999) Image size invariant visual cryptography. IEICE Trans Fundam Elect Commun Comput Sci E82-A(10):2172–2177
19. Koga H, Iwamoto M, Yamamoto H (2001) An analytic construction of the visual secret sharing scheme for color images. IEICE Trans Fundam 1:262–272
20. Koga H (2002) A general formula of the $(t, n)$-threshold visual secret sharing scheme In: (ASIACRYPT'02). LNCS, vol 2501. Springer, New York, pp 328–345
21. Krause M, Hu S (2003) Determining the optimal contrast for secret sharing schemes in visual cryptography. Comb Probab Comput 12(3):285–299
22. Kuwakado H, Tanaka H (2004) Size-reduced visual secret sharing scheme. IEICE Trans Fundam E87-A(5):1193–1197
23. Lin CH (2002) Visual cryptography for color images with image size invariable shares. Masters thesis. National Central University, Taiwan
24. Lukac R, Plataniostis KN (2004) Color image secret sharing. IEE Electron Lett 40(9):529–530
25. Naor M, Shamir A (1995) Visual cryptography. In: Proceedings of EUROCRYPT'94. LNCS, vol 950. Springer, New York, pp 1–12
26. Nakajima M, Yamaguchi Y (2002) Extended visual cryptography for natural images. In: WSCG conference, pp 303–412
27. Viet DQ, Kurosawa K (2004) Almost ideal contrast visual cryptography with reversing. In: Topics in Cryptology—CT-RSA, pp 353–365
28. Weir J, Yan WA (2010) A comprehensive study of visual cryptography. Trans Data Hiding Multimed Secur 5: 70–105
29. Wu C, Chen LA (1998) study on visual cryptography. Masters thesis. National Chiao Tung University, Taiwan
30. Wu XY, Wong DS, Li Q (2009) Threshold visual cryptography scheme for color images with no pixel expansion. In: Proceedings of the second symposium international computer science and computational technology (ISCSCT'09), pp 310–315
31. Yang CN, Laih CS (2000) New coloured visual secret sharing schemes. Des Codes Cryptogr 20:325–335
32. Yang CN, Chen TS (2008) Colored visual cryptography scheme based on additive color mixing. Pattern Recognit 41(10):3114–3129
33. Zhou Z, Arce GR, Crescenzo GD (2006) Halftone visual cryptography. IEEE Trans Image Process 15(8):2441–2453

# Chapter 6
# Various Applications of Visual Cryptography

## 6.1 Watermarking Applications

### 6.1.1 Watermarking

Watermarking is a technique to protect the copyright of digital media such as image, text, music, and movie [2, 4, 8, 9]. A watermarking scheme combines cover images with a watermark which is hard to be detected and removed, and the owner of the image can prove his copyright by extracting the watermark from the watermarked image [12, 14, 16, 22]. Generally, a watermarking scheme should meet the below criteria:

- **Imperceptibility**. It is hard to detect the differences between the original cover images and the watermarked ones by our Human Visual System. The imperceptibility is perfect if the watermarked images are identical/indistinguishable to the original cover images.
- **Robustness**. The watermark still can be extracted even the watermarked image suffers from various attacks.
- **Security**. Only the owner of the cover images can extract the watermark from the watermarked image.
- **Blindness**. The original cover images are not required for extracting the watermark. Hence, extra space is not required for storing the cover images.

Currently, most of the watermarking schemes are based on the transform domain techniques, including the Discrete Fourier Transform (DFT), the Discrete Cosine Transform, and the Discrete Wavelet Transform (DWT) [9, 12, 16, 21], because they provide better performance with respect to the robustness than that based on the spatial domain.

Watermarking schemes [12] for digital images suffer a lot of attacks that aim at severing the relationship between the watermarked image and the watermark, such as compression attack, blurring attack, sharpening attack, scaling attack, cropping attack, distortion attack, and noise attack.

© Springer International Publishing Switzerland 2015
F. Liu and W.Q. Yan, *Visual Cryptography for Image
Processing and Security*, DOI 10.1007/978-3-319-23473-1_6

The torus automorphism [19] is used to convert an image to a chaotic image shown in Eq. 6.1. It only fits square images and it can be extended to be applied on general size images. However, in order to simplify the discussion, we only discuss the watermarking scheme for square images, we should point out that the scheme can easily be extended for cover images of general size.

$$\begin{pmatrix} x_{i+1} \\ y_{i+1} \end{pmatrix} = \begin{pmatrix} 1 & 1 \\ k & k+1 \end{pmatrix} \cdot \begin{pmatrix} x_i \\ y_i \end{pmatrix} \ mod \ N \tag{6.1}$$

The model of watermarking can be viewed as an information transmission model [17, 18], where the cover image is the channel and the watermark is the message [12]. The attacks of the watermarking scheme add error pixels (noise) to the watermark (message). For some attacks, the error pixels may be aggregated, for example, the cropping attack. The torus automorphism can scatter the error pixels to the entire image uniformly. Taken the cropping attack with 25 % of the cover image being cropped as an example, after the torus automorphism process, there is on average one error pixel in each four pixels, and hence we may have a chance to correct the error pixel by the information of the remaining three correct pixels.

Watermarking schemes based on the transform domain technique often have better robustness. In this chapter, we will use the two-level DWT, where the decomposition of an image by using two-level DWT is shown in Fig. 6.1. By using the two-level DWT, the original image is first decomposed into four sub-bands that are normally labeled as LL1, LH1, HL1, and HH1. The LL1 sub-band is further decomposed into four sub-bands labeled as LL2, LH2, HL2, and HH2. The LL sub-band comes from low-pass filtering in both directions and it looks most like the original image. The LL sub-band contains most of the information of the original image. The remaining sub-bands are called detailed components. The sub-bands LH, HL, and HH represent horizontal, vertical and diagonal details, respectively.

The transform domain technique can extract the feature image of the cover image [22]; hence, watermarking schemes based on the transform domain technique often have strong robustness against compression attacks that apply transform domain techniques, such as the JPEG compression. Many watermarking schemes in the literature also applied the transform domain technique to enhance their robustness.

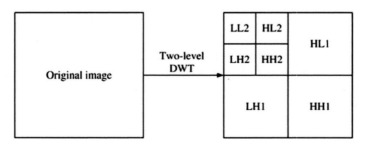

**Fig. 6.1** Two-level DWT

The attacks of the watermarking scheme add errors (noise) to the watermark (message). Hence, it is natural for us to use the error correcting code technique to reduce the errors [5, 12]. In this chapter, we make use of (8, 2, 5) Cordaro–Wagner Code, where the code length is 8, with two information bits and the minimum distance between the codes is 5. The (8, 2, 5) Cordaro–Wagner Code is maximum distance separable (MDS) code that can correct two errors. The four codewords of (8, 2, 5) code are as follows {00000000, 10110111, 01001111, 11111000}. Note that there are many kinds of MDS error correcting codes. One reason that we choose (8, 2, 5) Cordaro–Wagner code is for simplifying the programming, another reason is that this code can correct $(2/8) = 25\%$ errors which is comparable to the 25 % cropping attack.

The attacks of the watermarking scheme are equivalent to adding noise to the watermark. As we apply the chaos technique in this watermarking scheme, the noise will be uniformly scattered in the extracted watermark image [22]. Hence, we can make use of some noise reduction technique for digital images to improve the visual quality of the extracted watermark.

## 6.1.2 Visual Cryptography

Visual cryptography (VC)-based watermarking schemes have been proposed in recent years [7, 15, 16]. The advantages of VC technique for watermarking are that: first, it can achieve large embedding capacity, that is, it can embed a large watermark (an image) into the cover images; second, it can achieve high security; third, it has the ability to share a secret image between multiple users. However, its robustness is a disadvantage. In this session, in order to enhance the robustness of the VC-based watermarking schemes, we apply the transform domain technique, chaos technique, noise reduction technique, and error correcting code technique [5].

For most VC-based watermarking schemes in the literature [7, 8, 16, 20], each cover image corresponds to a secret image that is registered to a trust authority (TA) (the arbitrator). When the number of cover images is large, it will be a heavy burden for the TA to store all the secret images. We note that an owner may have the copyright of multiple images. If we only generate one secret image for all the images he owns, it will reduce the burden of TA significantly.

Furthermore, besides the case that an owner owns multiple images, there may be the case that an image is owned by multiple owners, which may be caused by several reasons, for example, the image is created by multiple photographers collaboratively. The ownership of a portrait may be shared by the persons in the portrait and the portraitists. For these cases, it is not efficient if we apply a watermarking scheme for each owner and each image, respectively. Hence, a watermarking scheme that can deal with multiple images and multiple owners will bring much convenience.

Compared with the known VC-based watermarking schemes in the literature [16, 20], the advantages of our scheme are as follows: first, our scheme has strong robustness; our scheme then can protect multiple cover images for multiple owners at a time and generates only one secret share, which reduce the storage space of the secret images for TA; third, the imperceptibility of our scheme is perfect; finally, our scheme is secure, which is guaranteed by the security model of the VC.

The model of our scheme includes three kinds of participants: the owners of the cover images who want to protect their copyright of the cover images, the attackers who want to illegally use the cover images, and a TA who will arbitrate the ownership of the cover images when a dispute occurs [14]. Generally, we assume that, $t$ owners own $n$ images, and there is only one TA where $t$ and $n$ are positive integers.

The watermarking scheme contains two algorithms: the embedding algorithm and the extracting algorithm. In the embedding algorithm, the owners generate $n$ watermarked images, a secret share and $t$ key images. They publish the watermarked images and the watermark, register the secret share to the arbitrator (the TA) secretly and distribute the key images to the owners secretly. After the watermarked images are published, the attackers may modify and illegally use them. In such a case, the legal owners need to show their evidences (the key images) to the arbitrator to claim their copyright of the watermarked images [14]. In the extracting algorithm, an extracted watermark can be extracted from the attacked image, the secret share and the key images together. By comparing the extracted watermark and the original watermark, the arbitrator can judge whether they own the copyright of the attacked images or not [14].

**Algorithm 6.1**. The embedding algorithm
**Input:** $n$ cover images $I_1, \ldots, I_n$ and a watermark image $W$.
**Output:** The watermarked images, a secret share $S$ that is registered to TA and $t$ key images $K_1, \ldots, K_t$ that are distributed to the owners.

**Step 1**. Apply two-level DWT to obtain the feature images of the cover images $FI_1, \ldots, FI_n$, where $FI_1, \ldots, FI_n$ are the low sub-band $LL_2$ of the cover images $I_1, \ldots, I_n$, respectively.
**Step 2**. Convert the feature images $FI_1, \ldots, FI_n$ into binary images $BI_1, \ldots, BI_n$. The conversion can be realized by setting a threshold $\delta$, and the pixels with gray values that are larger than $\delta$ are set to 1, the rest are set to 0.
**Step 3**. Convert the watermark image $W$ into a chaotic image $W_T$ by applying the torus automorphism with parameter $k$ for $i$ rounds.
**Step 4**. Encode the chaotic image $W_T$ into $W_E$ by using the $(8, 2, 5)$ Cordaro–Wagner code.
**Step 5**. Generate $t$ random key images $K_1, \ldots, K_t$ for $t$ owners, where the size of each key image is identical to the size of $W_E$.
**Step 6**. Generate the secret share $S$ by applying the $(n + t + 1, n + t + 1)$-VCS based on XOR operation, where $W_E = S \otimes BI_1 \otimes \cdots \otimes BI_n \otimes K_1 \otimes \cdots \otimes K_t$, that is, $S = W_E \otimes BI_1 \otimes \cdots \otimes BI_n \otimes K_1 \otimes \cdots \otimes K_t$.
**Step 7**. Publish $I_1, \ldots, I_n$ and $W$ as the watermarked images and the watermark, register $S$ to TA secretly and distribute $K_1, \ldots, K_t$ to the owners secretly.

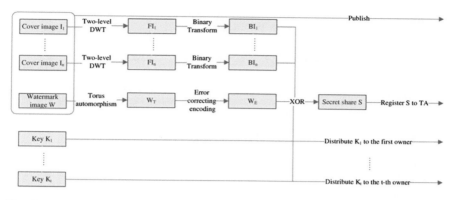

**Fig. 6.2** The embedding algorithm

The flowchart of the embedding algorithm is shown in Fig. 6.2. The security of the scheme is guaranteed by the security of VCS. Note that the key images $K_1, \ldots, K_t$ are random images that are distributed to the owners secretly, that is, the attackers do not have any information about $K_1, \ldots, K_t$. The secret share $S$ is generated by $S = W_E \otimes BI_1 \otimes \cdots \otimes BI_n \otimes K_1 \otimes \cdots \otimes K_t$. According to the security of VCS, because the attackers do not have $K_1, \ldots, K_t$, the attackers have no way to get any information about $S$ either, that is, the attackers cannot claim the ownership of the cover images.

Step 5 can also be realized by generating $t$ keys (such as passwords), and by taking the $t$ keys as seeds of a pseudorandom number generator, one also can generate $t$ key images $K_1, \ldots, K_t$. In such a way, the owners only need to remember a password rather than to take a key image. Note that, by applying the XOR-based extended VCS [1, 13], the key images $K_1, \ldots, K_t$ and the secret share $S$ can be meaningful images rather than noise-like shares.

According to the embedding algorithm, the watermarked images are identical to the cover images. Hence, the imperceptibility of our scheme is perfect. And it only generates one secret share for multiple cover images and multiple owners, and hence it saves storage memory of the secret shares for TA.

**Algorithm 6.2.** The extracting algorithm.
**Input** The attacked images $I'_1, \ldots, I'_n$, the secret share $S$ and $t$ key images $K_1, \ldots, K_t$.
**Output** An extracted watermark image $W'$ and compare it with the original watermark $W$ to get the value of accuracy ratio (AR).

**Step 1.** Apply two-level DWT to obtain the feature images of the attacked images $FI'_1, \ldots, FI'_n$, where $FI'_1, \ldots, FI'_n$ are the low sub-band $LL_2$ of the attacked images $I'_1, \ldots, I'_n$, respectively.
**Step 2.** Convert the feature images $FI'_1, \ldots, FI'_n$ into binary images $BI'_1, \ldots, BI'_n$. The conversion method is the same as that of the embedding algorithm.

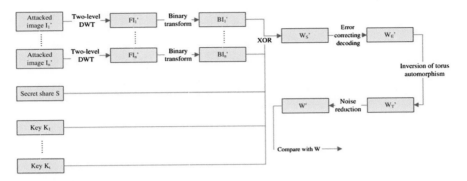

**Fig. 6.3** The extracting algorithm

**Step 3.** Obtain the secret share $S$ from TA, and obtain the $t$ key images $K_1, \ldots, K_t$ from the owners.

**Step 4.** Generate the $W_S'$ by the following equation $W_S' = S \otimes BI_1' \otimes \cdots \otimes BI_n' \otimes K_1 \otimes \cdots \otimes Kt$.

**Step 5.** Decode the $W_S'$ into $W_E'$ by using the (8, 2, 5) Cordaro–Wagner code.

**Step 6** Generate $W_T'$ by applying the inversion of the torus automorphism.

**Step 7.** Reduce the noise in $W_T'$ by using a median filter to get the extracted watermark $W'$.

**Step 8.** Compare the watermarks $W$ and $W'$ by calculating the value of AR.

The flowchart of the extracting algorithm is shown in Fig. 6.3.

**Simulation.** In order to evaluate the performance of our scheme, we give three kinds of simulations in this section. First, we give the simulation results of our scheme which has only one cover image and one owner. We then give a slightly more complicated simulation that has two cover images and two owners. Last, we give the simulation results of our scheme over a large number of cover images. We also provide the comparisons of robustness and effectiveness with some known VC-based watermarking schemes in the literature [7, 16].

We make use of the peak signal-to-noise ratio (PSNR) to measure the differences between the original image and the attacked image. Smaller PSNR indicates more differences between the original image and the attacked image. Two identical images will result in an infinite PSNR. Usually, the attacked image can be viewed as the original image that suffers an image quality loss, and the loss of image quality is considered to be acceptable if the PSNR is about 20 to 25 dB. Typically, PSNR is defined as follows:

$$PSNR = 10 \log_{10} \frac{255^2}{MSE} \qquad (6.2)$$

where $MSE = \frac{1}{N^2} \sum_{i=0}^{N-1} \sum_{j=0}^{N-1} (I_{ij} - I_{ij}')^2$, $I_{ij}$ and $I_{ij}'$ are the pixels of the original image and the attacked image. The AR is used to evaluate the similarity between the original watermark and the extracted one, which is defined as follows:

**Fig. 6.4** Test images for the first simulation. **a** Cover image. **b** Watermark. **c** Key image. **d** Secret share

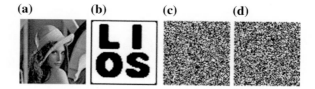

(a)  (b)  (c)  (d)

$AR = CB/NB$. $NB$ is the number of the original watermark bits, and $CB$ is the number of correct bits between the original watermark and the extracted one. $AR$ is expected to be as large as possible, and it is perfect when it reaches 1.

For the first simulation, the values of $PSNR$ and $AR$ are denoted by $PSNR_1$ and $AR_1$, respectively. For the second simulation, the values of $PSNR$ for the two cover images are denoted by $PSNR_{21}$ and $PSNR_{22}$, respectively (to simplify the discussion, we apply the same attack on both cover images), and the value of $AR$ is denoted by $AR_2$. For the third simulation, we calculate the average PSNR and average AR for a large number of cover images, where the values of average $PSNR$ and average $AR$ are denoted by $PSNR$ and $AR$, respectively.

We use the Matlab to perform the simulations. For the first simulation, the test images are shown in Fig. 6.4, where $a$ is the cover image with size $512 \times 512$, and $b$ is the watermark with size $64 \times 64$, $c$ is the key image with size $64 \times 64$ and $d$ is the secret share that registered to TA with size $64 \times 64$. For the second simulation, the test images are shown in Fig. 6.6, where $a$ and $b$ are the cover images with size $512 \times 512$, and $c$ is the watermark with size $64 \times 64$, $d$ and $e$ are the key images with size $64 \times 64$ and $f$ is the secret share that registered to TA with size $64 \times 64$. For the third simulation, the cover images are downloaded from the http://images.google.cn by using the following popular keywords 'area code, cars, dictionary, Facebook, game, Google, image, img, international, movie, myspace, news, photo, picture, song lyrics, sports, theme, topic, travel, world, weather, YouTube, and www together with the constraint keywords 'filetype:jpg image size: $512 \times 512$. The total number of cover images is 10238. The watermark, the key image and the secret share are the same as the first simulation in Fig. 6.4 (Fig. 6.5).

We simulate nine simple attacks on the cover images. These attacks are quite common in the internet environment. The simulations of these attacks are shown in Figs. 6.6 and 6.7. In this section, $a_1$ is the JPEG compression attacked image with qualify factor 5 %; $a_2$ is the JPEG compression-attacked image with qualify factor

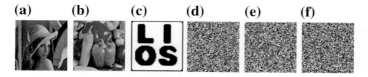

(a)  (b)  (c)  (d)  (e)  (f)

**Fig. 6.5** Test image for the second simulation. **a** and **b** Cover images. **c** Watermark. **d** and **e** Key images. **f** Secret share

a1: JPEG attack 5%                        a2: JPEG attack 10%

a3: blurring attack                       a4: sharpening attack

a5: scaling attack                        a6: cropping attack 10%

a7: cropping attack 25%                   a8: distortion attack

a9: noising attack                        a10: other image

**Fig. 6.6**  Attacked images and their extracted watermarks

10%; $a_3$ is the blurring attacked image that is generated by using a averaging filter with parameter 11 on the cover image (i.e., the Matlab source code is AttackImage = filter2(fspecial('average', 11), CoverImage)); $a_4$ is the sharpening-attacked image that is generated by using a multidimensional filter $H = [121; 000; 121]$ on the cover image (i.e., the Matlab source code is *AttackImage = imadd (CoverImage, imfilter(CoverImage, H)))*; $a_5$ is the scaling attacked image that is generated by reducing the cover image to size $64 \times 64$ and then enlarged to size $512 \times 512$; $a_6$ is the cropping attacked image with 10 % of the cover image being cropped; $a_7$ is the cropping attacked image with 25 % of the cover image being cropped; $a_8$ is the distortion attack that is generated by pinching and spherising the cover image; $a_9$ is the noising-attacked image that is generated by adding the salt and pepper noise with parameter 20%; $r$ is a different image(s). We give Fig. 6.7 for the results of the third simulation. According to Fig. 6.7, the proposed scheme has strong robustness against

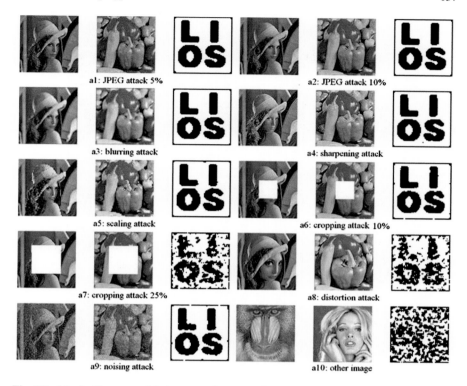

**Fig. 6.7**  Attacked images and their extracted watermarks

attacks $a_1, \ldots, a_9$. Because the AR value of an unwatermarked image is around 0.5, and the AR values of a watermarked image are close to 1, it is easy to identify a watermarked image from unwatermarked images.

**Comparisons**. We draw a comparison between the robustness between the proposed scheme and some known VC-based watermarking schemes in the literature that also gave the corresponding simulations. The comparison is mainly focused on the following common attacks: JPEG compression attack, blurring attack, sharpening attack, cropping attack, scaling attack, and noising attack. As different schemes made use of quite different attacked images, we only give an approximate comparison for the values of AR in Table 6.1, where $(QF)$ is the quality factor of JPEG compression and $(A)$ is the amount of noise. From the results in Table 6.1, it is clear that our scheme has better robustness.

We also give a comparison on the effectiveness between the proposed scheme and some known VC-based watermarking schemes in the literature. The comparison is mainly focused on the following properties: robustness, imperceptibility, blindness, security, multiple users, and multiple cover images. From the results in Table 6.2, it is clear that only the proposed scheme satisfies all the aforementioned properties,

**Table 6.1** Comparison of robustness

| Attacks | Ours | Ref 1 | Ref 2 | Ref 3 | Ref 4 | Ref 5 | Ref 6 | Ref 7 |
|---|---|---|---|---|---|---|---|---|
| JPEG (QF) | 1(10%) | 0.91(80%) | 0.7452(20%) | 0.9775(25%) | 0.9951(25%) | 0.996(50%) | 0.9817(20%) | 0.996(10%) |
| Blurring | 0.99927 | 0.8872 | 0.8447 | 0.8032 | 0.9761 | 0.988 | 0.9204 | 0.996 |
| Sharpening | 0.99805 | 0.8955 | 0.803 | 0.8398 | 0.9797 | 0.981 | 0.9439 | 0.986 |
| Cropping (10%) | 0.99707 | 0.9597 | n/a | n/a | n/a | n/a | 0.7475(10%) | n/a |
| Cropping (25%) | 0.93042 | n/a | 0.8691 | n/a | n/a | n/a | n/a | n/a |
| Scaling (1/64) | 0.99707 | 0.883 | n/a | 0.7717 | 0.9766 | n/a | n/a | 0.983 |
| Noising (A) | 0.99609 | n/a | n/a | 0.8948(10%) | 0.9944(10%) | 0.992 | 0.8977(10%) | 0.994 |

**Table 6.2**  Comparison of effectiveness

| Attacks | Ours | Ref 1 | Ref 2 | Ref 3 | Ref 4 | Ref 5 | Ref 6 | Ref 7 | Ref 8 | Ref 9 | Ref 10 | Ref 11 |
|---|---|---|---|---|---|---|---|---|---|---|---|---|
| Robustness | Yes | Yes | Yes | Yes | Yes | Yes | Yes | Yes | Yes | Yes | Yes | Yes |
| Imperceptivity (P: Perfect D: Degraded) | P | P D | P | P D | P D | P D | P | P | P | P | P | P |
| Blindness | Yes | Yes | Yes | Yes | Yes | Yes | Yes | Yes | Yes | Yes | Yes | Yes |
| Security | Yes | Yes | Yes | Yes | Yes | Yes | Yes | Yes | Yes | Yes | Yes | Yes |
| Multiple users | Yes | No | Yes | No | No | No | No | No | No | No | No | No |
| Multiple cover images | Yes | No | No | No | No | No | No | No | No | No | No | No |

**Fig. 6.8**  Average accuracy ratios for attacks $a_1, \ldots, a_{10}$ for the third simulation

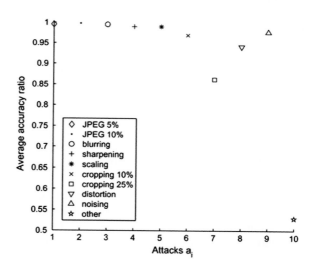

wherein Table 6.2(P) and (D) mean perfect and degraded imperceptibility, respectively.

Figure 6.8 is about average accuracy ratios for attacks $a_1, \ldots, a_{10}$ for the third simulation.

## 6.2  Resolution Variant Visual Cryptography

Resolution variant visual cryptography takes the idea of using a single share of visual cryptography (VC) to recover a secret from an image at multiple resolutions [11]. That means, viewing the image on a one-to-one basis and superimposing the share will recover the secret. However, if the image is zoomed, using that same share we can recover other secrets at different levels. The same share is used at these varying resolutions in order to recover a large amount of hidden secrets [10, 24, 25]. This process is quite similar to watermarking an image, whereby nothing can be seen while fully zoomed out, but as the zoom level is increased the watermark becomes visible. This would also be associated with a recursive style of secret sharing [6]. This type of secret sharing scheme would be appropriate for recovering specific types of censored information, such as vehicle registration numbers within certain types of images. Within this section, we present a new VC scheme that allows the user to recursively hide many secrets within a high resolution image. We use specially crafted shares to support the idea of multiple secret recovery at multiple resolutions [23].

There are two main contributions that are presented in this section. The first deals with embedding VC shares within the license plate location within an image [3, 26]. This would improve upon and provide a practical example of the work discussed within. This is a potential application for VC which uses the content of an image, rather than the full image itself. The second involves creating a recursive multiple resolution VC scheme which allows many smaller secrets to be hidden within one large share [6, 10]. Each of the secrets can be recovered irrespective of any type of zooming. However, when combined with a zoom function, for example, within Google Maps, the secret recovery becomes clearer at each level.

## 6.2.1 License Plate Embedding

Many techniques are available which assist in locating and detecting license plates [3]. The automatic license plate recognition (ALPR) technique used would be most appropriate for our type of application [26]. Using the system proposed within, we can automatically determine which characters make up the plate. Some false positives do occur, however, although this system works very well with a very wide range of license plates.

After the license plate area has been determined and the license number identification has been recorded, a Gaussian blur effect would typically be used within this area in order to obscure the identification number [26].

When viewing the final images after blurring, it is clear that the identification numbers are unrecognizable. We replace the typical Gaussian blur with a pixelated blur filter with an area of $21 \times 21$. This provides sufficient blurring which removes the salient points of the license plate, rendering it unreadable. Our scheme takes advantage of this blurring technique by embedding a VC share within this area.

As the area is already blurred, making any changes to it will not reduce the overall image quality and presents a perfect location to add some extra data. Our scheme works as follows: Using ALPR, we can determine the size of the area that contains the license plate along with determining the license plate identification number. After determining the identification, we can create an image of the appropriate size (based on the size of the area to be blurred) which contains this identification number. We

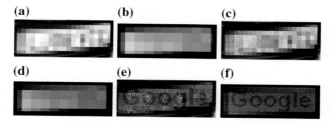

**Fig. 6.9** Obscuring license plates and accurately recovering them using VC. **a** License plate 1 pixelated. **b** License plate 2 pixelated. **c** License plate 1 VC. **d** License plate 2 VC. **e** License plate 1 recovered. **f** License plate 2 recovered

then use this image as the VC secret, generate two shares and embed share one within the license plate region.

Due to the versatile nature of VC, it is possible to create a set of shares such that two or more people must be present in order to recover the license plate number. This also makes it more difficult for assailants to recover the license plate data for their own personal use [26].

An example of license plate obscuring or filtering can be viewed within Fig. 6.9. From the results it is clear that using these VC techniques, the potential is there for removing license plate details from vehicles, while being able to restore them.

### 6.2.2 Multiresolution VC Scheme

The scheme works as follows. The smallest secret is chosen and a (2, 2) set of shares are created. We notate these shares as for share one based on secret one, for share two based on secret one. Using each of the shares, the next level of larger shares corresponding to the next secret is generated. This is the recursive part of the scheme [6]. First, we must determine the ratio that is being used to create these shares. This allows us to correctly construct the next set of shares. The original secrets we chose were of size $128 \times 128$, $256 \times 256$, and $512 \times 512$. This means that four images of secret one can fit inside secret two and four images of secret two can fit inside secret three, and so on. This means our ratio is 1/4.

After we have generated the first set of shares for secret one, we must set up two new images $N^1$ and $N^2$ which will become the new set of shares, within which we place parts of the previously created shares. These new images will become share one and share two of secret two and can be denoted by $S_2^1$ and $S_2^2$.

Within these new images, we split them up into different quadrants, $N^1_{q_1 q_2 q_3 q_4}$ and $N^2_{q_1 q_2 q_3 q_4}$. There are four of them because of the factor used. That means that each of the quadrants is of the same size as the previous shares that were generated. They can be expressed thus:

$$N^1 = \begin{pmatrix} q_1 & q_2 \\ q_3 & q_4 \end{pmatrix} \tag{6.3}$$

$$N^2 = \begin{pmatrix} q_1 & q_2 \\ q_3 & q_4 \end{pmatrix} \tag{6.4}$$

The new shares $S_1^2$ and $S_2^2$ are built up as follows: $S_1^1$ is placed into $q_1$ of $N^1$, $S_2^1$ is placed into $q_4$ of $N^2$. As the second secret is already known, we randomly generate the remaining quadrants of each of the new images.

This results in the following new shares:

$$S_1^2 = \begin{pmatrix} S_1^1 & R_2 \\ R_3 & R_4 \end{pmatrix} \tag{6.5}$$

$$S_2^2 = \begin{pmatrix} R_1 & R_2 \\ R_3 & S_2^1 \end{pmatrix} \tag{6.6}$$

where $R_1, R_2, R_3, R_4$ represent the randomly generated remainder of the share. This process is repeated for any remaining secrets using the same recursive steps [6]. The results can be viewed within Fig. 6.10. Three secrets have been hidden within the set of shares [10, 25]. As the second share is moved up to the left, the second hidden secret can be viewed. When this process is repeated we can obtain the original, smallest secret. Figure 6.10a–c represents the three secrets to be hidden within the final set of two shares. The final two shares, share 1 and share 2 can be examined in Fig. 6.10d and 6.10e respectively. Each of the recovered secrets is presented within Fig. 6.10f, 6.10g and 6.10h, respectively.

The supplementary red lines were added to assist the reader in viewing the corresponding regions of the share that contain the secrets. Using our multiresolution sharing scheme we can embed data within the image and then as we progressively zoom the image [11], we can use the same share to recover the data at different levels.

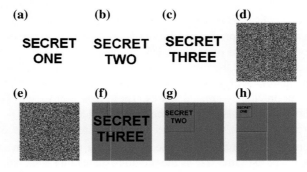

**Fig. 6.10** New recursive secret sharing scheme results. Three secrets. **a** Original secret 1 (128 × 128). **b** Original secret 2 (256 × 256). **c** Original secret 3 (512 × 512). **d** Final share 1 (1024 × 1024). **e** Final Share 2 (1024 × 1024). **f** Recover secret 3. **g** Recover secret 2. **h** Recover secret 1

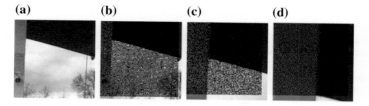

**Fig. 6.11** Multiple resolution secret recovery. **a** Section of the image with embedded data. **b** Recovering secret three. **c** Recovering secret two. **d** Recovering secret one

Figure 6.11 provides the results of this scheme. This illustrates the point that as the zoom level is increased, the smaller secrets become just as readable and clear as the largest secret prior to any zooming.

## 6.3  Exercises

(1) Compare the watermarking scheme using VCS with previous ones and list the advantages of the watermarking scheme using VCS.
(2) Which criteria should a watermarking scheme meet?
(3) Which applications can be generated by the features of VCS except those provided in this chapter?

## References

1. Ateniese G, Blundo C, Santis AD, Stinson DR (1996) Extended schemes for visual cryptography. Theor Comput Sci 250:1–16
2. Chang CC, Chuang JC (2002) An image intellectual property protection scheme for gray-level images using visual secret sharing strategy. Pattern Recognit Lett 23:931–941
3. Chang SL, Chen LS, Chung YC, Chen SW (2004) Automatic license plate recognition. IEEE Trans Intell Transp Syst 5(1):42–53
4. Chen TH, Tsai DS (2006) Owner-customer right protection mechanism using a watermarking scheme and a watermarking protocol. Pattern Recognit 39:1530–1541
5. Cordaro J, Wagner T (1967) Optimum (n, 2) codes for small values of channel error probability. IEEE Trans Inf Theory 13(2):349–350
6. Gnanaguruparan M, Kak S (2002) Recursive hiding of secrets in visual cryptography. Cryptologia 26(1):68–76
7. Hou YC, Chen PM (2000) An asymmetric watermarking scheme based on visual cryptography. In: IEEE intternational conference on signal processing, pp 992–995
8. Hsieh SL, Hsu LY, Tsai IJ (2005) A copyright protection scheme for color images using secret sharing and wavelet transformation. World Academy of Science, Engineering and Technology
9. Hsu CS, Hou YC (2005) Copyright protection scheme for digital images using visual cryptography and sampling methods. Opt Eng 44(7): 077003.1–077003.10
10. Hsu CT, Wu M (1999) Hidden digital watermarks in images. IEEE Trans Image Process 8:58–68

11. Jin D, Yan W, Kankanhalli MS (2005) Progressive color visual cryptography. SPIE J Electron Imaging 14(3)
12. Lin CY, Wu M, Bloom JA, Cox IJ, Miller ML, Lui YM (2001) Rotation, scale and translation resilient watermarking for images. IEEE Trans Image Process 10:767–782
13. Liu F, Wu CK, Lin XJ (2010) Some extensions on threshold visual cryptography schemes. Comput J 53(1):107–119
14. Lou DC, Tso HK, Liu JL (2007) A copyright protection scheme for digital images using visual cryptography technique. Comput Stand Interfaces 29:125–131
15. Naor M, Shamir A (1995) Visual cryptography. In: Proceedings of EUROCRYPT'94. LNCS, vol 950. Springer, New York, pp 1–12
16. Tai GC, Chang LW (2004) Visual cryptography for digital watermarking in still images. Pacific rim conference on multimedia LNCS 3332: pp 50–57
17. Thomos N, Boulgouris NV, Strintzis MG (2006) Optimized transmission of JPEG2000 streams over wireless channels. IEEE Trans Image Process 15(1):54–67
18. Tuyls P, Hollmann HDL, van Lint JH, Tolhuizen L (2005) Optimized transmission of JPEG2000 streams over wireless channels. Des Codes Cryptogr 37:169–186
19. Voyatzis G, Pitas I (1996) Applications of toral automorphisms in image watermarking. In: International conference on image processing 2: pp 237–240
20. Wang MS, Chen WC (2007) Digital image copyright protection scheme based on visual cryptography and singular value decomposition. Opt Eng 46(6):1–8
21. Wang MS, Chen WC (2009) A hybrid DWT-SVD copyright protection scheme based on k-means clustering and visual cryptography. Comput Stand Interfaces 31(4):757–762
22. Wang FH, Yen KK, Jain LC, Pan JS (2007) Multiuser-based shadow watermark extraction system. Inf Sci 177:2522–2532
23. Weir J, Yan WQ (2009) Sharing multiple secrets using visual cryptography. In: IEEE international symposium on circuits systems, pp 509–512
24. Weir J, Yan WQ (2009) Dot-size variant visual cryptography. In: Proceedings of IWDW'09, pp 136–148
25. Weir J, Yan W, Crookes D (2008) Secure mask for color image hiding. In: International conference on communications and networking in China, pp 1304–1307
26. Zheng D, Zhao Y, Wang J (2005) An efficient method of license plate location. Pattern Recognit Lett 26(15):2431–2438

# Glossary

**Visual Cryptography**  A secret sharing technique allows the sharing of a secret image among a number of participants.

**Visual Cryptography Scheme**  The VCS is a kind of secret-sharing scheme which allows the encryption of a secret image into $n$ shares that are distributed to $n$ participants. Any qualified sets of participants can reveal the secret image, and any forbidden sets of participants cannot obtain the secret image.

**General Access Structure**  A general access structure is a specification of qualified participant sets and forbidden participant sets which illustrates the access permission to secret information.

**Watermarking**  Watermarking is a technique to protect the copyright of digital media. A watermarking scheme combines cover images with a watermark which is hard to be detected and removed, and the owner of the image can prove the copyright by extracting the watermark from the watermarked image.

**Determinate Visual Cryptography Scheme**  DVCS is a kind of VCS that pixels in the secret image can be revealed correctly.

**Probabilistic Visual Cryptography Scheme**  PVCS is a kind of VCS that pixels in the secret image can only be revealed correctly with certain probability.

**Size Invaraint Visual Cryptography Scheme**  SIVCS is a kind of VCS that size of the secret image is identical to that of the share images.

**Extended Visual Cryptography Scheme**  EVCS is a kind of VCS that every participant can view an original image on his share. Any qualified sets of participants can reveal the secret image without trace of the original images, and any forbidden sets of participants cannot get information of the secret.

**Color Visual Cryptography Scheme**  Color visual cryptography is a kind of visual secret-sharing scheme in which the secret image and share images are with colors.

**Color Extended Visual Cryptography Scheme**  CEVCS is a special kind of EVCS which shares colored secret image. The generated shares of the scheme are meaningful and colorful.

**Aspect Ratio Invariant Visual Cryptography Scheme**  ARIVCS is a kind of VCS which preserves aspect ratio of the secret image invariant in the shares.

© Springer International Publishing Switzerland 2015
F. Liu and W.Q. Yan, *Visual Cryptography for Image
Processing and Security*, DOI 10.1007/978-3-319-23473-1

**Cheating Immune Visual Cryptography Scheme**   CIVCS is a kind of VCS which is designed to avoid cheating problems when the secret image is revealed.

**Progressive Visual Cryptography Scheme**   Progressive VCS is a kind of VCS with the property that clarity of the secret image is progressive when increasing the number of stacked shares.

**Flexible Visual Cryptography Scheme**   A flexible visual cryptography scheme denotes a kind of VCS which achieves any expected pixel expansion.

**Successful Cheating Method**   A SCM represents that the probability of cheating against a VCS is 1.

**Human Visual System**   Human visual system is part of the human central nervous system which detects and interprets information from visible light to create a representation of the surrounding environment.

**Binary Secret Sharing**   A secret sharing technique which shares black and white images.

**Visual Cryptography Model**   VCM is a specification of the implement method of VCS, which mainly consists of two models: "OR" and "XOR".

**Average Pixel Expansion**   APE denotes the average value of the total pixel expansions of the share images that each participant holds under the circumstance that participants may receive multiple share images with different pixel expansions.

**Color Model**   A color model is an abstract mathematical model describing the way that colors are represented as tuples of numbers.

**RGB**   An additive color model in which red, green, and blue light are added together in various ways to reproduce a broad array of colors.

**CMY**   CMY refers to the three colors: Cyan(C), Magenta(M), Yellow(Y) which make up a subtractive color model used in printing.

**Online Trustable Authorization**   The online trustable authorization is a online management mechanism which authenticates the identity of participants and authorizes the access to available resources.

# Index

**A**
Additive color model, 134

**C**
Cheating immune visual cryptography, 53
Color visual cryptography, 2, 131, 132, 136
Contrast, 42

**E**
Error diffusion halftoning, 84
Extended visual cryptography, 25, 37, 83, 109, 131

**G**
General access structure, 55

**H**
Human visual system, 97, 137, 138, 149

**I**
Information transmission model, 150

**M**
Multi-pixel encryption, 96, 97, 135, 136

**N**
Nozzles spray, 42

**P**
Pixel expansion, 40
Plane transformation visual cryptography, 35
Precise alignment, 24, 27
Print and scan, 25
Probabilistic visual cryptography, 14, 41, 83
Pseudorandom number, 116, 120, 123

**S**
Secret-sharing scheme, 131
Shareholder, 54
Size-invariant visual cryptography, 83, 96
Subtractive color model, 134
Superposition, 24, 25

**T**
Thin line problem, 50
Traditional visual cryptography, 35, 53, 83
Transparency, 33
Trust authority, 151

**U**
Universal quality index, 94

© Springer International Publishing Switzerland 2015
F. Liu and W.Q. Yan, *Visual Cryptography for Image
Processing and Security*, DOI 10.1007/978-3-319-23473-1

Printed in the United States
By Bookmasters